John Henry Wigmore *and the* Rules of Evidence

John Henry Wigmore and the Rules of Evidence

The Hidden Origins of Modern Law

ANDREW PORWANCHER

University of Missouri Press
Columbia

ISBN: 978-0-8262-2086-8 (hardcover : alk. paper)
ISBN: 978-0-8262-2311-1 (paperback : alk. paper)
Library of Congress Control Number: 2016937224

∞™ This paper meets the requirements of the
American National Standard for Permanence of Paper
for Printed Library Materials, Z39.48, 1984.

Typeface: Bembo

Publication of this volume has been supported with a gift from the
Kinder Institute on Constitutional Democracy.

STUDIES IN CONSTITUTIONAL DEMOCRACY

Jeffrey L. Pasley and Jay K. Dow, Series Editors

In partnership with the Kinder Institute on Constitutional Democracy, this series explores the history and development of American constitutional ideas and democratic practices both in the United States and as they have reverberated throughout the world. The volumes in this series showcase interdisciplinary scholarship that helps readers gain insight into both new and traditional themes in American politics, law, society, and culture, with an eye to both practical and theoretical applications.

(continued on next page)

(continued from previous page)

Bureaucracy in America:
The Administrative State's Challenge to Constitutional Government
Joseph Postell

The Myth of Coequal Branches: Restoring the Constitution's Separation of Functions
David J. Siemers

Reforming Legislatures: American Voters and State Ballot Measures, 1792–2020
Peverill Squire

Indeed you cannot hope to appreciate what your volumes on Evidence and later association with you at Northwestern meant to a half-trained practitioner in the rough-and-tumble of the Nebraska courts, searching for a legal science he could but feel must exist somewhere.

—Roscoe Pound to John Henry Wigmore, 1919

Contents

Illustrations

Acknowledgments

MY DEBTS ARE many. Gary Kass is the kind of acquisitions editor whom every scholar hopes for. He is charitable with his time, attentive to details, and full of helpful ideas. I was fortunate to cross paths with Justin Dyer several years ago at a workshop in Chicago. He has been a keen proponent of this project, and I thank him for bringing it to the attention of Jeffrey Pasley. The work that they do at the Kinder Institute should be a model for civic education nationwide. I am thrilled to publish this monograph in their new series "Studies in Constitutional Democracy," and especially honored to author one of the inaugural books. Sara Davis was instrumental in guiding this book to completion. I also appreciate the backing of Clair Willcox, editor in chief of the University of Missouri Press.

This book began as a doctoral dissertation at the University of Cambridge, and so I owe tremendous thanks to my supervisor, Michael O'Brien. It is a strange coincidence that on the day I mailed my finished manuscript to the publisher, Michael passed away. I regret that I was not more expeditious in bringing this book to fruition that he might have lived to see the project in its final form. I hope he would find this book worthy of the time that he invested in me. I am also grateful to Philip Gardner for his guidance in the early stages of my research. Martin Halliwell and Tony Badger read the manuscript with care; they made my viva voce a great experience.

The history students at Cambridge had a collaborative spirit and contagious passion for the subject. I would be remiss if I did not also mention my home in graduate school, Darwin College. The students there were diverse in their interests, international in their backgrounds, and sociable to the extreme, providing the best environment I could imagine for producing a dissertation.

I revised the manuscript into a book while a new faculty member at the University of Oklahoma. There, Kyle Harper was an unrelenting advocate for this project. I wish I could find more compelling language to express my gratitude to him for his enthusiasm. David Wrobel was a steady source of counsel. David Anderson, Wilfred McClay, and Luis Cortest merit special thanks. Financial support was provided from the Office of the Vice President for Research, Office of the Senior Vice President & Provost, College of Arts & Sciences, and Department of Classics & Letters at the University of Oklahoma.

Beyond OU, historians like Noah Feldman, Raymond Haberski, Mel Urofsky, and Vernon Burton offered their advice and encouragement. This book benefited tremendously from the thoughtful comments of Robert Burns and my anonymous reader. Kevin Leonard at the Northwestern University Archives and Lesley Schoenfeld at the Harvard Law School Library helped make my research trips fruitful. While I received help from many hands, any errors of fact or interpretation in this book are mine alone.

My friends were constant sources of support in these years. Dan was always a valuable sounding board, Eli generously hosted me during a research trip to Boston, Robby has a couch with a permanent impression of my body, Dustin was inexplicably excited for me, and Ben went so far as to relocate with me to England. Most of the actual writing of the manuscript took place during a year spent in Washington, DC—it was there that my roommate and old friend, Chad, had to hear about John Henry Wigmore daily, that Kiran proved a great writing partner as he worked on *Mud Creek Medicine*, and that Milich could always be counted on to eat my leftovers. These friends patiently listened and asked questions whenever I gave way to rambling about a seemingly obscure and long-dead legal figure. If their interest was sincere, I am appreciative. If it was feigned for my benefit, I am doubly so.

Researching Wigmore's pained relationship with his mother and father made me value my own parents all the more. The long path from dissertation proposal to published book was navigable because of their unwavering support.

I save my final expression of thanks for the most important professor in my life—my older sister, Kara. In our youth, she convinced me that I was adopted from Martians who would be retrieving me in short order. This was upsetting news at the time as I had grown accustomed to my earthly surroundings. Since then, Kara has more than redeemed herself for that troubling piece of misinformation. She is a friend and a mentor, always ready with an encouraging word. My greatest pleasure in writing this book is dedicating it to her.

Norman, OK

John Henry Wigmore *and the* Rules of Evidence

Introduction

JOHN HENRY WIGMORE came of age amid the severe dislocation of a quickly modernizing society. As a boy growing up in San Francisco in the 1870s, he bore witness to the most rapid urbanization of any community in American history. As a graduate student at an innovating Harvard Law School in the 1880s, he was among the first to receive modern professional education in the United States. As a young professor in his initial academic post in Tokyo in the 1890s, he lived in a Japan that had only recently emerged from its centuries of isolation and was aggressively emulating the advances of the West. And as the new dean of Northwestern Law in the early 1900s, he published *A Treatise on the System of Evidence in Trials at Common Law*, a reference work that would dominate the law of evidence in a country turning from its agrarian heritage toward an industrial future.[1]

A core function of the jury trial is to discriminate between truth and falsehood, and so the courtroom offers an instructive microcosm of the American struggle to establish credible knowledge amid the disorientation of modernity. One would imagine, then, that the law of evidence—which stipulates fact-finding in trials and thus speaks directly to epistemology—would be vital to the historiography on American legal thought. The academic literature *does* describe the contemporaneous rise of a modernist jurisprudence, often called legal realism, that reacted against an increasingly anachronistic philosophy of legal formalism. That master narrative, however, is silent on the law of evidence.[2]

While general histories of jurisprudence implicitly deny the relevance of evidence law to legal thought by omission, historical scholarship on the rules of evidence explicitly disaggregates the subject from modernizing trends. The sparse field of evidence law historiography is led by William Twining, who describes "Wigmore's divorce from the mainstream of American Legal Realism" and the "extraordinary isolation of the study of evidence from intellectual developments in other fields during the twentieth century." The "developments" to which Twining alludes include modernist jurisprudence and analogous trends in philosophy, history, and economics. As Twining writes of Wigmore, "The temper of his thought and many of his specific assumptions stand in quite sharp contrast to many of Wigmore's American contemporaries, for example, William James, Charles Beard, Thorstein Veblen, Oliver Wendell Holmes, Jerome Frank, and other apostles of the revolt against formalism." Echoing Twining's conclusions, Annelise Riles asserts that Wigmore "made his scholarly name as an expert in the field of evidence, and his serious and still-popular treatise is a standard performance in that formalist genre."[3]

It is the central thesis of this book that precisely the opposite is true: under the hegemonic influence of Wigmore's *Treatise*, the law of evidence embodied and promoted modern legal thought. By extension, evidence law incorporated the same modernist values that characterized the work of nonlegal progressives such as James, Beard, and Veblen. As a law student and young lawyer in the 1880s, Wigmore came under the tutelage of two giants of modernist jurisprudence—Massachusetts Supreme Judicial Court justice Oliver Wendell Holmes Jr. and Harvard Law School professor James Bradley Thayer. Wigmore internalized their philosophy of law over the next two decades and ultimately translated their modernist insights into concrete rules of evidence. After the 1904–1905 publication of the four-thousand-page *Treatise*, the most renowned figures of modern legal theory—including Harvard Law School dean Roscoe Pound, Supreme Court justice Benjamin Cardozo, and intellectual provocateur Jerome Frank—looked to Wigmore's tome as a lodestar of legal modernism.[4]

The *Treatise*, then, was more than just a useful reference work for practitioners that would govern jury trials for the better part of the twentieth century. It helped catalyze a new era in American law. Wigmore's prolific correspondence with the leading lights of the legal world reveals the centrality of personal relationships to this intellectual development. Behind the judicial decisions and law review articles lay a dense network of mentor-protégé connections that as much as any idea gave birth to modern legal thought.

While my book dissents from current scholarship on the law of evidence, it also contributes to a recent and substantial revision of the master narrative of contemporary legal thought. Before turning to the revision, I will first recapitulate the contours of the master narrative. According to the historiography, rapid modernization between the 1880s and 1930s prompted two diametrically opposed schools of legal theory: 1) "formal legal thought," also known as "classical legal thought," and, 2) "modern legal thought," often called "progressive legal thought" or "legal realism."

Formalist thinkers idealized syllogistic judicial decisions, wherein judges discovered universal principles controlling clearly demarcated areas of law and applied these principles to individual cases with all the certainty of geometric proofs. Both guiding axioms and the categories to which they corresponded were considered natural and immutable. The logical integrity of a judge's decisions was highly prized. He served as a dispassionate medium through which the law facilitated justice. Formalists believed in a sharp separation between law and society, individually autonomous yet collectively harmonious. Government's proper role was to refrain from intervention in the inherently just distribution of rewards by the hand of the free market. In the formalist worldview, the individual rather than the collective constituted the organizing principle of law.[5]

Modernists accepted contingency and flexibility where the formalists had demanded certainty and universality. Absolutes were a fiction and the desire for them unhealthy. Instead of viewing legal principles and categories as innate and permanent, modern legal thought held that law was socially constructed. While formalist jurists exalted the individual, modernists prioritized the needs of society over those of the self. Many modernists called for social scientific research, not quixotic universals, to guide court decisions. Judges were to discard the public myth of their role as passive arbiters of justice who *discovered* law and instead serve openly as active agents of public policy who *created* law. Legal modernism criticized formalist judges for hiding their prejudices behind a false pretense to objectivity and a specious veneer of logic. Modernists saw judges as unavoidably fallible beings who nevertheless ought to exercise discretion and do so candidly. A modernist judge should employ balancing tests to reconcile competing values, doctrines, and policy concerns. The value of legal doctrine was to be determined by its consequences rather than its consonance with abstract principle. Lived experience should trump hollow sophistry. Expedience and practicality provided reason enough to establish, discard, or justify any given legal doctrine. Modernism understood the law as integral to—not independent from—the broader social fabric, and government as a benevolent force that could remedy the inequalities exacerbated by industrialization. Legal modernists also stressed relational analyses that looked to the connections between things rather than to their essential elements. Formal and modern legal thought, then, offered a neat set of binary oppositions.[6]

The master narrative depicts the judiciary as enraptured with formal legal thought from the 1880s until the late 1930s. As formalist judges chased the illusory ideal of a closed, complete, and universal system of interlocking legal principles, their decisions betrayed a disregard for real-world outcomes. Formalists were mired in the conceptual framework of a rural-agrarian society and unwilling to countenance the new imperatives of an urban-industrial world. By the end of the 1930s, formal legal thought collapsed under the weight of its anachronism. Throughout these decades of formalist reign, modern legal thought gradually developed as a stark alternative to the dominant legal theory. In the generation preceding World War I, iconoclastic protomodernists such as Holmes, Thayer, and Roscoe Pound issued the initial criticisms of the formalist model and laid the basis for a modern philosophy of law. Through the 1920s and into the 1930s, a new generation of progressive jurists seized on their insights, developed a full-fledged modernist jurisprudence, and accelerated the demise of formal legal thought.[7]

A nascent revisionist school debunks much of the preceding narrative. The revisionist literature illustrates that formal legal thought was largely a fiction that modernists created to caricature and discredit their conservative opponents. Several of the jurists whom historians identify as leading formalists in actuality espoused the very modernist views that they allegedly opposed. Holmes and Pound were not isolated prophets of modernity but spokesmen for many of their contemporaries in the legal fraternity. Core modernist beliefs—such as the necessarily discretionary nature of adjudication, the integrated relationship of law and society, and the imperative for law to accord with social ends—were widespread before the 1930s. While true that a conservative judiciary sometimes impeded progressive legislation, the bench's often-sluggish recalibration of the law to modern needs did not equate to a mythical formalist agenda. The revisionist school acknowledges that legal thinkers in the late nineteenth century did not articulate *every* modernist tenet; they expressed little interest in social scientific approaches to law, for example.[8]

By recovering the full-throated modernism of a figure who—and branch of law that—historians dismiss as formalist, my book further questions the very existence of formalism. Modernism replaced not formalism but a disorderly legal system that had been characterized by the dearth of any organizing philosophy. When I use the phrase "the formalist model," I am referring to a straw man against which modernists railed.

This study is also an investigation into the sociology of knowledge. The reform of evidence law to accord with the demands of an urban-industrial society was part of a significant moment in American history when rapid modernization required many fields to establish credible knowledge in new ways. As Wigmore pushed the law of evidence across the threshold into modernity, intellectual life saw the advent of pragmatism in philosophy, challenges to classical economic theory, innovative modes of historical analysis, and an increased premium on experimental science. These varied disciplines sought to make sense

4

of a thoroughly novel social reality and shared modernist tendencies with the law of evidence. However, this study argues for correlation but not causation between the law of evidence and modernism in other fields. Indeed, Wigmore was largely indifferent to nonlegal modernism despite its affinity with his own work.[9]

There is an important difference between Wigmore and nonlegal modernists such as William James, Charles Beard, and Thorstein Veblen. In philosophy, history, and economics, modernists were influential but by no means the only voices. Wigmore alone enjoyed unchallenged dominance in his respective field. The success of his *Treatise* illustrates how modernist values could not merely inform but monopolize an important realm of American civic life.[10]

The history of evidence law complicates our understanding of the legacy of pragmatism in particular. Evidence doctrine shared the cardinal values of pragmatism, including its emphasis on the contingent instead of the permanent and the consequences of ideas rather than their internal logic. Historians have long agreed that pragmatism's influence waned with the onset of the Second World War. Pragmatism may have fallen from favor in wider *intellectual* circles, but its values continued to determine *institutional* norms in American jury trials well past the Second World War. This nuanced conception of pragmatism's history is possible only when intellectual history reaches beyond the history of intellectuals to include the intellectual foundations of our workaday institutional practices.[11]

This book further captures just how tight-knit the elite clique that pioneered modern legal thought really was. While historical scholarship illustrates that the routes to intellectual modernism were many, Wigmore's story suggests that the path to *legal* modernism was remarkably uniform. If the most influential modernists of the early twentieth century were associated with a handful of pre-eminent law schools, then those who came of age in the late nineteenth were affiliated with just one. Oliver Wendell Holmes Jr., Louis Brandeis, Learned Hand, Roscoe Pound, as well as Wigmore—all studied at Harvard Law and all were protégés of James Bradley Thayer. Benjamin Cardozo was perhaps the only legal modernist who was born before 1885 and did not follow this course yet still rivaled in significance these Harvard-trained Thayer acolytes.[12]

Historians frequently and rightfully caution that "legal realism" does not refer to a monolithic body of thought, and I offer the same disclaimer regarding "modern legal thought." Those jurists whom I call "modernists" often entertained sharp disagreements on any number of issues, and not every modernist subscribed to every modernist tenet. Still, "modernism" is neither arbitrary nor devoid of meaning in American legal history. The term is useful as an analytical tool because it allows us to focus on those views that progressive legal thinkers and practitioners often had in common despite their differences. The various precepts of modern legal thought hang together; if a judge or professor or lawyer subscribed to one, he likely subscribed to others. For example, an anti-universalist ethic that called for case-by-case flexibility necessarily entailed a faith in the discretion of the bench, as did a belief in the propriety of balancing tests. A worldview that saw law as a social construct served to legitimate this kind of judicial discretion because it was easier to justify the regulation of legal rights when they were not considered natural. Moreover, if the distinction between law and society was artificial, then it was logical to conclude that the dichotomy of the individual and the collective was false as well.[13]

★ ★ ★ ★ ★

John Henry Wigmore remains among the most misunderstood academics in American history. The historical record demands a radical reappraisal of his role in the birth of modern legal thought. Amid the tumult and uncertainty of a new century, his *Treatise* was, at heart, an effort to confront the fundamental question: "What is truth?" When measured by direct institutional effects, Wigmore's answer was the most influential of his generation.

Wigmore's Life

JOHN HENRY WIGMORE was born on March 4, 1863, in San Francisco, California. He was named for both his father, John, a self-made Irishman in the lumber business, and his mother, Harriet, a genteel woman of English origin. Wigmore had an older half brother, Alphonso, and eleven younger siblings, six of whom survived into adulthood. One of Wigmore's sisters, Beatrice, described him as "the apple of Mother's eye, and we children were accustomed to hear our brother John Henry spoken of as a great man." Harriet delighted in dressing her favorite child in traditional Scottish garb, "sash, sporran, kilt, and all." Wigmore's academic talent was evident from an early age. Although his father wanted him to attend public school, Harriet insisted that their son enroll in the prestigious private school, Urban Academy. There, Wigmore throve academically, so much so that his younger brother Francis found it difficult to emulate his "reputation for erudition and phenomenal attainments."[1]

Wigmore would be well situated as an adult to adapt evidence law to an urbanizing society in no small part because of his childhood in San Francisco. While much of America experienced unprecedented urbanization in Wigmore's lifetime, nowhere was its process more accelerated and its effects more acute than in his hometown. The nearby discovery of gold in 1848 incited a fantastic period of growth in San Francisco perhaps rivaled only by Denver. An expansion of the rail lines allowed the city to diversify its economy, merge into the national marketplace, and avoid the fate of the ghost town. In the decades of Wigmore's childhood, San Francisco exploded from 56,802 residents in 1860 to 233,959 in 1880. A population that Boston had achieved over 250 years, San Francisco amassed in merely 25. If waves of immigrants flooded American shores in general during these years, then San Francisco experienced a tsunami—in 1880, over 100,000 of the city's inhabitants were foreign-born.[2]

At the end of his high school education, Wigmore planned to attend the nearby University of California at Berkeley, but as Beatrice recalled, "Mother was under the spell of the New England men and women of letters of the time, and nothing would do but that [John Henry] must go to Harvard." Unsettled at the thought of her firstborn so far from home, Harriet moved the Wigmore family to Massachusetts in 1879 to join her sixteen-year-old son on this new stage of his life. Only Alphonso remained in San Francisco to manage the family's lumberyard.[3]

At Harvard, Wigmore performed with distinction, and the experience galvanized his confidence in his intellect. The family returned to San Francisco after Wigmore earned his bachelor's degree, and there the recent college graduate spent a year working for his father, only to reappear at Harvard in 1884 for law school. This time Wigmore came to Cambridge alone. At the end of his first year of graduate study, he ranked first in a class of sixty-one students.[4]

Wigmore's tenure at Harvard Law informed his later efforts to accord the law of evidence with the needs of a rapidly professionalizing America. Under the stewardship of an enterprising dean, C. C. Langdell, Harvard Law School catalyzed modern professional education in the United States at the very time that Wigmore attended. Professionalization was both a symptom and agent of modernization. Amid the complexities of modern life, the professional wielded his expertise to help the layman navigate uncertain times. The term "professional" is a historically contingent one, but in Wigmore's day it generally meant persons who had acquired specialized training, skills, and knowledge, and who shouldered fiduciary responsibilities. To be sure, professionals were hardly novel at the time. Common law courts, for instance, had admitted scientific expert testimony since the late eighteenth century. Still, the rapid changes in American society in the late nineteenth and early twentieth centuries accelerated the division of labor and thereby increased the premium on expertise. University-based training, rather than apprenticeship, was an important element of professionalization.[5]

Langdell served as dean from 1870 to 1895 and turned Harvard Law into a paragon of professional education that other American law schools strove to emulate. He established legal research and teaching in the academy as a full-fledged profession. Langdell's case method of instruction recast classroom pedagogy from a rote exercise to an analytical endeavor. In both the admission of students and the hiring of faculty, he made significant strides toward an academic meritocracy. During his tenure, Harvard Law also enriched its library holdings, which were crucial for research, and created a national network of alumni.[6]

Wigmore's role in founding the *Harvard Law Review* in 1886 underscores his eager participation in the school's rapid professionalization. Academic journals were conspicuous symbols of professionalization; they embodied the professoriate's newfound commitment to research, nationalized academic discourse, reflected a culture of specialization, and enforced putatively meritocratic standards. Upon the fiftieth anniversary of the inception of the *Harvard Law Review*, Wigmore recalled that he had shared with his fellow students a "conviction that the Harvard Law School had a message for the professional world." Referring to the group that originated the *Review*, Wigmore explained, "We *knew* that our Faculty comprised scholars of the highest standards and accomplishments in their fields. . . . We *knew* that their pioneer work in legal education was not yet but ought to be well appreciated by the profession. We yearned to see the fruits of their scholarship in print." Only twenty-three years old, Wigmore had internalized the ethic of professionalization that defined Langdell's school.[7]

During these law school years, Wigmore met the woman who would become his wife, Emma Hunt Vogl. Wigmore's sister described her as the daughter of a "scholarly gentleman who had come to New England from Prague." Louis B. Wehle, who later worked with Wigmore, remembered Emma as "a strikingly pretty woman." A friend, Lawrence Egbert, "had heard her spoken of as a 'perfectionist.' Younger women seemed to think of her with a kind of fearful respect." Still, Egbert "was deeply impressed with his constant attentiveness to her and the depth of her affection for him." A longtime intimate of the Wigmores, Agnes F. Bradley, similarly remarked, "It was never possible to think of one of them without the other, such complete unity was theirs."[8]

Wigmore received his law degree in 1887. After working in private practice in the Boston area for two years, he and Emma announced that they were moving to Tokyo. He had been offered a visiting professorship in Anglo-American law at Keio University. This far-flung path in his early adulthood caused tension between Wigmore and his family. John and Harriet wanted their son to settle permanently in San Francisco and join the family business, but it became increasingly clear that Wigmore had set his own course. Wigmore's parents were also piqued that he chose to reject the Episcopalian denomination to which they were so devoted. It is unclear why Wigmore severed his ties to Episcopalianism. His religious views were opaque. He maintained a deep interest in the Bible but never attended church. Wigmore also believed in a deity but not in an afterlife. Once, rather enigmatically, he remarked to one of Northwestern's trustees over lunch, "If I were a Catholic I should be quite content: I would never leave it." John and Harriet's absence from their son's wedding in September of 1889 was one indication of a widening breach. The Wigmore family always kept Harry's

Fig. 1: Wigmore at his graduation from Harvard Law School. Northwestern University Archives Photographic Collection.

room, with a view of the Golden Gate, just as he had left it as a boy—perhaps a comforting reminder of an earlier day when the parents still had some control over their son.[9]

It was just prior to Wigmore's departure for Japan that he was contacted by Albion Small, a leading modernist in the field of sociology. Modernism was gaining traction not just in law but also sociology, philosophy, economics, and history. Amid the sweep of urbanization and industrialization, time-honored verities proved increasingly obsolete. Intellectuals in a variety of disciplines grasped for new methods of establishing credible knowledge. Some philosophers, economists, historians, and sociologists embraced modernist values analogous to those in evidence law. Rebuking the false security of universal truths, they emphasized flux and contingency. Dismissing abstract logic, they embraced concrete experience and real-world consequences. Rejecting an atomized vision of society, they understood institutions and people as woven into a common social fabric. An umbrella term like "modernism" glosses over the differences between diverse thinkers writing in distinct genres. Still, scholars in these various fields articulated a number of related intellectual positions, and I use "modernism" as an analytical term to refer to these commonalities.

Small—who would soon found at the University of Chicago the first-ever department of sociology—exhorted Wigmore to consult the findings of Lester Ward, a pioneering sociologist of modernist inclination. Ward taught at Brown University and served as the first president of the American Sociological Association. "You are doubtless familiar with Lester F. Ward's . . . *Dynamic Sociology*," Small presumed. "It is a work that has seemed to fall flat, but a few men are beginning to appreciate it." He added, "I would make that book my point of departure."[10]

In *Dynamic Sociology*, the first sociology textbook in the United States, Ward explored a modernist theme that would resurface in Wigmore's *Treatise*: legal concepts were socially constructed rather than innate. Despite the constructivist parallels between Ward and Wigmore, it appears that Wigmore never used *Dynamic Sociology* in his own work. Small's scholarship also exerted little impact on Wigmore. Their sparse correspondence suggests a cordial relationship of negligible import to the development of American modernism. This kind of disciplinary insularity was typical of Wigmore and indeed the legal academy writ large.[11]

As a professor of law at Tokyo's Keio University in the early 1890s, Wigmore cultivated a modernist ethic that would characterize his later approach to the law of evidence. Arriving in 1889, he bore witness to a novel period of Japanese history known as the Meiji era, which ran from 1868 to 1912. Previously, under the Tokugawa shogunate, Japan had largely isolated itself from the outside world for over 250 years and maintained a feudal society. In sharp contrast, Meiji Japan pursued an aggressive agenda to shed the vestiges of feudalism and modernize (i.e., Westernize) as rapidly as possible. The Japanese government sought to identify the leading nation in any given field (especially in science, technology, and industry) and solicit experts from that country to train Japanese students in their respective specialties.[12]

The Japanese were particularly eager to recalibrate their legal system along Western lines. Toward the end of the Tokugawa years, Japan had brokered a number of treaties with Western powers that permitted foreign trade and travel in designated ports. Central to these agreements was the practice of extraterritoriality, in which a foreign country enjoyed legal jurisdiction over its nationals in Japan and thereby protected its citizens from feudal law. The Westernization of Japanese law, therefore, not only reflected the dominant zeitgeist of the Meiji era but also was the only means through which Japan could revise its treaties and free itself from extraterritoriality.[13]

As early as the 1860s, the Japanese recruited Westerners to formulate modern legal codes. In the 1870s, the French legal scholar M. G. Boissonade created criminal codes that went into effect in 1881, and he then drafted a civil code that became law in 1893. The German jurist Herr Otto Rudorff created the Law of Organization of Courts, codified in 1890. In the American periodical *Scribner's Magazine*, Wigmore related how Japan employed Western architecture for its new Parliament buildings, an imitation indicative of "the potent wish to equip the nation with such of the outward insignia of Western constitutional methods so that the Japanese demand for treaty revision cannot in decency be refused by the Western powers." Now governed primarily by French and German law, Japan successfully rid itself of extraterritoriality in the 1890s.[14]

Despite the preeminence of continental law in Japan, the common law still had considerable prestige. It was in this context that Wigmore secured his teaching post in Anglo-American law in 1889 at Tokyo's Keio University, a leading center for the study of the West. Keio was founded by one of Japan's most prolific Westernizers—Fukuzawa Yukichi (1835–1901). A member of the first Japanese mission to the United States in 1860, Fukuzawa became enamored of the United States and had three of his sons educated there. Wigmore once described Fukuzawa as "Horace Mann, Horace Greeley, and Ralph Waldo Emerson combined in one personality."[15]

After Harvard University president Charles William Eliot recommended Wigmore for the visiting professorship at Keio, the latter began diligent preparations for his tenure abroad. Wigmore started to teach himself the language. He read two decades' worth of an English-language newspaper about Japan and the entirety of the American-Japanese diplomatic annals. Just days after their wedding, Wigmore and his new bride left Boston for Tokyo. As their ship, the SS *Gaelic*, approached the island nation, the Japanese scenery left a deep impression on the twenty-six-year-old Wigmore: "We passed close to the shore, and the little cloves, green sward, and fairy trees made one and all of us, feel over and over again, that it was a journey into fairyland."[16] After taking a train to Tokyo, the Wigmores were greeted by a crowd of Keio students. Emma recounted how her husband gazed upon "the mass of youthful faces about him, and set them almost wild by waving his hat."[17]

Wigmore was instrumental in designing Keio's law curriculum and served as the only full-time professor of law at the university. In that day, Japanese law faculties were generally comprised of adjunct instructors. Beyond the prohibitive expense of hiring full-time professors, law schools found that the foreign-trained Japanese lawyers suitable for such positions opted for highly coveted government stations. Wigmore assumed a substantial course load, including classes on torts, evidence, equity, and Roman law.[18]

To what must have been the pleasure of the Japanese, Wigmore emerged as a vocal opponent of extraterritoriality. In the American publication *The Nation*, he expressed an unequivocal conviction that "Japan may surely claim that the long-standing indictment against her be quashed without delay, and that her judicial autonomy be once more restored." Wigmore recognized that "forty years ago" the "feudal framework in the government of the country" provided "the basis of a claim of exterritorial jurisdiction." He insisted, however, that the Japanese had since cast off feudal law "like a rotten scaffold which had been left about a complete mansion and finally falls at a tremor of the earth." Acutely aware that the abrogation of extraterritoriality was, for the Japanese, "a question of redeeming national honor," Wigmore assured his readers that "Japan has laws equal to the best of Europe" with "judicial officials" that measure "more than favorably with English and French courts."[19]

Although Wigmore was a consummate symbol of Meiji Westernization—an American professor teaching common law and playing shortstop on what may have been Tokyo's first baseball team—he eagerly turned his attention to Japanese history. Upon his arrival, Wigmore "was anticipating with professional interest the opportunity of making some acquaintance with the law of Japan,—not the newly imported Codes, fresh from foreign workshops, but the indigenous law, the law of the people, representing the sum of the ideas of justice which had grown up amid this unique civilization of the East."[20] Drawing on the common law as a reference point for understanding its Japanese counterpart, Wigmore, in his words, "came under the spell of what is called Comparative Law."[21]

Historians recognize Wigmore's comparative research as seminal in the corpus of American legal scholarship. According to Jerome Hall, "In the United States . . . professional comparative law may be said to have begun with Wigmore." Annelise Riles likewise refers to Wigmore as "one of the most active practitioners of comparative law of all time." Moreover, David S. Clark describes him as a "major American comparatist with a worldwide reputation."[22]

Wigmore's interest in Japan's legal history was almost as remote to Japanese jurists as it was to American scholars. In 1892, Wigmore lamented, "the last thing that the ordinary Japanese law student thinks of is records of the legal ideas indigenous to his country." Wigmore noted that it was "to a very few scholars . . . that Japan must look to rescue her inheritance from the oblivion into which the mental revolution of the last two decades has plunged it." The following year, he published a study of Japanese legal education in the American legal journal *Green Bag* and asked, "Where does the native Japanese law come in? It does not come in at all." Among Japanese students, Wigmore reported, "there is a positive contempt for the ideas and customs of the past generation. . . . They have not yet learned to value the inheritance of their past, and they cannot be persuaded to take up its study." Decades later, Wigmore remembered how "the new Occidental legislation was occupying all thoughts of the Japanese people, including the students, and no interest was shown in their own native institutions."[23]

Wigmore was especially keen to research Japanese legal history because he viewed the Tokugawa era as singularly susceptible to "scientific" analysis. At the twilight of his life, Wigmore reflected on Japan's exceptional appeal in this respect. "In the laboratory methods of natural science," he explained, "one of the chief methods of tracing causes is to isolate each hypothetical element and to observe its reactions in that isolation under controlled conditions." However, instances of isolation "in the annals of legal history are rare" because societies constantly interacted. Therefore, "the isolation of Japan during the Tokugawa two-and-a-half centuries, in its independent island civilization . . . makes that country an almost unique field for the study of legal development."[24]

Although Wigmore exalted laboratory science as an epistemic model for legal study, he conceded that the analogy was far from exact. "The perpetual handicap for the student of comparative legal ideas," he acknowledged, "is the impossibility of ever observing the living idea in all the systems that are to be compared." By way of contrast, "the inorganic sciences do not suffer from this handicap. The electron can be studied in the laboratory of any country."[25] In other words, Wigmore could draw, however loosely, from the methods of laboratory science without making pretenses to comparable levels of certainty.

Although the Meiji era is remembered for the Westernization of Japan, in fact Japanese law shaped its American counterpart thanks to Wigmore. The modernist values that would characterize his *Treatise* on evidence he first identified as traits of Japanese legal history. This early exposure to legal modernism was conspicuous in Wigmore's 1892 contribution to *Green Bag*, "The Legal System of Old Japan." In this article, he examined Japan's feudal law with reference to the Anglo-American common law. Wigmore first described the common law as prone to "making generalizations into hard-and-fast rules" and to "eliminating in individual cases a variety of important moral considerations." He then contrasted Japan's indigenous legal culture with his own:

> The chief characteristic of Japanese justice as distinguished from our own may be said to be this tendency to consider all the circumstances of individual cases, to confide the relaxation of principles to judicial discretion, to balance the benefits and disadvantages of a given course, not for all time in a fixed rule, but anew in each instance.[26]

Emphasis on particularity, deference to the bench, distaste for rigid principles, balancing tests—all would emerge as core themes in his treatment of evidence doctrine (although here his commentary remained descriptive rather than normative). It is perhaps not without irony that the qualities of Japan's premodern legal system would prove well suited to a rapidly urbanizing and industrializing America.

Wigmore was quick to preempt criticism that the flexibility of the Japanese system rendered it capricious. "It would not be fair to infer from this that the courts of old Japan could have been no better than the tents of an Arab Sheikh," he pleaded. "On the contrary, there was in Japan a legal system, a body of clear and consistent rules, a collection of statutes and of binding precedents." In the event that a suit came to court, Wigmore reported, "there was, of course, an important foundation of customary law and of statutes from which all parties thought as little of departing as we do from the Constitution; but these rules were applied to individual cases with an elasticity depending upon the circumstances."[27] The young American comparativist had distilled an important lesson from his investigation of Japan's feudal law that he would carry with him for the rest of his life—flexibility in a legal system need not degenerate into arbitrary justice.

The various modernist elements that Wigmore uncovered in Japanese legal history found recurring expression in his body of comparative work. For instance, he embraced an anti-universalist ethic that eschewed epistemic certainty. Wigmore understood that one language could not perfectly translate into another and so the recovery of Japanese legal history in an English text was ineluctably inexact. He first acknowledged this difficulty in his 1892 publication, *Materials for the Study of Private Law in Old Japan*. In the Japanese Ministry of Justice, Wigmore had uncovered a number of largely unknown Tokugawa-era legal sources, and he subsequently raised funds from the Asiatic Society of

Japan to produce a multivolume English-language translation. In the course of this project, Wigmore came to appreciate the unavoidable fallibility of the translation process. "Those who understand Japanese and Chinese will know how useless it is to expect a purely literal rendering," he relayed. "The nature of these languages, or rather, the modes of thought and expression, do not permit it. They are elliptical where we should be exact, and prolix where we should be brief."[28]

In her essay on Wigmore's role as a comparativist, Annelise Riles argues that his scholarship stressed the "*commonalities*" between Japanese legal development and other countries, and so amounted to "a celebration of universalism." To be sure, Wigmore recognized congruous elements between legal systems, but he was equally keen to highlight their differences. Wigmore's comment in his article on Japanese feudal law that "it is in Japan that we may find the extreme antithesis to the Anglo-Saxon conception of justice" is hardly a celebration of universalism. A later article on a legal concept called the "pledge-idea" explicitly warned against universalistic approaches: "There is no intention of suggesting the notion that the development of the pledge-idea might *a priori* have been expected to be the same in all systems, or that for any other legal idea the form or the expedients or the progress must be or is likely to be identical among various peoples."[29]

If anything, Wigmore embraced a cultural relativism that offered a marked contrast to the concept of universal values. In 1893, he wrote of Japan, "It is not difficult to find fault with the ways of its people, in legal education or in other activities; but the doubt always remains whether it is really a fault that we find. By our standards something may fall short; but there is a constant residuum of doubt whether we have any right to apply those standards."[30] Be it an embrace of flexible legal guidelines, a recognition of the limits of comparative epistemology, or an emphasis on the diversity of foreign systems of law, Wigmore consistently articulated an anti-universalism at this early stage of his career.

Alongside an anti-universalist orientation, Wigmore situated legal development in a broad social context. In his work on the Tokugawa-era legal sources, he provided an "introductory survey" that exposed the reader to "the life of the community" where legal "customs prevailed and these precedents ruled." Wigmore covered topics as diverse as "religious organization," "commercial houses," "guilds," "transportation," "money, banks, and commercial paper," and the "rice trade."[31]

Analogously, he turned his attention to the current relationship between Japan's culture and law in "The Legal System of Old Japan." Here, Wigmore described Japanese society's "deep-seated opposition to whatever implies clash, clatter, shock, roughness, strain, in any shape, and an inclination to make everything quiet, smooth, easy, harmonious." "If I have seemed to digress in illustrating this," he clarified, "it is because this quality in one of its manifestations had so great an influence on the administration of justice." For instance, the Japanese aversion to confrontation fueled a widespread conviction "that every dispute should, if by any means possible, be smoothed out by resort to private or public arbitration" rather than a full-fledged lawsuit.[32]

In addition to an anti-universalistic ethic and focus on social context, Wigmore's early immersion in the culture and history of Japan cultivated his preference for privileging of the actual over the theoretical, of lived experience over a priori assumptions. Wigmore embraced this particular aspect of legal modernism in 1891 in his first major contribution to Japanese legal history, *Notes on Land Tenure and Local Institutions in Old Japan*. The raw material for this work came from the notes of an American physician, Duane B. Simmons, who had practiced medicine in Japan for much of his adult life and passed away before completing a text on Japanese feudal history. Wigmore arrived in Japan shortly after Simmons's death and was tasked with the culmination of the latter's project. After praising Simmons for having taken the "first steps in the study of local institutions in old Japan," Wigmore asserted that the source material for the book "may be taken to represent, in any given instance, the actual practice among the people, rather than the theoretical rule."[33] At this very early stage of his career, Wigmore displayed a modernist's sensitivity to the distance between theory and practice.

In the same vein, he commented in his piece on Japanese legal education that "it is a superstition of the home-keeping citizen that the ordinary traveler gains a knowledge of the character and institutions of the peoples he visits. Where the journey has prolonged itself into a sojourn of a few years," it is assumed that "the cup of the sojourner's wisdom must be filled, and there is no question that may not be asked of him. But experience speedily dissipates this superstition."[34] Wigmore had seen firsthand how concrete experience could dismantle fallacious albeit commonly held assumptions. It was this combination of deference to experience and skepticism of a priori suppositions that would inform Wigmore's approach to the law of evidence.

Wigmore exemplified a functional approach to knowledge when he drew from his historical inquiries to render moot a contentious debate about the future of Japan's commercial law. During Wigmore's tenure at Keio, the Japanese questioned whether they should enact a proposed commercial code, modeled after European law, or adopt a code consistent with Japan's legal heritage. By demonstrating that much of Japan's feudal law dovetailed with its modern European counterpart, Wigmore successfully exposed the false dichotomy that had incited the debate. He related how "Japanese commerce possessed, with scarcely an exception, the fundamental mercantile institutions and expedients with which Western commercial law deals." Wigmore further assured his readers that we are "without support, when we assume that the new Code brings in notions and rules novel to the people or opposed to their traditions of commerce." On the contrary, "we have no cause to anticipate friction from putting into force a modern commercial Code in a nation which has for two centuries possessed nearly every leading institution and expedient therein regulated."[35] When Wigmore later turned his attention to the production of an original treatise on evidence, he followed this instrumentalist model and culled from Anglo-American legal history lessons for immediate application.

Wigmore appreciated how Japanese feudal law prized expediency and practicality rather than abstract principles. In his survey of the subject, Wigmore found that a key function of the judiciary had been "to arrange a given dispute in the most expedient way, to sacrifice legal principle to expediency." He related how "the greatest fame was achieved by those magistrates who" had demonstrated "good sense in apportioning practical justice." Wigmore's scholarship on Japan also revealed his belief in legal categories as constructed rather than natural. He warned in the introduction to *Materials*, "let no one suppose that this table of contents may be freely used as a guide to the cases and statutes on the different topics." As "cases are found grouped together which have a superficial likeness only," it followed that his scheme of classification was "a rough one only."[36]

Wigmore's study of Japanese legal education offered a hint of an additional theme that would emerge with greater salience in his work on evidence law—advocacy of judicial discretion. Referring to the selection of law school administrators, he detailed how "Japan proceeds on the Confucian principle, which we, in our politics at least, would do well to follow more closely: Rules count for little; find a good man, put him in office, and trust his discretion."[37] The deference toward administrators that Wigmore now endorsed was the very attitude he would later display toward the bench in his canonical *Treatise*.

Wigmore turned down Keio's offer of a three-year contract extension and in 1892 left Japan to search for a position at an American university. In his words, Wigmore "hoped on returning to the United States to become a professor of Comparative Law. But President Eliot pointed out to me that there was no American interest in that subject, and no opening for it in law schools."[38] For the remainder of his career, the law of evidence occupied the center of Wigmore's scholarly pursuits, although his work in that domain reflected the many lessons he had gleaned from his study of Japan.

Wigmore landed at the Northwestern University School of Law in 1893. As a new faculty member, he found himself in a city urbanizing on a greater scale, if not a quicker pace, than his hometown. Chicago of the 1890s was rife with all the hopes and hazards of metropolitan life. In these years, the city built the first iteration of its elevated railroad, established itself as a robust center of commerce, and proudly hosted the Columbian Exposition. Yet Chicagoans also suffered from frequent epidemics, severe overcrowding, and industrial conflict.[39]

At Northwestern Law, Wigmore discovered an institution that rivaled his alma mater in its enthusiasm for professionalization. Northwestern president Henry Wade Rogers was centrally concerned with the university's professional schools, and none attracted his attention more than the law school. A former dean of the University of Michigan Law School, Rogers served as acting dean of Northwestern Law from 1892 to 1898 and implemented many of the changes that Harvard Law had initiated. Like Langdell, he increased the number of full-time faculty members and lengthened the law degree from two years to three.[40]

In his early days at Northwestern, Wigmore taught topics as varied as torts, evidence, and quasi contracts. He ascended to the deanship in 1901 before his fortieth birthday. Building on Rogers's culture of professionalization, Wigmore increased standards for admission to and graduation from the law school, developed a course on "The Profession of the Bar," and established the law library as a major center for legal research in the Midwest. Wigmore's emphasis on professionalization was not lost on his students. As one pupil, Charles Elder, recalled, "he held forth the ideal of the expert, the individual who by mere knowledge would be in demand as an adviser, or an advocate."[41]

In physical appearance, Wigmore possessed an "erect, military bearing."[42] Elder described his professor's "light brown hair parted evenly above a high symmetrical forehead, gray eyes," and "a light brown moustache." "He invariably wore a standing collar with rounded wings, a black satin four-in-hand tie, loosely tied, and dark clothes," Elder recollected.[43] In truth, Wigmore was too cerebral to pay much attention to his appearance; his wife was responsible for his immaculate presentation.[44]

Wigmore was widely known for his urbane and congenial disposition. Anne George Millar, a local teacher, related that he was "endowed, like a prince of the fairy-tales, with the magic gift of charm." One colleague, Edwin Austin, remembered the Northwestern dean as possessed of a "rare talent for human friendship" and another, Jerome Hall, said Wigmore had "an unusual capacity for social intercourse." A student of Wigmore's who later taught at

Northwestern Law, Fred Fagg Jr., recalled the dean's "genial smile, nimble wit, and mild manner."[45]

Yet many of Wigmore's fervent admirers also conceded his many faults. They noted that "he was sensitive to criticism and quick of temper" and "seldom admitted an error."[46] A Northwestern trustee who had once been Wigmore's pupil, William MacChesney, met with the ire of his old professor when he offered a donation to the university through the board of trustees rather than a Law School committee. Wigmore exploded at MacChesney, "I will see to it that you will never be known in connection with this Law School Building now."[47] That MacChesney desired to allocate funds for a Wigmore Chair of Evidence did little to cool the dean's temper.

Perhaps Wigmore's most salient characteristic was his remarkable productivity. He wrote forty-six original volumes, edited another thirty-eight, and organized the translation and editing of nine on the Tokugawa shogunate of Japan—nearly one hundred books in all. When lined on a shelf, the aggregation of his scholarship stretches an astounding eighteen feet. Wigmore's tendency to work on multiple projects at once helps explain his output; when he would grow restless with one scholarly activity, he would immediately redirect his energies to another. Wigmore's longtime secretary, Sarah Morgan, depicted her boss "as indefatigable, utilizing every spare moment." Francis Wigmore similarly remembered his older brother as always "engaged in some form of mental activity, never just sitting or reclining inactively."[48]

In 1902, Oliver Wendell Holmes Jr. expressed concern that the young dean was overworked. "Nothing I am sure will stop your continued success except the possibility that you run your machine too hard," warned the recent nominee to the US Supreme Court. "Don't do it—have fixed hours—*don't work at night*." Suspecting that Emma shared his misgivings, Holmes added, "I wish that I could reinforce and make you feel what I doubt not your wife says to you. I am most serious in my feeling and thought about it." In fact, Emma was in no small way responsible for her husband's professional success. "Her ever-present determination, and perhaps anxiety was to preserve his health and to try to see to it that nothing whatsoever should be allowed to interfere with his life work," Francis Wigmore recalled of his sister-in-law.[49]

Holmes's letter arrived just as Wigmore was in the midst of crafting the most enduring indication of his work ethic—his exhaustive treatise on evidence. Laurence Egbert, a professional associate of Wigmore's, remarked that "anyone who has even glanced at those magnificent authoritative tomes entitled 'Wigmore on Evidence' knows that the man Wigmore had unbelievable persistence and terrific drive." Robert Wynass Miller was a student

AN EPOCH MAKING TREATISE ON THE

LAW OF EVIDENCE

By JOHN H. WIGMORE

DEAN OF THE LAW SCHOOL OF NORTHWESTERN UNIVERSITY

☞ The fullest treatment of this great subject ever offered.

☞ It cites more than 40,000 cases and contains over 9,000 Statutes, parts of Statutes, and Code Sections.

☞ Its 4,000 large octavo pages comprise as much matter as eight ordinary volumes.

Full particulars, together with Specimen Pages are contained in the pages of this pamphlet.

LITTLE, BROWN, AND COMPANY, Publishers

Fig. 2: Box 228, Folder 6, Wigmore Papers.

at Northwestern Law during Wigmore's preparation of the first edition of the *Treatise* and remembered in vivid detail the intensity with which the dean focused his energies on his life's magnum opus. "Aided by numerous cigarettes," Miller recalled, "he applied himself to the work which was to give him imperishable fame." Although the smoking room in the old courthouse where Wigmore labored "was not the quietest place in the world," he remained "wholly undisturbed by the activity around him." "With the absorption there attended an air of sureness and serenity," added Miller, "as of one who possessed the certainty that what he was doing would be in perfect fulfillment of his design." When Wigmore finished this first edition of the *Treatise*, Emma was hesitant to trust its security to the mail, so she copied, by hand, the entirety of the tome.[50]

Wigmore's treatment of evidence doctrine reflected his early exposure to and keen grasp of urbanization. For instance, he argued in his *Treatise* that urbanization challenged traditional legal notions of reputation. A party's "neighborhood-reputation" in a small, agrarian town where people knew each other well possessed appreciable credibility—but less so, if at all, in a large urban center. "In communities of more primitive conditions," maintained Wigmore, "where social life continues stable amid constant and fixed surroundings, the neighborhood-reputation is unquestionably of some value." Conversely, "amid the isolated individualism and kaleidoscopic changes of the metropolitan horde no neighborhood-reputation is likely to exist."[51] In the maelstrom of sweeping urbanization, Wigmore consciously sought to accord evidence law with the reality of the breakdown of the traditional community.

Wigmore's support for professionalization also informed his approach to the law of evidence. For instance, in his *Treatise* he advocated the admission of professional scholarship in court at a time when only two jurisdictions allowed scientific treatises. This position rested on Wigmore's understanding—born from his experience on the *Harvard Law Review*—of professional communities of scholars and the manner in which they ensured the legitimacy of academic knowledge:

> The writer of a learned treatise publishes primarily for his profession. He knows that every conclusion will be subjected to careful professional criticism, and is open ultimately to certain refutation if not well-founded; that his reputation depends on the correctness of his data and the validity of his conclusions; and that he might better not have written than put forth statements in which may be detected a lack of sincerity of method and of accuracy of results.[52]

Since the academic professions were structured to safeguard against inaccuracies, reasoned Wigmore, courts could safely admit the fruits of scholarly labor as evidence.

In a similar example, Wigmore lamented that courts did not admit abstracts of title unattached to the testimony of their authors. He argued in the *Treatise* that evidence law should countenance the credibility of such abstracts because they "are ordinarily expected to be tested by other professional persons" through "examination and collation" and "so far as they have survived this test unquestioned, they stand approved and accepted by the profession as trustworthy."[53] For Wigmore, the professional community endowed knowledge with authority. This, too, was a central component of modernism—it was not the individual who discovered truth but the collective that created it.

An important element of professionalization was the creation of associations that developed standards, debated professional issues, and represented the interests of their respective fields to society at large. Within the law, the formation of the American Bar Association (ABA) in 1878 and contemporaneous founding of state bar associations were central to these ends. As historian Samuel Haber explains, "the American Bar Association stood at the head of the profession in the important work of creating the lawyers' professional self-understanding."[54] Over the course of his long career, Wigmore assumed leadership roles within the ABA. For instance, he was integral to the creation of the association's Section on Legal Education and he chaired a Committee on Reorganization of the ABA.[55] In an era when professionals increasingly identified with national and not just local networks of colleagues, Wigmore argued, "What the Association now needs, most of all" is "to activize [*sic*] its latent national power with maximum effect."[56] In 1932, the ABA would award Wigmore its prestigious annual medal for "typifying a life devoted to the service of your profession."[57]

Insofar as bar associations devised codes of ethics, they participated in a core activity of professionalization—self-policing. The legitimating rationale of this feature of professionalization was that only specialists possessed the requisite expertise to judge the quality of fellow practitioners. This element of professionalization influenced Wigmore's treatment of the law of evidence in his *Treatise*. He was particularly keen to defer to the conventions of doctors. "To deny the competency of a physician who does not know his facts from personal observation alone is to reject medical testimony almost in its entirety," he concluded. "The law must recognize the methods of medical science. It cannot stultify itself by establishing, for legal remedies, a rule never considered necessary by the medical profession itself."[58] In an age when professions increasingly insulated themselves from external policing and defined themselves by internal codes, Wigmore displayed a conspicuously modern deference to professional norms.

In the realm of legal education, Wigmore made explicit the links between professionalization and modernization. He argued in the *Tennessee Law Review* that state bars should admit only those possessed of a college degree because the dynamism of modern times demanded that legal practitioners acquire a broader education than high school could provide: "The law has ceased to be static. . . . It is now in a state of flux. Economic and social conditions are changing, and Law must adapt itself to the change." Given "the innumerable new methods in transportation, banking, production, invention, medicine, social control, and engineering," it is necessary "that the lawyer, if he is to maintain his pristine position as a leader in the community, must at least know as much as these men of other occupations." Wigmore concluded that "to do this, he must prepare by going to college." This predilection was wholly consistent with another common aspect of professionalization in the United States—the situating of the university as the focal point of training and credentialing.[59]

Wigmore was just as passionate about his own pedagogy at Northwestern as he was legal education generally. He took great joy in adding a theatrical flair to his classroom. A student described him as "an actor on the stage of legal learning." Once, a porter at the law school entered Wigmore's class and handed a note to Michael Clarke, a student. Clarke then gathered his belongings and began to exit the room when Wigmore interrupted:

"Mr. Clarke, what do you mean by breaking up my class in this manner?"

"I have a note from Mr. Crossley, secretary of the school, asking me to come to the office immediately," Clarke explained.

"A note from Mr. Crossley?"

"Yes."

"Hm-m-m, let's see that note."

Clarke handed Wigmore the note and the professor began to read aloud:

"Mr. Michael Clarke, immediately upon receipt of this letter please leave the class room and come to this office. (Signed) Frederick B. Crossley Secretary of the Law School."

Wigmore began to interrogate the bemused student. "Now, Mr. Clarke, did you ever see Mr. Crossley sign his name?"

"No."

"Did you ever carry on a long correspondence with him which purported to bear his signature?"

"No."

"Now, as a matter of fact, I wrote that letter myself, [and] signed Mr. Crossley's name." The day's lesson on establishing the authenticity of handwriting had begun.[60]

Another student of Wigmore's, Stuart S. Ball, found that his teaching conveyed many core elements of legal modernism. Wigmore, for instance, subscribed to a conception of law as integral to, rather than autonomous from, society. "Closely related to his emphasis upon interrelation of history and law," wrote Ball, "was the Dean's implicit view that the latter was a robust part of society's everyday life." Wigmore also espoused an anti-universalist ethic that eschewed categorical principles, rights, and doctrines. As Ball noted, "The Dean never assumed in his teaching that the law was a collection of certainties and absolutes." What's more, Wigmore rejected abstraction while emphasizing lived experience in the classroom. "The subject of his attack," recounted Ball, "were rules which have faulty logic behind them, or which are supported by a logic out of touch with reality."[61]

As a consequence of his *Treatise*'s dominance in the practice of evidence law, Wigmore's status in legal academe steadily rose. Rival institutions such as Yale and Columbia eagerly recruited him, but Wigmore was intent on staying at Northwestern. He successfully leveraged competing offers to secure higher salaries for his faculty, expand the law library, and increase facility funding.[62]

Wigmore was not a political partisan. He involved himself as a young man in local Republican politics and later identified as a conservative Democrat. Possessed of a mild reformist streak, Wigmore expressed interest in municipal issues such as parks and public transport.[63] A student once expressed to Wigmore a deep disillusionment with society and an attendant conviction that "nothing but a revolution would settle matters." Wigmore assured the disaffected pupil that "it would do no good to scrap everything that had gone before as we would have to build it from the bottom again with all the mistakes,—the thing to do was to tinker away and try to correct the mistakes little by little."[64] This brand of moderation aptly characterized Wigmore's approach to legal progress. As another student noted of the dean, "he stood decidedly for actual judicial open-mindedness, legal reform, and efficient government, but of an orderly nature with a due consideration of existing law, and the lessons of history."[65]

Wigmore's premium on moderation in jurisprudence did not extend to his attitude about World War I. He viewed the war as a Manichaean struggle of good against evil and had no tolerance for any loyal opposition. "To him it was a time for action, and discussion became taboo," recalled a fellow scholar, Manley Hudson. "What many others view as grey was black to him; he saw white where others rested on their doubts." From 1917 to 1919, Wigmore served in the military for the Judge Advocate General's Office in Washington, DC, where he rose to the rank of colonel. His primary activities involved revising the rules of evidence for courts-martial and assisting the Selective Service Administration. He also advised Woodrow Wilson on judicial nominations. On Northwestern's campus, Wigmore fostered a culture that made conscientious objecting difficult and drew criticism from free speech proponents. Students and colleagues alike were aware that Wigmore's preferred mode of address back at Northwestern was "Colonel," a title that endured for the rest of his life.[66]

In many respects, Wigmore's rigidity surrounding the war seems unlikely. He served as the second president of the American Association for University Professors (AAUP), an organization dedicated to the protection of academic freedom. Moreover, Wigmore was highly cosmopolitan; he traveled globally and could read a dozen languages as disparate as Arabic, Russian, and Japanese. Most importantly, he subscribed to a legal philosophy that eschewed absolutism.[67]

Yet in other respects, Wigmore's jingoism is not surprising. He was hardly the only professor associated with the AAUP to readily abandon the organization's creed amid the hysteria of the war. His very early years at Northwestern offered a harbinger of his later authoritarian attitude. In an 1894 letter to his Harvard mentor, James Bradley Thayer, Wigmore described his own mindset toward educational reform in militant terms. The young scholar reported to Thayer that the Northwestern faculty was "happily united in almost all its policy and is congenial and harmonious in a way that" rendered "the task of the legal missionary here a very agreeable one." "Domestic happiness and unity," added Wigmore, "is an important prerequisite for successful external warfare." Although "warfare" was only a metaphor in this context, when read literally, Wigmore's message about unity echoes with an eerie prescience. Northwestern Law faculty member Francis Philbrick offered something of an explanation for the dissonance between the balanced component of Wigmore's intellect and his dogmatic streak. "On subjects involving no emotionalism he reasoned with directness, simplicity, and peculiar clarity," Philbrick observed. Yet when the dean dealt with topics susceptible to "emotionalism," he was "strangely lacking objectivity and logical consistency."[68]

Wigmore's jingoism persisted after the war as he coerced his students into signing a loyalty pledge and proved unsympathetic to the civil liberties of political dissidents. A conspicuous example of his postwar intolerance was his strident indictment of Oliver Wendell Holmes Jr.'s famous dissent in *Abrams v. United States* (1919), notwithstanding the fact that Holmes was an important mentor to Wigmore. In this case, the US Supreme Court upheld the conviction of anarchists who had conspired to publish pamphlets advocating a general strike in American ammunition factories during World War I. Holmes issued a dissent in support of the defendants that laid the basis for modern free speech theory and endures as a classic in the annals of modern legal thought.[69]

Wigmore roundly criticized Holmes in the pages of Northwestern's law review. This breach was rooted partly in their distinct understanding of the facts and partly in divergent philosophical approaches. Regarding the facts of the case, Wigmore perceived a threat where Holmes did not. Holmes saw no danger to "the success of the government arms" from "the surreptitious publishing of a silly leaflet by an unknown man." Conversely, Wigmore believed that because the war hinged on the provision of munitions, the dissidents struck at the very heart of the war effort. He maintained that "there was danger in a single day's lapse at a single factory or a single work-bench." Wigmore characterized Holmes's dissent "as blind to the crisis—blind to the last supreme needs of the fighters in the field, blind to the straining toil of the workers at home, obtuse to the fearful situation." In melodramatic fashion, Wigmore theorized that had a majority on the Court sided with Holmes, the case "would have ended by our letting soldiers die helpless in France."[70]

If Holmes and Wigmore had merely entertained different views of the facts, then their disagreement would have little bearing on Wigmore's relationship with modernism. However, Holmes's dissent and Wigmore's article offer markedly distinct philosophies. In Holmes's words, "Persecution for the expression of opinions seems to me perfectly logical," albeit unconstitutional. "If you have no doubt of your premises or your power, and want a certain result with all your heart, you naturally express your wishes in law, and sweep away all opposition." Consistent with his anti-universalist ethic, Holmes pleaded that we should never be so certain of our position that we deny a voice to others who may correct us. As Holmes had written privately to Wigmore four years earlier, "Certainty is not a test of certitude." Wigmore, however, presented the war as a clear-cut struggle between right and wrong: "It was a supreme moral issue. There was but one side to take; and America took it." Wigmore eagerly embraced the very absolutism that Holmes so acutely feared.[71]

Although Holmes and Wigmore entertained distinct approaches to certainty in this instance, they both privileged the collective over the individual—albeit in very different ways. In one of the most famous lines in constitutional history, Holmes prophesized, "When men have realized that time has upset many fighting faiths, they may come to believe even more than they believe the very foundations of their own conduct that the ultimate good desired is better reached by free trade in ideas." In Holmes's view, society could only make use

27

of the best ideas when exposed to them all. Wigmore's article offered a stark contrast. "Where a nation has definitely committed itself to a foreign war, all principles of normal internal order may be suspended," he declared. "Liberty of speech may be limited or suppressed, so far as deemed needful for the success-ful conduct of the war." Wigmore had turned Holmes's communalist logic on its head. Whereas Holmes legitimated liberty because it enhanced the public welfare, Wigmore advocated the infringement of individual rights because they supposedly threatened the common good.[72]

Holmes was taken aback by Wigmore's upbraiding. "Wigmore in the *Ill. Law Rev.* goes for me *ex cathedra* as to my dissent in the *Abrams case*," he relayed to the English jurist Sir Frederick Pollock. Holmes characterized Wigmore's commentary as "sentiment rather than reasoning" and concluded that "he has grown rather dogmatic in tone." Yet Holmes did not let this public disagree-ment dampen his private friendship with Wigmore. Expressions of mutual af-fection continued to pass between Evanston and Washington for many more years until Holmes's death. In one indication that these two friends viewed professional disagreements with a degree of levity, the justice good-naturedly ribbed the dean about another case: "On Monday [I] delivered a dissent that you will abhor."[73]

Wigmore's illiberal patriotism was further evident in a highly public dis-agreement with the esteemed Harvard Law professor Felix Frankfurter. Like Wigmore, Frankfurter was a Holmes acolyte who made important contribu-tions to legal modernism. Frankfurter would later serve as an adviser to Franklin Roosevelt and ultimately join the US Supreme Court. The dispute between Wigmore and Frankfurter revolved around the Sacco-Vanzetti case, among the most highly publicized and controversial criminal cases in American history. On April 15, 1920, two assailants in South Braintree, Massachusetts, mortally wounded a factory paymaster and his security guard, stole over $15,000 (about $180,000 in today's dollars), and then made their escape in a getaway car. The authorities questioned and charged Nicola Sacco, a cobbler, and Bartolomeo Vanzetti, a fish peddler. As Italian immigrants with ties to a fringe anarchist movement, Sacco and Vanzetti struggled to secure a fair trial amid the culture of fear that characterized Red Scare America. Moreover, the prosecution found an ally in the overtly biased presiding judge, Webster Thayer. From the bench, Thayer spouted immaterial declamations about patriotism and permitted the prosecution to coach its witnesses from the stand. Despite dubious evidence against the defendants, in July of 1921 the jury convicted Sacco and Vanzetti after only three hours of deliberation.[74]

Initially the Sacco-Vanzetti case attracted limited attention and seized the imagination largely of the far left. It was not until after the defendants were sentenced to death in 1926 that Sacco and Vanzetti moved to the center of public consciousness, both in the United States and abroad. Just prior to the sentencing, the defendants issued dramatic addresses in the courtroom that censured the proceedings and affirmed their innocence. Copies of their speeches circulated worldwide, and the two men became symbols of victimhood. Mainstream legal figures and journalists soon joined artists, poets, and intellectuals in decrying the imminent execution of Sacco and Vanzetti.[75]

Frankfurter was among the most prominent and respected Americans to join the fray on behalf of the convicted. In a lengthy analysis of the trial in the *Atlantic Monthly*, he contended that the proceedings had been patently unfair and expressed his disbelief that Sacco and Vanzetti could have committed a crime that bore the mark "of highly professional banditry." Responding to Webster Thayer's refusal to grant a retrial, Frankfurter commented, "In modern times Judge Thayer's opinion stands unmatched for discrepancies between what the record discloses and what the opinion conveys."[76] With his Harvard pedigree and sober analysis of the legal process, Frankfurter proved instrumental in rendering support for Sacco and Vanzetti palatable to moderates on both sides of the Atlantic.

Wigmore was incensed by Frankfurter's article. "I am going to make a counter offensive by telling of the facts which he has suppressed," Wigmore informed Webster Thayer in a letter. "I want thereby to take away any popular sympathy his account may have excited." Wigmore requested some written materials for his forthcoming rebuttal to Frankfurter and assured the judge, "of course I should not name my authority for any information you might send."[77]

Wigmore's response to Frankfurter, published in the *Boston Evening Transcript*, provoked a prompt rejoinder by Frankfurter, followed by yet another round of rebuttals in the press. Where Frankfurter saw grave errors, Wigmore felt assured that Sacco and Vanzetti had received a fair trial. Wigmore's criticism turned personal—he refused to refer to Frankfurter by name and instead pejoratively labeled him "the contra-canonical critic." Frankfurter was *contra*-canonical because, according to Wigmore, his publication in the *Atlantic Monthly* violated "Canon 20 of the American Bar Association's Code of Professional Ethics," which prohibited lawyers from commenting in newspapers about pending cases. Wigmore also strongly disputed what he characterized as Frankfurter's narrative of "the typical bitter prosecutor, out for a conviction, smashing into the case this illegal and prejudicial evidence, with the support of the hostile judge, and foreclosing the case a hopeless one from the start." In Wigmore's view, Frankfurter's accusations were nothing more than "a mean libel."[78]

Frankfurter was reticent to attack Wigmore's character in kind. "I shall continue to leave vituperation to Dean Wigmore while I stick to the facts," he offered bluntly in the *Boston Herald*. Although Frankfurter may "have left all personal animadversions to Dean Wigmore," he felt compelled to defend not only Sacco and Vanzetti but himself as well. "At no time," Frankfurter concluded his rejoinder, "have I had any other interest, or been subjected to any other influence, than my sense of justice and my devotion to the just administration of the criminal law, to the fair name of our courts and to the honor of this commonwealth."[79]

Wigmore received a number of letters from Massachusetts judges, lawyers, and law school deans in support of his position.[80] As Judge Thayer himself gratefully wrote, "Your answer to Prof. Frankfurter came at a time when my burdens were tremendously heavy to bear." He credited Wigmore for giving him a "heart filled to its very limit with gratitude and appreciation for what you have done."[81] The prominent National Civic Federation asked Massachusetts governor Alvan Fuller to sponsor a public debate between Wigmore and Frankfurter to help him decide whether or not to grant clemency, but the governor demurred.[82] While Frankfurter never had an opportunity to argue with Wigmore in person, the former considered himself the unequivocal victor in this controversy. "When Wigmore tried to attack me he was just pulverized," Frankfurter recalled many years later.[83]

Frankfurter tried to repair his personal relationship with Wigmore after the incident, but Wigmore's animus never abated. Northwestern University president Walter Dill Scott seemed to imply to Wigmore that he should temper his tone by noting that Frankfurter had done just that. "You will be interested to know that Felix Frankfurter made statements concerning you in Chicago day before yesterday all of which were complimentary," Scott wrote in a letter only a few weeks after Frankfurter's final rebuttal appeared in print. "Friends of Northwestern who were present greatly appreciated this attitude of mind on the part of Professor Frankfurter." But Wigmore had no remorse. What Frankfurter considered a professional disagreement, Wigmore interpreted as a difference of character. In writing to J. Edgar Hoover about Frankfurter's *Atlantic Monthly* article, Wigmore relayed, "I know enough of him personally to know how biased his account is."[84]

It might appear at first that this dispute has some bearing on Wigmore's approach to evidence law—after all, critics of the verdict stridently questioned the integrity of the trial's fact-finding procedures. However, Wigmore's diatribe against Frankfurter was, in Wigmore's own words, "not . . . a detailed analysis of the Sacco-Vanzetti evidence," but "a statement of the reasons why" Frankfurter's "article in the *Atlantic Monthly* is wholly devoid of credit."[85] Wigmore's commentary, then, bespeaks a knee-jerk antagonism to Frankfurter's sympathy for political dissidents rather than a reconsideration of modernist values in evidence doctrine.

Wigmore's disagreements with other modernists had only an *apparent* bearing on Wigmore's relationship with modernism. In 1923, Wigmore and his colleague Albert Kocourek edited a volume of essays entitled *The Rational Basis of Legal Institutions*, which prompted a disparaging critique in the *Columbia Law Review* from Columbia Law scholar and esteemed modernist Underhill Moore (1879–1949). Historian William Twining cites Moore's "savage attack" as evidence of "Wigmore's divorce from the mainstream of American Legal Realism." In fact, Moore's review grossly distorted Wigmore's position.[86]

Moore accused Wigmore of essentializing rationality—a stance that Wigmore had already rejected nearly two decades earlier in his *Treatise*. According to Moore, an end is "rational in so far only as it is a means to another end." Moreover, in Moore's analysis, there were no ultimate ends: "Ultimates are phantoms drifting upon the stream of day dreams." So if rationality referred only to a legal institution's ability to serve an end, and ends were always transient rather than ultimate, then rationality was a contingent social construct. Moore elaborated on what he perceived as the fatal flaw for Wigmore and Kocourek: "The problem, then, that loomed so obscurely before the editors, was not one of rational ends, but rather, What are the means to legal institutions and to what proximate ends are legal institutions means?"[87]

Yet Wigmore had defined rationality in the *Treatise* as a construct. In his words, rationality consisted of "prevailing standards of reasoning" at any given time; it was not some abstract and universal notion. Because Wigmore saw rationality as a social construct, he posited that the distinction between "rational and non-rational modes of proof is after all not between the use of scientific reasoning and the employment of superstitious ordeals; it is rather between employing the best standards we know and those which we realize are not the best." That is, there was no ideal standard of rationality against which to measure legal rules, only the most reasonable methods of the day. "There have been, in the history of our modes of proof," Wigmore recounted, "separate epochs, in each of which we progressed from what we were aware to be the inferior to what we had come to know as better; and this in a broad sense is the significance of the principle that the law of evidence is based on the employment of rational standards."[88] For Wigmore, rationality as a concept was always a product of time and place, not some "phantom" notion of the "ultimate" that Moore ascribed to Wigmore's book.

Certainly, some of the criticisms in the review amounted to a legitimate difference of opinion between Moore and Wigmore. Moore, for instance, advocated the utility of "modern psychology, biology, social psychology, anthropology, and sociology" in legal studies.[89] Wigmore, however, was somewhat incredulous of the social scientific study of law. These divergent attitudes toward the social sciences are best understood as part of a dispute between modernists who shared much else in common.

John Dewey, a giant of philosophical modernism, praised Moore's caustic review of Wigmore's *Rational Basis*. "The general type of thought you criticize is certainly the great intellectual enemy at present," Dewey relayed to Moore. Yet Dewey's criticism cannot be taken very seriously because he acknowledged to Moore, "I haven't seen the book."[90] Had Dewey read the work, he might have realized that Wigmore's brand of modernism worked in parallel to Dewey's own in the field of philosophy. Dewey's unfounded disapproval of Wigmore points to the wall that too often separated legal modernism from analogous intellectual developments in other fields.

But the fault was not Dewey's alone—Wigmore would not have described himself as part of a far-reaching interdisciplinary modernist movement. Indeed, just as Dewey failed to appreciate Wigmore's modernism, so too did Wigmore appear to deride Thorstein Veblen, a major figure in economic modernism. Veblen was a colleague of Dewey's. Both taught at Chicago around the turn of the twentieth century, and they later joined forces to found the New School for Social Research in New York, an institution dedicated to academic freedom and social reform through scholarly research.[91] Ostensibly, Wigmore criticized Veblen in a letter to Holmes, and although the letter is lost, Holmes's extant response offers a fair indication of Wigmore's opinion. "I note with pleasure your remarks on Veblen," Holmes wrote. "He is a great bore, and in my opinion not at all the profound philosopher he thinks he is. His Theory of the Leisure Class struck me when I read it years ago as taking 400 pages to say what didn't need or deserve more than 40."[92] Given the tenor of this exchange, it is little surprise that nowhere in the *Treatise* did Wigmore's limited engagement with nonlegal modernists surface. As Wigmore crafted the law of evidence, scholars such as Dewey and Veblen simply did not register.

Wigmore may have been disinclined to unearth the implicit modernist parallels between law and other fields, but he was amenable to the ideas of philosophers, economists, and sociologists if and when they turned their attention to law. Wigmore's *Rational Basis* offers a prime example of his familiarity with legally focused scholarship by nonlegal modernists; the collection featured work by Lester Ward, Albion Small, and, interestingly enough, Veblen and Dewey. To be sure, *Rational Basis* possessed some decidedly antimodernist material from the likes of John Locke and Herbert Spencer because the goal of the volume was to sample a wide range of thought. But the sympathies of Wigmore and his coeditor, Kocourek, lay with the modernists. "The pragmatic method," they wrote (using the philosophical term for modernism), "in a field so vast in time and area, is of course the least available and perhaps the most dangerous; yet it is also the most useful and the most needed; and a few passages are based on that method."[93] This endorsement from the editors further belies the legitimacy of Moore's critique.

In 1929, Wigmore stepped down as dean and officially retired from the faculty five years later, although he continued to teach at Northwestern and retained the title "Dean Emeritus."[94] He had taken a long hiatus from original research in comparative law during his deanship, only to dedicate much of the last fifteen years of his life to the study of foreign legal systems. This second round of comparative work reflected Wigmore's enduring commitment to understanding law with reference to the environment in which it developed. In 1928, he published a three-volume study, *Panorama of the World's Legal Systems*. A somewhat whimsical book filled with pictures, *Panorama* was designed "to interest the professional public (lawyers, and students of law and political science) in the world's legal systems outside our own." From Mesopotamian to maritime and Egyptian to ecclesiastical, Wigmore surveyed a diverse range of legal systems and highlighted the import of social context. "The individual rules and institutions," he insisted, "are bound and related together as the gross product of the social and political life of a particular race or people."[95]

Similarly, in a two-part article that appeared in 1931 and 1932 in the *Tulane Law Review*, Wigmore emphasized "that a legal institution can be fully comprehened [*sic*] only in the light of the social, economic, religious, political, racial, and climatic circumstances which surround it." He then criticized his own study of the pledge-idea, published thirty-four years prior, for neglecting this kind of holistic treatment: "In my exposition no account was taken of the differing economic, social, religious or other conditions of the various peoples and countries which could explain the variations found in their respective laws." Wigmore found that others had fallen short as well. "We can of course equip ourselves," he offered, "with a background of the social and ethical and economic facts and ideas in which the system of law thrives at a particular period. This is a truism, but apparently it needs to be constantly inculcated."[96]

Wigmore again seized the opportunity to highlight the integrated relationship between law and society after returning to Japan in 1935 to resume his earlier work on the Tokugawa shogunate. The Japan Cultural Society had solicited Wigmore to expand *Materials for the Study of Private Law* into a comprehensive sixteen-volume English-language translation of the Tokugawa-era legal sources. Now seventy-two years old, Wigmore spent two months in Japan and arranged for translators thereafter to send him drafts continually for the series. He would revise these proofs in Chicago and ship them to Japan for eventual publication. This process proceeded unhindered until World War II, when Allied bombing threatened the safety of the documents. The society's translators packaged the sources in rucksacks and successfully ensconced them in an isolated hamlet until the war's end. Although *Law and Justice in Tokugawa Japan* was not completed until the 1980s—long after Wigmore's death—Wigmore had penned a preface for the series in 1941 that stressed the relevance of social circumstances in legal history. "In these trial records," he relayed, "not only the legal life is pictured, but also the whole domestic, social, agricultural and commercial life."[97]

Wigmore's interest in comparative law worked in tandem with his belief in the merits of professionalization. Reflecting on the lessons gleaned from his decades of study of foreign legal systems, he related in the *Tulane Law Review*, "My favorite theme is that the development of a system of law has never taken place except through the formation of a professional class—whether that professional class be religious or secular, official or unofficial."[98] Wigmore acted on this finding and promoted the professionalization of comparative and international law. He served as the first chairman of the ABA Section on International and Comparative Law, partook in the International Congress of Comparative Law in 1932, and emerged as a vocal exponent of both the League of Nations and the Permanent Court of International Justice. With respect to the latter, Wigmore received endorsements the world over to serve as a judge but asked that his name be removed from consideration.[99]

Fred Fagg—Wigmore's former student and later colleague—came to appreciate the extent of Wigmore's fame when the two attended a hearing of the United States Supreme Court in the 1930s. "It was interesting to note," Fagg reflected, "how quickly the justices spotted the visitor from Northwestern and with what dispatch the pages were sent down to invite him to tea or dinner. Six invitations arrived within the first five minutes after the court convened."[100] Nor was Wigmore's renown limited to the judicial branch of government. President Franklin D. Roosevelt relied on Wigmore to advise him about the emerging field of air travel law.

The end came abruptly for John Henry Wigmore. On April 20, 1943, the still-active eighty-year-old attended an editorial meeting for the *Journal of Criminal Law and Criminology* in Chicago. Afterward, Wigmore climbed into a taxicab that soon collided with another vehicle. He sustained a fracture in his skull and died within a few hours. Shortly thereafter, the childless Emma confided to a younger woman whom she regarded as a niece, "Uncle Harry and I were too much one person and when that taxi-cab killed Uncle Harry, he killed Aunt Emma, all but a mere fragment that is trying, not very successfully, to carry on." The summer after burying her husband in Arlington National Cemetery, Emma joined him there.[101]

Intellectual Influences

Wigmore's *Treatise* was a consummate expression of modern legal thought. He did not develop his ideas in a vacuum. Extensive in his reading and well connected in his professional relations, Wigmore appropriated others' ideas for his tome whenever he found them useful. Three figures stand out among the rest as particularly influential on Wigmore—James Bradley Thayer, Oliver Wendell Holmes Jr., and Jeremy Bentham. While the last of these jurists died more than thirty years before Wigmore's birth, the other two enjoyed close personal and intellectual ties to the author of the *Treatise*. Thayer, Holmes, and Bentham all articulated core tenets of modern legal thought that Wigmore in turn amalgamated and translated into concrete evidence doctrine.

James Bradley Thayer

James Bradley Thayer was born in 1831 in Haverhill, Massachusetts, into a family of modest means. Thanks to the beneficence of an affluent widow, Thayer attended Harvard for his bachelor's degree. After returning to Harvard to study law and graduating first in his class, Thayer worked as an attorney in Boston for nearly two decades. He later joined the faculty at Harvard Law School, where he taught from 1874 until his death in 1902, and was, for a time, one of only four full-time faculty members. Thayer's life was marked by the presence of a number of progressive thinkers. He was a childhood friend of the Cambridge intellectual Chauncey Wright. In the 1860s, a young Oliver Wendell Holmes Jr. came under the tutelage of Thayer. The future Supreme Court justice Louis Brandeis was a favorite student of Thayer's, and Thayer relied on Brandeis to teach his evidence course when otherwise preoccupied with research.[1]

Thayer was instrumental in shaping the modernist cast of Wigmore's thought. Wigmore's estrangement from his own family led him to seek out a father figure in Thayer, who inspired in his protégé a veneration bordering on hero worship. In a letter to Thayer's widow written shortly after his death, Wigmore described his connection to her husband in religious terms—he referred to Thayer as his "master and father-confessor" and himself as a faithful "disciple." "It was a good word of his," Wigmore related, "which helped me at almost every stage in the profession; and to him, more than to any one man, I was indebted for action which brought me advancement."[2]

Indeed, Thayer had continually encouraged Wigmore from the earliest stages of his career. When Wigmore was only twenty-five and embarking on an academic life in the late 1880s, Thayer wrote, "I am truly glad that you are making yourself favorably known." In another letter dated 1889, Thayer asked Wigmore to "remember that I shall always be glad to hear from you and of you and always ready to say or do anything which may help you." And a few years later, Thayer offered, "Let me know if I can help you in any exigency." These words of support from such an eminent scholar meant a great deal to the young Wigmore, who said that he never considered an evidentiary issue "without imagining what [Thayer] would think of it."[3]

As Wigmore's career progressed through the 1890s, he frequently consulted Thayer on a range of academic issues. Often, Wigmore sought clarification on a historical point or advice in revising an academic article. He also looked to Thayer as an authority on the reform of legal education. Lamenting the "desperately Philistine" approach of most educators, Wigmore lauded Thayer in 1895 for the "exalted tone" and "high standards" of a recent speech by Thayer on the subject. Moreover, Wigmore highly valued Thayer's recommendations for law faculty at Northwestern.[4]

Wigmore relied heavily on Thayer's teaching materials in his own evidence classes. In 1892, Thayer published a casebook for students, *Cases on Evidence*; Wigmore assured the author that, "My men [i.e., students] have enjoyed extremely the *Cases on Evidence*." When Thayer produced a second edition in 1900, Wigmore conveyed to Thayer his appreciation of the revised text. "I was deeply impressed, on turning over its pages, with the immense amount of detailed care spent in the revision," relayed Wigmore. "It is indeed a new book, for every page seems to have been given some breath of new life." Praising the "copious citations" and other "new minor conveniences," Wigmore concluded, "It will all be a decided advantage for students and teachers." Not only did Wigmore use *Cases on Evidence* in the classroom, but he would also reference it in his *Treatise*.[5]

Thayer, in turn, drew from Wigmore in developing curricular materials for his Harvard students. In a letter dated 1899, Thayer commended Wigmore for his "excellent article on *Confessions*." Referring to his own students, Thayer informed Wigmore, "I shall turn my men loose on it. . . . This seems to me one of the best and neatest things you have done. I wish you would print it in a pamphlet and send a copy to every judge in the country." Thayer was also struck by Wigmore's revision of *Greenleaf*, the dominant reference work on evidence prior to the appearance of the *Treatise*. He reassured Wigmore, "You have done all that can be to rehabilitate your learned author." A few months later, Thayer reported, "I am constantly referring my men to your new *Greenleaf*." In fact, Thayer referenced Wigmore's *Greenleaf* in the second edition of *Cases on Evidence*. Wigmore's reaction to these citations was indicative of his adulation for Thayer: "I certainly did not for a moment dream of this compliment."[6]

In the midst of this intellectual exchange, one work in particular left an indelible mark on Wigmore and served to condition his thought along modernist lines—Thayer's *Preliminary Treatise on Evidence at the Common Law* (1898). A work of both history and theory, this treatise was "preliminary" in that it was the first installment of what was supposed to be a much grander enterprise. Thayer hoped to translate insights from this initial, and relatively academic, work into a full-throated evidence treatise for practitioners that would modernize the increasingly outdated rules of evidence (he would pass away before bringing his vision to fruition). In Thayer's view, the time was "ripe for the hand of the jurist" to initiate "a full historical examination of the subject," culminating, eventually, in "a restatement of the existing law and with suggestions for the course of its future development." The first four chapters of the book focused on the development of the trial, particularly the jury trial. The rest of the *Preliminary Treatise* was largely concerned with exposing substantive law that masqueraded as evidence law.[7]

Wigmore's correspondence with Thayer reveals the profound effect of the *Preliminary Treatise* on the younger scholar. In a letter addressed to Thayer shortly after the appearance of the monograph, Wigmore insisted, "Any other book on Evidence could be spared . . . but not this. I only wish that every judge who is to write an opinion on the law of evidence could be required to read this book." In Wigmore's view, the time had come for a wholesale overhaul of the rules of evidence. "The crying need of today is clear thinking; and there will be no clarifier more potent than your Preliminary Treatise," he exclaimed. "As an achievement merely in the writing of history, it would be unique and pioneer, but I do not know when a mark of history ever bore so immediately and practically upon concrete improvement in current practice." It comes as little surprise, then, that Wigmore cited the *Preliminary Treatise* dozens of times in his own *Treatise*.[8]

The *Preliminary Treatise* possessed many elements of the modernist agenda that directly informed Wigmore's treatment of evidence law. For instance,

Thayer expressly privileged experience over logic. His comment that "the law of evidence is the creature of experience rather than logic" was a clear echo of Holmes's famous aphorism, "The life of the law has not been logic: it has been experience." Thayer railed against the incursion of abstract reasoning on legal doctrine, just as Wigmore would six years later in the *Treatise*. In the first pages of the *Preliminary Treatise*, Thayer remarked that the law of evidence "is not concerned with nice definitions, or the exacter [*sic*] academic operations of the logical faculty. It is attending to practical ends." He lamented that "a bastard sort of technicality has thus sprung up, and a crop of fanciful reasons for anomalies destitute of reason, which baffle and disgust a healthy mind." On the subject of the parol evidence rule, which prevented parties from admitting evidence that contravened the terms of a contract, Thayer criticized the "mere rules of procedure, and reason, and logic which overloads it." The notion that logic could "overload" an area of law reflects the standard modernist concern that a fetish for logical form had come at the expense of common sense.[9]

In a critique that anticipated Wigmore's, Thayer chastised the judiciary for obscuring the reality of law behind a façade of logic. According to Thayer, judges denied that they legislated from the bench because such a notion was "not quite in harmony with the general attitude of the common-law courts and their humble phraseology in disclaiming the office of legislation." In actuality, he asserted, adjudicating amid "ever-changing combinations of fact" forced the bench to "constantly legislate" and "it is best that this be openly done." Thayer further dismissed as pure fantasy the expectation that formalistic modes of judicial analysis would result in the uniform application of the law. "Judges, and whole benches of them," he observed, "may decide such questions differently, while perfectly agreeing on the rule of law and keeping within it." In Thayer's view, the legal fraternity had to countenance the hard realities of legal practice rather than seek refuge behind the comforting fictions of legal theory.[10]

Thayer maintained that where logic had led the legal fraternity astray, experience could guide the law in more sensible directions. In a broad sense, Thayer's entire treatise, with its emphasis on legal history, embodied his faith in experience as a tool to shape doctrine. Turning to a specific example, Thayer noted that courts often employed "reasonableness" as a legal standard for behavior, and he directed the legal system to rely on "its fund of general experience" to determine the limitations of this ambiguous term. Similarly, the interpretation of documents "may depend on no legal rule, but only on the rules, principles, or usages of language and grammar, as applied by sense and experience." Thayer also noted that juries often had to "estimate damages and to act upon expert testimony" by "bringing into play that general fund of experience and knowledge" from which "they must in all cases draw." He was keen, however, to draw a distinction between the mental gymnastics of farcical logic and legitimate logical analyses derived from experience. "The law furnishes no test of relevancy," Thayer declared. "For this, it tacitly refers to logic *and* general experience" [emphasis added]. Wigmore would later voice the same contention that logic and experience were ultimately reconcilable.[11]

In addition to the primacy of experience, Thayer advocated an anti-universalist approach. To qualify, Thayer did maintain that "certain great principles" should govern evidence law, but he saw these principles as flexible guidelines rather than categorical dictates. For Thayer, certainty was quixotic. The law of evidence, he maintained, could never achieve "exact results; it deals with probabilities and not with certainties; it works in an atmosphere, and not in a vacuum; it has to allow for friction, for accident and mischance." He praised the "more elastic procedure of the English courts," which offered a contrast to the rigidity of their American counterparts.[12]

The influence of Thayer's anti-universalism on Wigmore is evident in their parallel treatments of the parol evidence rule. Thayer reviewed a dissent relating to parol evidence authored by the English judge Lord Chief Justice John Holt (1642–1710). Holt had argued that the meaning of a will should derive only from its terms and not from evidence of the circumstances in which the will was formulated. In Thayer's estimation, Holt had lapsed into a false sense of absolutism unresponsive to the contingencies of the real world. "The Chief Justice," wrote Thayer, "here retires into that lawyer's Paradise where all words have a fixed, precisely ascertained meaning." While "men have dreamed of attaining" an "absolute security," "the fatal necessity of looking outside the text in order to identify persons and things tends steadily to destroy such illusions and to reveal the essential imperfection of language." In his own discussion of parol evidence in the *Treatise*, Wigmore quoted this very passage from Thayer. Chiding the opinion of another English judge who presumed that "certainty of interpretation can be had," Wigmore was drawn to the same conclusion as Thayer: "It is a dream of the impossible."[13]

Alongside his emphasis on experience and his anti-universalist ethic, Thayer believed that law was part of the broader social fabric. For example, he situated the transition from legal practice premised on supernatural beliefs to more rational methods in the context of monarchical authority. "Where royal power was vigorous," Thayer recounted, "it required safer and directer ways of settling those matters of fact on which its revenues depended than the rude, superstitious, one–sided methods which were followed in the popular courts." In another instance, Thayer explained the origins of judicial notice of almanacs with reference to the proliferation of holidays (judicial notice was a convention by which a judge could admit an alleged fact without evidence). "The multitude and multiplication of saints and saints' days" as well as "the intricacies attending upon the notion of movable feasts" both rendered it difficult "to find out the details of the calendar for any given year; so that the courts were assisted by written and printed tables of more or less authority." Wigmore cited this section of the *Preliminary Treatise* in his own discussion of the admission of almanacs. Thayer further indicated his belief in the interdependence of law and society when he expressed optimism that the communications revolution of his own era would herald the rapid expansion of "enlightened modes of proof." Noting the endurance of outdated legal conventions, Thayer reflected, "Perhaps it will be otherwise as the superior and elect minds of our race come to find an audience among the men of their own day—a thing more and more happening as swift means of communication make all men neighbors." Although Wigmore relied heavily on Thayer's work, Wigmore ultimately made much more of an effort than did his mentor to situate legal developments against the backdrop of sweeping social forces.[14]

Yet another modernist tendency in the *Preliminary Treatise* was its call for increased judicial discretion. "In our own administration of the law of evidence," warned Thayer, "too many abuses are allowed, and the power of the courts is far too little exercised in controlling the eager lawyer in his endeavors to press to an extreme the application of the rules." He lauded "rules regulating the examination of witnesses" because "fortunately they allow much more discretion to the judges in administering them than is found in most of the rules of evidence." Thayer further advocated that, contrary to contemporary practice, the determination of the existence of a particular foreign law should be a matter for the judge rather than the jury. Regarding judicial notice, he insisted, "it is an instrument of great capacity in the hands of a competent judge; and is not nearly as much used, in the region of practice and evidence, as it should be." In his own endorsement of expanded judicial notice, Wigmore quoted this very portion of the *Preliminary Treatise*.[15]

While Thayer called for greater judicial discretion in the procedural realm of evidence law, he was explicit about the need for restraint from the bench in substantive law. Thayer contended, "It would never do to submit to the free control of the judges, through rules of court, the great mass of substantive law that now lies disguised under the name of the law of evidence." Thayer's sentiment here had origins in a *Harvard Law Review* article that he had authored in 1893 and that endures as his best-known contribution to American law. In that piece, Thayer first delineated the quintessential modernist argument that judges should abstain from striking down social welfare legislation in the exercise of judicial review. For Thayer, a law was valid not if the judge personally believed in its constitutionality but if *anyone* rationally could. His principle of judicial restraint "recognizes that, having regard to the great, complex, ever-unfolding exigencies of government, much which will seem unconstitutional to one man, or body of men, may reasonably not seem so to another; that the constitution often admits of different interpretations." According to Thayer, the bench cannot invalidate legislation "merely because it is concluded that upon a just and true construction the law is unconstitutional." A judge can only disallow a legislative act "when those who have the right to make laws have not merely made a mistake, but have made a very clear one,—so clear that it is not open to rational question."[16]

Holmes thrust Thayer's theory of judicial restraint into the center of American jurisprudence in 1905 when Holmes used Thayer's reasoning in a famous dissent. In *Lochner v. New York*, the Supreme Court invalidated a New York law intended to protect the health of bakers by limiting their working hours to sixty per week. Traditionally, historians have characterized the *Lochner* decision as the epitome of formal legal thought because it prevented the legislature from interfering in the free market and thus putatively embodied the "night watchman" ideal of the state. Indeed, "*Lochner*-era jurisprudence" has served as a synonym for formal legal thought.[17]

Other scholars dispute this conventional understanding of *Lochner*. They note that, in the majority opinion, Justice Rufus Peckham did *not* frame the case in terms of the absolute liberty of the individual to contract his labor against the creeping power of the state. Peckham readily conceded that "a fair, reasonable and appropriate exercise of the police power of the State" to enact health regulations would pass constitutional muster. In the case before him, however, Peckham concluded that "the limitation of the hours of labor as provided for in" the New York labor law bore "no direct relation to, and no such substantial effect upon, the health of the employee as to justify us in regarding the section as really a health law." So while the high court may have been unconvinced of the dangers posed to bakers, neither did it sanctify the free market as inviolable.[18]

Nevertheless, Holmes blasted the majority for arbitrarily reading laissez-faire into the Constitution. In one of the most celebrated dissents in American legal history, he announced, "This case is decided upon an economic theory which a large part of the country does not entertain." The Constitution, Holmes insisted, was agnostic on the question of economics. "The Fourteenth Amendment does not enact Mr. Herbert Spencer's Social Statics," he wrote, referring to the British scholar's 1851 book that argued laissez-faire was of a piece with natural law. For Holmes, a judge's personal economic views ought to have no bearing on the law: "I strongly believe that my agreement or disagreement [with laissez-faire] has nothing to do with the right of a majority to embody their opinions in law." By arguing that the bench had no authority to substitute its idiosyncratic beliefs for the judgment of the legislature, Holmes here offered, without citing Thayer, a direct application of his mentor's theory of judicial restraint (even if Holmes had created something of a straw man).[19]

In fact, Wigmore had anticipated Holmes's reasoning the previous year in the *Treatise*. Attributing to the bench "a righteous desire to check at any cost the misdoings of Legislatures," Wigmore rebuked efforts to make the judiciary "a second and higher Legislature." He felt that a democracy thrived by electing good representatives rather than "trusting a faithful Judiciary to check an evil Legislature." "The sensible solution is not to patch and mend casual errors by asking the Judiciary to violate legal principle and to do impossibilities with the Constitution," argued Wigmore, "but to represent ourselves with competent, careful, and honest legislators, the work of whose hands on the statute-roll may come to reflect credit upon the name of popular government."[20]

When Wigmore revisited the subject of judicial review later in the *Treatise*, he turned his attention specifically to the relationship between "economic science" and the Constitution. Whereas Thayer argued that a piece of legislation with any credible purchase on rationality passes constitutional muster, Wigmore pushed Thayer's logic further by suggesting that the bench should not strike down even brazenly irrational laws. "If the Legislature can make a rule of evidence at all," he proffered, "it cannot be controlled by a judicial standard of rationality, any more than its economic fallacies can be invalidated by the judicial conceptions of economic truth. Apart from the Constitution, the Legislature is not obliged to obey either the axioms of rational evidence or the axioms of economic science." In his general deference to the legislature and in his view that the law sanctions no specific economic theory, Wigmore articulated the very analysis that traced its origins to Thayer and would soon achieve lasting fame with Holmes.[21]

Consistent with legal modernism, Thayer's *Preliminary Treatise* demonstrated a suspicion of innate categories and treated classification as a contingent and somewhat arbitrary enterprise. For instance, he rejected any natural distinction between "law" and "fact." This dichotomy was particularly relevant for the rules of evidence because law was the domain of the judge while fact ultimately rested with the jury. Thayer understood that discriminations between law and fact were historically fluid. He related how in cases of negligence, courts had once considered the question of whether "one conformed to the standard of the prudent and reasonable man" to be a legal rather than factual inquiry. In his own day, Thayer reported, "questions of reasonable conduct" were now "clearly recognized as a question of fact for a jury."[22]

Wigmore's discussion of the opinion rule in the *Treatise* bespeaks Thayer's influence on the issue of classification. This particular doctrine prohibited witnesses from offering inferences that the jury could draw on its own. Thayer conceded, "In a sense all testimony to matter of fact [*sic*] is opinion evidence; *i. e.*, it is a conclusion formed from phenomena and mental impressions." Finding, then, the distinction between "fact" and "opinion" an arbitrary one, Thayer instead relied on a consequentialist test: "Any rule excluding opinion evidence is limited to cases where, in the judgment of the court, it will not be helpful to the jury. Whether accepted in [these] terms or not, this view largely governs the administration of the rule." Wigmore's analysis parroted Thayer's. "There is no virtue in any test based on the mere verbal or logical distinction between 'opinion' and 'fact,'" Wigmore argued. "No such distinction is scientifically possible. . . . Nearly everything which we choose to call 'fact' either is or may be only 'opinion' or inference." Ultimately, the constructed nature of legal categories was a much more prevalent theme in Wigmore's *Treatise* than in Thayer's.[23]

Practicality was another recurring motif in Thayer's treatise. "The peculiar character and scope of legal reasoning," Thayer contended, "is determined by its purely practical aims and the necessities of its procedure and machinery." On the topic of litigation, he wrote, "It must shape itself to various other exigencies of a practical kind, such as the time that it is possible to allow to any particular case, the reasonable limitations of the number of witnesses, the opportunities for reply, and the chance to correct errors." Moreover, the law's "special limitations, exclusions, and qualifications" all "spring from the practical aims of a court of justice and the practical conditions of its work." Thayer also praised the jury system for elevating pragmatism as an organizing principle of law: "The jury system has reacted upon [judges], and upon the body of law which they administer, in a way to keep forever in the foreground, in determining matters of fact, the thought of convenience, and of easily applied principles of practical sense." In determining which party shouldered the burden of proof, Thayer announced, "Now, and at all times, the tests of justice and practical convenience are legitimate ones." This emphasis on practicality would readily characterize Wigmore's work.[24]

Thayer frequently appraised evidence rules based on their effects rather than their internal logic. While he endorsed the doctrine "that *prima facie* the language of a document shall have its natural and proper meaning," Thayer still insisted that it was possible for the court "to make words bear other meanings than the usual and proper ones, in order to avoid absurd or unreasonable results." In another instance, Thayer dismissed the import of semantics and instead maintained, "The important question in any particular instance is what is the effect and operation of the rule, not what its name is." On the topic of litigation, he suggested, "It must adjust its processes to general ends, so as generally to promote justice, and to discourage evil, to maintain long-established rights, and the existing governmental order." This was precisely the kind of outcome-based philosophy that Wigmore would employ in the *Treatise*.[25]

While Wigmore sometimes took issue with Jeremy Bentham's ideas in the *Treatise*, any departure from Thayer was much less outspoken. Bentham, like Wigmore, had produced a monumental treatise on evidence practice; Thayer, by contrast, wrote a comparatively brief meditation on history and theory. As a result, there were simply more occasions for Wigmore to disagree with Bentham. Another potential explanation for this discrepancy concerns Wigmore's relationship with Thayer; Wigmore may have been reticent to openly criticize the ideas of a man who had not only mentored him but who had died only recently. It is a matter for speculation how Thayer's sequel to the *Preliminary Treatise*, had he ever finished it, would have dovetailed with or diverged from Wigmore's. Thayer had done considerable legwork in the preparation of the next volume, but it is difficult to decipher his master plan from his handwritten notes.[26]

Although Wigmore proved reticent to critique Thayer in the *Treatise*, during Thayer's life, his protégé frequently acknowledged in correspondence their differences of approach. At first Wigmore was sheepish about distancing himself from his former professor. In 1898, he confessed to Thayer, "on matters of classification and analysis, I am sometimes unfortunate enough to find myself taking a different attitude from yourself." Two years later, referring to Thayer's casebook, Wigmore belatedly offered "a suggestion which I wanted to make before this, but did not have the courage to advance." Wigmore went on to recommend a "larger selection of cases on the Examination and Impeachment of Witnesses" and added, somewhat obsequiously, "I hope you will not think me to be intruding with this suggestion." Thayer proved quite amenable to Wigmore's advice and implored, "Pray give me any other hints. I wish I had written to you before." Soon after, Thayer assured his former student, "It would be a real favor if you would let me have good criticism." Eventually, Wigmore traded his deferential language in favor of more direct feedback. Responding to Thayer's suggested historical development of two legal doctrines, Wigmore offered bluntly in a 1902 letter, "I doubt the significance you suggest." It appears that the disciple had finally stepped out from the long shadow of his father-confessor. According to the historical record, this was the last letter that Wigmore ever sent Thayer. Within three weeks, Thayer would be dead, his treatise forever unfinished, and Wigmore left on his own to steward evidence law into the twentieth century. Two years later, Wigmore published his *Treatise*, dedicated, of course, to "the great master"—James Bradley Thayer.[27]

Oliver Wendell Holmes Jr.

Oliver Wendell Holmes Jr. (1841–1935) was the father of modern legal thought. Generations of jurists looked to Holmes as a lodestar, his body of scholarship and dicta as a rich repository of wisdom to guide them in their reformation of American law. With the exception of sociological jurisprudence, he articulated every major component of the modernist agenda. Holmes was, perhaps, the greatest legal thinker in American history.

Holmes was born in Boston on March 8, 1841. His father, Oliver Wendell Holmes Sr., was the superlative well-rounded New England gentleman. A gifted orator, novelist, Harvard anatomy professor, founder of the *Atlantic Monthly*, and poet, the elder Holmes towered over his ambitious son. Holmes Jr., following in the tradition of his father and grandfathers, enrolled in Harvard in 1857. As domestic political strife degenerated into civil war, Holmes found himself drawn to the abolitionist cause and enlisted in the Union military while he was still an undergraduate. He sustained a near-fatal shot to the chest at Ball's Bluff and narrowly escaped death once again when a bullet pierced his neck at Antietam.[28]

Disabused of his romantic perception of war, Holmes returned to Boston in 1864 and entered Harvard Law School. He joined a local law firm two years later where he drafted contracts and developed a specialty in admiralty law. Unfulfilled by legal practice, Holmes found intellectual engagement as a contributor to and then editor of the *American Law Review*. Throughout the 1870s, Holmes continued to practice law and publish academic work. In 1880, Holmes's scholarly development culminated in a series of lectures (delivered without notes to a packed audience) that he soon collated into a book that would achieve canonical status—*The Common Law*. After accepting a full-time professorship at Harvard Law School in 1882, Holmes resigned only three months later when Massachusetts governor John Lang offered him a seat on the state's supreme judicial court.[29]

Holmes served on the Massachusetts high court for twenty years, the final three as chief justice. Life on the bench failed to enthrall the cerebral Holmes, so he continued to lecture and produce scholarship in search of stimulation that he despaired of finding in the courthouse. At Boston University in 1897,

Holmes delivered his best-known address, "The Path of the Law," which became famous for its contention that law was merely politics, an exercise in the balance of competing social interests. When a vacancy opened on the United States Supreme Court in 1902, President Theodore Roosevelt heeded the recommendation of Senator Henry Cabot Lodge, a childhood friend of Holmes, and nominated the Massachusetts chief justice; all three men were alumni of the Porcellian Club at Harvard.[30]

Holmes served for thirty years as a Supreme Court justice. He possessed a remarkable ability to analyze a complex case quickly and formulate a pithy decision. His writing evinced the same literary flair that had earned him the title of class poet at Harvard. Known as "The Great Dissenter," Holmes became the darling of young progressives for minority opinions that recognized the rights of organized labor and the prerogative of state legislatures to attenuate the effects of capitalism. Ironically, Holmes sided with the capitalists in his personal views, but he also believed that the Constitution failed to endow him with the authority to invalidate social welfare legislation. On the platform of the nation's highest court and with the vocal support of loyal acolytes, Holmes earned a national reputation in his final decades that exceeded even that of his celebrated father. The ninety-one-year-old Holmes retired in 1932 as the oldest justice in the Court's history. When he died three years later, the justices of the Supreme Court carried the coffin of the Civil War veteran. He was laid to rest in Arlington National Cemetery.[31]

Like Wigmore, Holmes came under the tutelage of Thayer early in life. Thayer was a partner at the law firm where Holmes worked in the years just after the Civil War. During this time, James Kent, the grandson of the famous American jurist of the same name, asked Thayer to prepare a new edition of his grandfather's classic work, *Commentaries on American Law*. Thayer solicited Holmes's assistance and thus provided the young lawyer with his first major publishing opportunity. A decade later, Thayer was in the audience for Holmes's lecture series that led to the publication of *The Common Law*. Impressed with Holmes's performance, Thayer recommended him to Governor Long for the judiciary. After Long initially passed over Holmes, Thayer, with the help of Louis Brandeis, raised the funds for a new professorship for Holmes at Harvard Law. In other words, no one did more than Thayer to facilitate Holmes's early ascension in the legal community.[32]

Sixty years after Thayer's death, the recent Supreme Court retiree Felix Frankfurter reflected on Thayer's tremendous influence: "Both Holmes and Brandeis influenced me in my constitutional outlook, but both of them derived theirs from the same source from which I derived mine, namely, James Bradley

Thayer." Notably, in "The Path of the Law," Holmes lauded Thayer's historical approach, later praised his *Preliminary Treatise*, and drew on Thayer's theory of judicial restraint in his celebrated *Lochner* dissent. The overlap between the jurisprudential views of Holmes and Wigmore is hardly surprising in light of this shared intellectual lineage.[33]

Holmes's impact on Wigmore took place in the context of a close personal connection that spanned nearly fifty years. Wigmore and Holmes began exchanging letters in 1887, when Holmes informed the twenty-four-year-old Wigmore, "I have read your articles on Boycotting and Interference with Social Relations with much interest and hope that as soon as I get through sitting with the full court you will give me an opportunity to talk with you about them." Holmes went on to praise Wigmore's "historical examination" as "a first rate piece of work." No doubt, such a compliment from a justice on the Massachusetts Supreme Judicial Court was a great source of encouragement and pride for the young Wigmore.[34]

Holmes continued to read Wigmore's academic work and encouraged the aspiring scholar throughout Wigmore's earliest years in academia. In 1891, Holmes wrote Wigmore, "All I can say is to thank you, to express my belief in the value of your publication. . . . I shall always hear with interest of your work and shall hope for and anticipate your success." A few years later, Holmes assured Wigmore, "You have every good wish from me in this career which you have begun with so much promise and success." Wigmore, in turn, thrived on Holmes's support. When Holmes expressed interest in Wigmore's work on Japanese law the following year, the young law professor responded, "It gave me great pleasure to hear that the subject attracted your notice." Wigmore lamented that "the science of comparative law arouses no interest except among a very few scholars like yourself," and so he was "glad for every trifle of encouragement." In 1893, Holmes caught Wigmore near Young's Hotel in Boston and asked the budding academic to join him for lunch at his window table in the hotel restaurant. Wigmore was distressed over his own career, but Holmes's reassurance fortified Wigmore's faith in himself. Nearly four decades afterward, Wigmore recalled the meal in a birthday letter to Holmes. "Other utterances of yours have had national influence," Wigmore observed, "but your words on that day have been like apples of silver to *me*; and on this your anniversary I like to repeat to you this acknowledgement of your influence upon your admiring disciple."[35]

Holmes's visit to Northwestern Law School in 1902 is the most illustrative example of both Holmes's deep investment in Wigmore and Wigmore's acute veneration of Holmes. Northwestern Law was set to move into the Tremont

House, where Abraham Lincoln had challenged Stephen Douglas to their famous debates. Holmes acceded to Wigmore's request to serve as the guest of honor. It was the first and only time that Holmes traveled west of the Allegheny Mountains. Eager to impress the Supreme Court's latest nominee, Wigmore had hung up a portrait of Holmes in the law school. "It will be an inspiration to our young men," Wigmore relayed to Holmes, "as they look up from the perusal of good Massachusetts opinions." With Thayer only recently laid to rest, Holmes was all the more important a mentor to Wigmore.[36]

Wigmore prepared an elaborate ceremony to honor Holmes's appearance at the dedication of the new law building. On October 20, 1902, the university trustees headed a procession, followed by the faculty, then federal and state judges, alumni, and finally, Holmes, flanked by Wigmore and Judge O. H. Horton, vice president of the board of trustees. Colonel Frank O. Lowden, president of the alumni, asked that Holmes sign and date a glass panel with a diamond pencil to commemorate his visit. Lowden presented the pencil as a gift to Holmes, but Wigmore was eager to keep the memento and even asked Holmes to return it after the visit. "Possessing as yet but few traditions, yet keenly appreciating their helpfulness, we were determined to preserve all that pertains to the Holmes tradition," Wigmore explained to Holmes. For his part, Holmes was happy to indulge his fervent admirer: "I am glad that you sent for it as I would much rather the College should have it than I."[37]

It is little surprise that Wigmore took pains to secure a seemingly trivial keepsake with which to remember the occasion; Holmes had effusively praised Wigmore in his keynote address at the ceremony. Originally, Holmes expressed reluctance to speak much, but Wigmore was keen for the Massachusetts chief justice to say something. Referring to the elder Holmes's prolific reputation for oratory, Wigmore aimed to flatter the younger Holmes and observed, "Truly, the father's gift of utterance has descended." Holmes acquiesced and delivered two speeches, one that had a lasting impact on Wigmore, then dean of the law school. "I never have had an opportunity to give public expression to my sense of the value of the work of your accomplished dean," Holmes announced to the gathering. "I wish now to express my respect for his great learning and originality and for the volume and delicacy of his production." In a letter to the wife of English jurisprudent Frederick Pollock, Holmes revealed that his generous comments were more than just polite. "As I soaped the Dean I was sure of having one nearer in my favor," he recalled. "But I said no more than I meant. The next pleasantest thing to be intelligently cracked up oneself is to give a boost to a younger man who seems to deserve it, and who has not yet had much public recognition." As an indication of the enduring pride that

Northwestern University
School of Law

RESPECTFULLY REQUESTS YOUR PRESENCE AT A
RECEPTION IN HONOR OF THE

HONORABLE OLIVER WENDELL HOLMES
CHIEF JUSTICE OF THE SUPREME JUDICIAL COURT OF MASSACHUSETTS
AND NOMINATED TO BE ASSOCIATE JUSTICE OF THE
SUPREME COURT OF THE UNITED STATES

ASSISTED BY THE

FEDERAL AND STATE JUDGES IN CHICAGO

ON THE OCCASION OF THE

DEDICATION OF THE NEW QUARTERS
OF THE SCHOOL

MONDAY EVENING OCTOBER TWENTIETH
ONE THOUSAND NINE HUNDRED AND TWO
AT HALF PAST EIGHT

NORTHWESTERN UNIVERSITY BUILDING
LAKE AND DEARBORN STREETS
CHICAGO

Fig. 3: Box 65, Folder 25, Wigmore Papers.

Wigmore felt, he had Holmes's speech reprinted thirty years later, upon the justice's retirement from the Supreme Court, for Northwestern Law students and alumni.[38]

In the midst of this genial and nurturing relationship, Holmes greatly influenced Wigmore's conception of the law and, indirectly, his treatment of evidence doctrine. In particular, Holmes's seminal book, *The Common Law* (1881), was profoundly important in directing Wigmore (as well as the broader legal fraternity) in a modernist direction. Its opening passage is perhaps the most famous in any American book on law and set the terms for the modernist enterprise for the next sixty years. Here appeared Holmes's timeless maxim, "The life of the law has not been logic: it has been experience." Holmes continued, "The felt necessities of the time, the prevalent moral and political theories, intuitions of public policy, avowed or unconscious, even the prejudices which judges share with their fellow-men, have had a good deal more to do than the syllogism in determining the rules by which men should be governed." In other words, Holmes called for analysis that penetrated past the veneer of logic expressed in judicial decisions to the substratum of practicalities, policies, and prejudices that truly informed legal doctrine—all key elements in Wigmore's approach to evidence law. Holmes stressed the importance of understanding law in a broad social context because "the law embodies the story of a nation's development through many centuries, and it cannot be dealt with as if it contained only the axioms and corollaries of a book of mathematics." In fact, Wigmore would do much more than Holmes to contextualize legal history.[39]

Any mention of *The Common Law* requires some qualification. Despite Holmes's bold and sweeping introductory remarks, reviews of the book indicate that his ideas were not truly iconoclastic at the time but indicative of a nascent movement. Moreover, the remainder of the book—which covered topics as varied as torts, contracts, and criminal law—did not rigorously apply modernist philosophy. For instance, Holmes focused on the substance of legal doctrine with little concern for external factors. *The Common Law*, then, was important primarily for the influence of its opening paragraphs.[40]

Wigmore distinguished himself from other students of *The Common Law* in two ways. First, he appreciated the full significance of Holmes's contribution well before most other jurists. While the legal community came to consider *The Common Law* one of the classic texts in American law only by the 1920s, Wigmore grew enamored of the book when Holmes was a little-known state judge and Wigmore still a law student. He once relayed to Holmes, "I do not forget the thrill with which I first read The Common Law in 1886." After finishing the book, Wigmore fell ill, and his classmate Joe Beale lent Wigmore his lecture notes. To express his gratitude, Wigmore presented Beale with a copy of *The Common Law*. When Holmes retired from the US Supreme Court, Wigmore indicated to Holmes that "your standard of learning in 'The Common Law' gave the first push to my latent urgings." The second noteworthy reason for Wigmore's interest in *The Common Law* is that he internalized not only the broad precepts articulated in its introduction but also saw in the midst of its dense body the tools he needed to reform evidence law.[41]

Wigmore's application to evidence law of Holmes's tort principle exemplifies how *The Common Law* helped cultivate Wigmore's modernism. Torts comprise an area of civil law concerning the legal responsibility of one party for harm done to another in circumstances not involving contracts. In the latter half of the nineteenth century, the explosive growth of factories, railroads, and new technologies created novel kinds of injuries, and older conceptions of torts proved increasingly inadequate. In *The Common Law*, Holmes argued that courts should employ a flexible reasonableness standard in assessing the liability of defendants; if "the ideal average prudent man" could not have foreseen the injury, then the tribunal should not hold him liable. In discussing this standard, Holmes indicated a preference for case-by-case analyses rather than universal dictates: "The featureless generality that the defendant was bound to use such care as a prudent man would do under the circumstances, ought to be continually giving place to the specific one, that he was bound to use this or that precaution under these or those circumstances." For Holmes, context mattered. The source of his reasonableness standard was experience. "The tendency of a given act to cause harm under given circumstances," he declared, "must be determined by *experience*" [emphasis added]. This standard was part and parcel of a broader theory of torts that prized the real-world outcome rather than logical integrity of legal doctrine. Holmes also organized torts in a functional rather than syllogistic classification scheme. In other words, his tort theory in general and his reasonableness standard in particular were integral to Holmes's far-reaching modernist agenda.[42]

Wigmore seized on Holmes's tort analysis and teased out its normative implications for evidence law. Consider Wigmore's approach to the dilemma of reconciling the internal standard of intent with the external standard of action in the domain of legal acts. To use Wigmore's example, "Doe and Roe go through the form of marriage, Doe secretly intending it in jest, but Roe seriously." The disconnect between Doe's intention and action raised the question of whether Doe's internal desire to jest or external performance of marriage dictated the legality of the act. Wigmore refused to choose between either standard. With anti-universalist zeal, Wigmore declared, "We are to accept neither solution in this absolute form. . . . No practical system of law could be content with either, applied in rigid uniformity." For Wigmore, there was no essential element in volition or expression that provided guidance; "it is rather a question of the relation between the two elements." In formulating a solution, Wigmore advised that "the general doctrine of legal acts" use "the test of *negligence, i. e.* responsibility resting on a volition having consequences which ought reasonably to have been foreseen." Wigmore afforded Holmes full credit: "For tortious responsibility, its phrasing was first broadly given in the epoch-making book of Mr. Justice Holmes, The Common Law." Following Holmes, Wigmore defined reasonableness with reference to both experience and the idiosyncratic demands of individual cases. A standard of reasonable foresight, wrote Wigmore, hinged "on varying experience in different epochs and communities and in different kinds of transactions." In borrowing from Holmes's conceptual toolbox, Wigmore employed many different elements of the modernist enterprise.[43]

Wigmore found Holmes's negligence standard fruitful for his treatment of evidence doctrine; Wigmore had long expressed interest in and enthusiasm for Holmes's approach to torts. In 1894, Wigmore sent Holmes a lengthy letter praising the justice's recent article on the subject. "I write this now," Wigmore related, "in the ardor of pleasure at finding in the current Law Review that your great support can now be claimed for what has been for two or three years a solid conviction of mine, what I may call the tripartite division of tort-questions." "I have groaned in spirit at the difficulty of persuading the profession to accept this" position, Wigmore continued, "but now that you have said it, it must 'go,' and other men will be listened to where you have sanctioned the thesis they are advancing." Describing in some detail his own approach to torts, Wigmore referenced *The Common Law* as a source of guidance. For his part, Holmes warmly welcomed the admiration of the young Wigmore: "As far as I see we agree in our views substantially, and your kind expressions give me great pleasure." Wigmore, who had recently cited *The Common Law* in his own article on torts in the *Harvard Law Review*, soon produced two more articles that also drew heavily from Holmes's book. Not surprisingly, they quickly met with Holmes's approval: "In my turn I have been much pleased with your two last articles. They seem to me very sound and suggestive. If you ever come this way let me know it, I beg." By the time Wigmore applied Holmes's tort standard of reasonable foresight to the rules of evidence, he had been corresponding with Holmes about tort law for over a decade.[44]

The origins of Wigmore's support for judicial discretion further highlight how *The Common Law* informed the *Treatise*. Holmes may have advocated judicial deference to the legislature when it came to assessing the constitutionality of social welfare legislation, but he favored the expertise of the bench over the general experience of the lay jury. He first learned the value of expertise on the front lines of the Civil War, where soldiers schooled in battlefield tactics proved far more useful than amateur fighters. In *The Common Law*, Holmes indicated a preference for judicial discretion in a discussion of torts. Facts were the domain of the jury and law that of the judge, but reasonable foresight was both a factual and legal standard. While "there are many cases, no doubt, in which the court would lean for aid upon a jury," Holmes wrote, "as the circumstances become more numerous and complex, the tendency to cut the knot with the jury becomes greater." Referencing this passage, Wigmore displayed a similar willingness to remove questions of negligence from the juror and entrust them to the judge. According to Wigmore, when a "definite rule of law, more precise and concrete" than the reasonable foresight standard "has been framed for determining the effect of the person's conduct, this rule of law may, in the hands of the judge, conclude the question; and it may cease to be a question of fact for the jury to the extent that the rule of law applies." For Holmes and Wigmore, tribunals were vehicles for public policy, and the judge was more favorably positioned than the jury to accord the resolution of an individual case with the aggregate social welfare.[45]

Holmes's faith in judicial discretion influenced Wigmore's approach to evidence that tended to confuse the jury. Wigmore refused to impose an unconditional mandate excluding such evidence, and advised the justice system to take advantage of "a simple expedient"—"the discretion of the trial Court." "The whole objection in question," Wigmore explained, "is mainly (as Mr. Justice Holmes has neatly put it) 'a purely practical one, a concession to the shortness of life'; and it would be unworthy of the genius of our law if Courts should feel obliged to lay down a hard-and-fast rule of exclusion when such a simple expedient was at hand." Wigmore's invocation of the high priest of modern legal thought here underscores Wigmore's desire to rest his advocacy of judicial discretion on Holmes's body of work.[46]

Consequentialism was another jurisprudential value that Wigmore gleaned from Holmes's opinions and scholarship. One conspicuous example is found in Wigmore's discussion of a rule excluding evidence that "*disturb[ed] a plain meaning*" of the terms of a legal document. Unimpressed with most arguments in favor of this long-standing rule, Wigmore nevertheless appreciated the outcome-based reasoning of Holmes: "The real strength of the argument is rather found in the practical statement of Mr. Justice Holmes." Wigmore went on to quote an 1891 decision from Holmes where the justice had asserted, "You cannot prove a mere private convention between the two parties to give language a different meaning from its common one. It would offer too great risks if evidence were admissible to show that when they said 500 feet they agreed it should mean 100 inches, or that Bunker Hill Monument should signify the Old South Church." In other words, contracts would prove inoperable if courts constantly entertained doubts about unambiguous phrasing.[47]

Holmes made a similar point in his essay, "The Theory of Legal Interpretation." There, he advanced the position that when two parties disagreed on the meaning of the terms of contract, a "judge's interpretation of the words" must stand; otherwise, simply invalidating the contract "would greatly enhance the difficulty of enforcing contracts against losing parties." Holmes's results-oriented approach resonated with Wigmore, who quoted this "acute essay" by "the learned justice" in the *Treatise*.[48]

Holmes's renowned article "The Path of the Law" further impressed upon Wigmore the merits of consequentialism. "A body of law," announced Holmes, "is more rational and more civilized when every rule it contains is referred articulately and definitely to an end which it subserves, and when the grounds for desiring that end are stated or are ready to be stated in words." Wigmore chose this very quotation for the epigram of his *Treatise*.[49]

"The Path of the Law" voiced another theme that reverberated through Wigmore's rules of evidence—law as a social construct. Holmes sought to dispel the myth of law as some ethereal essence, a natural entity immanent within the universe. He warned that "nothing but confusion of thought can result from assuming that the rights of man in a moral sense are equally rights in the sense of the Constitution and the law." Despite the claims of the courts, the law was neither a "system of reason" nor a "deduction from principles of ethics or admitted axioms." In one of his most famous statements, Holmes then declared, "The prophecies of what the courts will do in fact, and nothing more pretentious, are what I mean by the law." Law is what judges do, nothing more.[50]

Modernists welcomed this reasoning because it was much easier to legitimate the regulation of legal rights if rights were constructs rather than inherent qualities of man. The dispute between progressives and conservatives over the legitimacy of "liberty of contract" illustrates the concrete stakes of redefining rights as constructed rather than natural. Some conservative judges exalted as a natural right the notion of "liberty of contract"—the idea that an employer and employee should remain at liberty to enter into a contract without interference from the state. From the progressive perspective, liberty of contract could have made sense as a principle if capital and labor possessed equal bargaining power. But in an industrializing America, the influx of immigrant laborers willing to work for subsistence wages meant that management was largely free to dictate the terms of employment. Congress and progressive state legislatures passed laws designed to mitigate this imbalance. In 1898, for instance, Congress forbade "yellow-dog" contracts, which had stipulated that employees of a given business could not join a union. Ten years later, the Supreme Court struck down Congress's prohibition on yellow-dog contracts as an unconstitutional encroachment on liberty of contract. If rights—including liberty of contract—were part of the natural order of the world, then judges were obliged to void legislation that interfered with the private sector. But if rights were merely social constructs, then the principle of liberty of contract had no more claim to legitimacy than a statute designed to regulate contracts. In fairness to the bench, most social welfare legislation in this era withstood judicial scrutiny. The minority of cases in which courts struck down progressive laws garnered outsized attention, which in turn made the judiciary seem more hostile to Progressivism than it was in reality.[51]

A constructivist understanding of law animated Wigmore's *Treatise*. In his view, the law was simply the judiciary's actual behavior. His classification of "simplicative rules" betokens Wigmore's constructivist view. These rules preemptively forbade evidence considered inimical to fact-finding. In organizing them according to their "actual operation," Wigmore concluded, "The final question always in the law of evidence is, What do the judges do?—and not, What do they say that they do? nor even, Why do they say that they do it?" In peeling back the layers of rhetorical sophistry and extracting the core of actual judicial practice, Wigmore loudly echoed Holmes's canonical aphorisms from "The Path of the Law."[52]

Wigmore wanted the bench to balance competing interests on a case-by-case basis—a stance informed by Holmes. In his 1894 article "Privilege, Malice, and Intent," Holmes rejected syllogistic reasoning and insisted on balancing tests. Judicial decisions, Holmes claimed, were merely social policy formulations involving a practical balancing of interests, even if judges were loath to admit it. "Questions of policy are legislative questions, and judges are shy of reasoning from such grounds." As a result, explained Holmes, decisions "often are presented as hollow deductions from empty general propositions." In reality, "the worth of the result, or the gain from allowing the act to be done, has to be compared with the loss which it inflicts. Therefore, the conclusion will vary, and will depend on different reasons according to the nature of the affair." In the words of one historian, Holmes's reasoning here constituted a revolutionary conceptual leap and "perhaps it is the moment we should identify as the beginning of modernism in American legal thought."[53]

That "Privilege, Malice, and Intent" had an immediate and profound effect upon Wigmore is evident in his effusive letter to Holmes praising the article just four days after its publication. "This is to express to you," wrote Wigmore, "my thankfulness at feeling that we have always with us a jurist—almost the only one—who can always be relied upon to penetrate to the innermost essentials of

legal reasoning." He exalted Holmes for clearing away "the arid waste of precedent by the higher criticism of careful analysis" and referred to him as "our
greatest American or English analyst and jurisprudent." While it is difficult to
draw a direct line between Holmes and any specific balancing test advocated by
Wigmore, given Holmes's seminal status in this domain and Wigmore's gushing
admiration of Holmes's article, it is reasonable to infer Wigmore's intellectual
debt on this count.[54]

Wigmore consistently brought an anti-universalist ethic to bear on the law
of evidence, a disposition likely inspired by Holmes's own rejection of absolutes. Holmes's classic statement of anti-universalism—"General propositions
do not decide concrete cases"—appeared in his *Lochner* dissent in 1905, yet his
disavowal of axiomatic truths dated back to the Civil War. On the battlefields of
Ball's Bluff and Antietam, Holmes experienced firsthand how an unmitigated
faith in one's own worldview made the violent enforcement of that view upon
others inevitable. In the 1870s, Thayer's childhood friend Chauncey Wright
further cultivated Holmes's nascent anti-universalism in an intellectual group
called the Metaphysical Club.[55]

As with balancing tests, there were no direct lines between Holmes's anti-
universalist declarations and Wigmore's revision of specific evidence rules because Holmes wrote very little about evidence. However, Wigmore would have
been familiar with Holmes's pithy proclamation from "The Path of the Law":
"The logical method and form flatter that longing for certainty and for repose
which is in every human mind. But certainty generally is illusion, and repose is
not the destiny of man." Moreover, Holmes's speech at the Northwestern Law
dedication in 1902 indicates that Wigmore had direct exposure to Holmes's
anti-universalist ethic at the very moment in which the young dean was crafting his evidence treatise. Aside from offering accolades for Wigmore, Holmes's
address concerned the idea of certainty. The law, Holmes reasoned, "would seem
commonplace to a mind that understood everything. But that is the weakness
of all truth. If instead of the joy of eternal pursuit you imagine yourself to
have mastered it as a complete whole, you would find yourself reduced to
the alternative of either finding" the "whole frame of the universe . . . a bore,
or of dilating with undying joy over the proposition that twice two is four."
Holmes's insight was that certainty was not only unobtainable but also undesirable. Wigmore would echo this repudiation of universality time and again in
his formulation of evidence law.[56]

Despite Wigmore's reverence for Holmes, he was nevertheless willing to criticize the reasoning of his mentor. Wigmore took issue, for instance, with *The
Common Law*'s distinction between voidable and void contracts (a party had

the option of invalidating a voidable contract, whereas void contracts had no legal force). Holmes was well aware of Wigmore's criticisms and took them in stride. In Holmes's Northwestern address, he acknowledged that while "I have come in for my share of criticism from" Wigmore, "also I have had from him words which have given me new courage on a lonely road." Holmes expressed a similarly appreciative attitude in a letter to Lady Pollock when he mentioned that Wigmore "generally has pitched into me—the young fellows are apt to try their swords in that way—but his implications are flattering and his work good." Embracing diversity of opinion was an agreeable chore for the justice who would famously declare in 1915 (in an article that Wigmore had solicited for Northwestern's law review), "To have doubted one's own first principles is the mark of a civilized man."[57]

Jeremy Bentham

Jeremy Bentham (1748–1832) was one of England's greatest legal philosophers. While at the University of Oxford, he listened to the lectures of the legendary professor Sir William Blackstone and there developed an antagonism to the arcane English legal system. Indeed, one of Bentham's first major works offered a lengthy rebuke of Blackstone's enormously influential treatise, *Commentaries on the Laws of England*. Although trained as a lawyer, Bentham never tried a case in court and instead opted for a monastic life of scholarship with an eye toward reform.[58]

Bentham's voluminous body of work—covering topics as diverse as legal procedure, animal rights, and economic policy—was unified under the principle of utilitarianism. In *A Fragment on Government* (1776), Bentham summarized the philosophy that would characterize his writings for the rest of his life: "*It is the greatest happiness of the greatest number that is the measure of right and wrong.*" His study of evidence law offered a systematic application of this utilitarian ethic. Bentham's most important contribution to the field of evidence was his *Rationale of Judicial Evidence*, written between 1802 and 1814, a work later edited by John Stuart Mill and finally published in 1827. Nearly all of Wigmore's numerous references to Bentham come from the *Rationale*. A massive treatise, it directed the legislator to provide statutory guidelines for judges presiding over legal fact-finding. Bentham chastised contemporary evidence law for its abstruse and overly technical design, which he saw as a ruse to serve the financial interests of the legal fraternity.[59]

A few passages from the *Treatise* poignantly capture Wigmore's reverence for the sharp-tongued Englishman. "No one can say," remarked Wigmore, "how long our law might have waited for regeneration, if Bentham's diatribes had not lashed the community into a sense of its shortcomings." Wigmore included Bentham among those "names of extraordinary panoply in the law," and remarked that "we might almost regard his condemnation of any rule as presumptively an index of its ultimate downfall." More specifically, Wigmore celebrated Bentham's rejection of an evidence rule that rendered inadmissible an entire testimony if marred by a single lie. This privilege, Wigmore explained, "was only abolished from the law (long after it had practically lost its social acceptance) as a result of Bentham's pungent criticisms." He also extolled Bentham for denouncing an analogous privilege against the production of documents for one's opponent. "Nothing was done, nor even thought of being done," reported Wigmore, "until Bentham's righteous indignation lashed the time-honored crudities of the ancient privilege, and stirred up the young reformers of the 1800s to aggressive action." In sum, Wigmore idealized Bentham as an iconoclastic prophet speaking out against the false idols of his day.[60]

Historians throughout the twentieth century largely echoed Wigmore's assumption that Bentham was the catalyst for posthumous nineteenth-century reforms to the English law of evidence. By way of contrast, C. J. W. Allen's scholarship demonstrates that the similarities between the arguments of reformers and those of Bentham led to a case of mistaken causal attribution. For instance, Parliament extended a witness's right to affirm the veracity of his testimony without taking an oath on the Bible. Although Bentham had advocated such a measure, in fact it was the waning need for religion as a social cohesive—combined with an increasing skepticism about faith—that facilitated the acceptance of affirmations in lieu of oaths. In other instances, Parliament flatly rejected Benthamite proposals, such as his suggestion to compel defendants to testify. While Allen acknowledges that some Parliamentary reformers were influenced, in part, by Bentham's work, Allen illustrates that the consummate utilitarian was far more marginal than traditional histories allow.[61]

If historians typically exaggerate Bentham's role in English evidence law, then they underestimate his significance to the American rules of evidence. Admittedly, in Bentham's own time, his influence in the United States was limited, although not for lack of effort. In 1776, Bentham appeared an unlikely figure to cultivate an appreciation for the United States; he ghostwrote a repudiation of the American claim to independence. In time, however, Bentham came to laud the United States as a paragon of his utilitarian ethic and an antipode to the oligarchies of Europe. He once confessed in a letter to Andrew Jackson that he was "at heart more of a United-States-man than an Englishman."[62]

Unhappy only to admire the United States from afar, Bentham eagerly solicited opportunities to cleanse American law of the residue of its Old World heritage. He wrote directly to President James Madison in 1811 and offered to create, pro bono, criminal and civil legal codes for the United States. Madison did not accept. Over the next several years, Bentham enlisted the support of his friend John Quincy Adams to disseminate his writings, as Bentham hoped to convince individual state governors to implement Benthamite codes in their jurisdictions. Simon Snyder, governor of Pennsylvania, and William Plumer, governor of New Hampshire, both proved sympathetic to Bentham's overtures, but neither was able to galvanize the support of his respective legislature. Bentham also tried to appeal directly to the American people in their newspapers with flattery: "On the ground of Constitutional law,—you who on that ground have so nobly shaken off the yoke of English law—the system you have is to all essentials a model for all nations." Despite these considerable efforts, he could find no stateside patrons for his complimentary services.[63]

Notwithstanding Bentham's disappointment, his acolytes in the United States scored some notable successes. In the early nineteenth century, the statesman Edward Livingston persuaded Louisiana to adopt a code informed by Bentham's work. Before Livingston's reforms, Louisiana was mired in a complex amalgam of Spanish and French law. Rather than introduce the common law to Louisiana (so as to harmonize its system with the other American states), Livingston created a statutory code consistent with Benthamite proposals and principles. In the mid-nineteenth century, David Dudley Field II forged advances in New York state law; he too was a follower of Bentham's teachings.[64]

Maine's John Appleton offers the most conspicuous example of Bentham's American influence. A justice on the state's supreme judicial court from 1852 until 1883, Appleton drew heavily and explicitly from Bentham in his mission to reform the law of evidence. Thanks to Appleton's efforts, in 1864, Maine became the first jurisdiction in any common law country to provide defendants with the right to testify. According to Allen, "such an obvious example of Bentham's influence on particular law reforms is lacking in England." By recovering the import of Bentham's ideas to Wigmore's thought, this book lends credence to Allen's implication that—at least in the realm of evidence law—Bentham played a greater role in the United States than in his native land.[65]

It is tempting to use "modernization" as an organizing principle for comparing Bentham and Wigmore. After all, many Bentham scholars explain the efficacy of his ideas in the context of Britain's transition to an urban-industrial society. Even if Bentham's posthumous influence was negligible, one can still argue for the importance of modernization as a motif in his writings. Still, there are limits to the usefulness of "modernization" as a tool for comparison of Bentham and Wigmore. Some historians have situated Bentham within a

Weberian model of modernity that emphasized "a neatly organised pyramid of power," "rational criteria of appointment, promotion and hierarchy," and "uniformity, clarity, order and consistency . . . in both law and administration." Yet modernization in the Weberian sense only partially applies to Wigmore. He may have valued professionalization, but Wigmore also derided any quest for uniformity, clarity, and consistency as hopelessly quixotic. Max Weber himself specifically identified the common law, with its indeterminacies, as a poor fit for his model.[66]

In the end, Wigmore was neither a straightforward Benthamite transplanting the principle of utilitarianism to American soil nor a modernizer of the variety associated with Weber. Wigmore did, however, find in Bentham an approach toward evidence law that was consistent with the modernist values he had gleaned from Thayer and Holmes. Content to borrow from Bentham when it served his purposes, Wigmore disregarded the rest.

Turning to the parallels between Bentham and Wigmore, a pragmatic ethic that prized expedience was one of Bentham's most salient characteristics, and a number of evidentiary topics demonstrate how he shaped Wigmore's own approach to evidence law. For instance, they both critiqued the legal system for failing to facilitate greater pretrial discovery, the process by which each party collects and informs the other of its evidence. Bentham called for a robust "anticipative survey of the contents of the budget of evidence," which would allow a judge to exclude preemptively evidence that was "either irrelevant, or unnecessary, or unavailing," and thus spare the tribunal the effort "attached to the production" of the needless evidence. Citing Bentham, Wigmore voiced similar distress over "the limitations of the orthodox bill of discovery," which unwittingly endowed parties with either a "blind faith in the strength of their cause" or a "misguided assumption that the facts forming its defects and weaknesses are unknown to the adversaries and that their concealment to the last moment will heighten the chances of success." A more exhaustive discovery, claimed Wigmore, would afford a great "advantage to justice; because parties entertaining either belief without foundation would be disabused of it at an early moment" and "would perceive the uselessness of further contest in court." For civil cases, Wigmore hoped that actual trials would serve only as remedies of last resort.[67]

First Bentham and then Wigmore saw opportunities to expedite the judicial process in the admission of documents, underscoring their common ethic of practicality. Bentham noted that a party could challenge the authenticity of every document to delay the trial and increase the lawyers' fees in the hopes "of forcing his injured adversary out of the field of litigation by the pressure of expense." As a redress, Bentham proposed that the tribunal charge such additional expenses to the party questioning the document's authenticity, a policy designed to discourage frivolous challenges. Bentham further advocated the provisional admission of contested documents, which would be subject to "subsequent authentication." In the same vein, Wigmore proposed an "expedient for facilitating the proof" of documents in the form of "some sort of judicial admission." Wigmore related that "it was Bentham (as usual, one might say) who seems first to have proposed this measure."[68]

A shared instrumentalist orientation is further evident in their calls for official registers—yet another Benthamite cause that Wigmore resuscitated. Bentham bemoaned the incursion of "religious policy" on the credibility of official registers, such as the substitution of registrations of baptism for registrations of birth. According to Bentham, religious institutions had "deteriorated the whole mass of genealogical preappointed evidence." Referencing Bentham, Wigmore too stressed the importance of registers that recorded "the facts of birth, marriage, and death, with their times and places and the persons' names"—all "facts of pivotal importance in legal controversies." While some jurisdictions had made progress on this front, many others relied on "church registers of all sorts." "This indiscriminate sanction, liberal as it is, can be regarded only as a makeshift," Wigmore contended, "and fails to provide proper safeguards for the permanence and accuracy of records." Neither Bentham nor Wigmore was an opponent of religious denominations per se, but each possessed greater faith in the secular institutions of civil society.[69]

Bentham's belief in balancing tests also conditioned Wigmore's thought. Bentham called on judges to apply a perpetual balancing test that weighed the probative value of an article of evidence against its potential detriment. Potential bars to evidence came in three primary forms: vexation, expense, and delay. According to Bentham, the bench had to exclude relevant evidence that tended to vex the tribunal, exact undue expense on the litigants, or unfairly delay the administration of justice. In Bentham's ideal courtroom, judges applied this balancing test to all evidentiary submissions. Wigmore followed with his own triad of balancing considerations: (1) "confusion of issues," wherein the evidence would confuse the jury, (2) "unfair surprise," wherein one party would be surprised by the evidence and unable to respond adequately, and, (3) "undue prejudice," wherein the evidence would have a prejudicial effect on the jury.[70]

Wigmore derived his approach to limiting witnesses from Bentham's balancing method. Bentham recognized that each new witness had the potential either to illuminate the truth or merely to confuse the jury and delay the proceedings. He suggested, therefore, that the bench weigh the "collateral inconvenience in the shape of vexation, expense, and delay" against "the probability of direct mischief . . . for want of the evidence proposed to be excluded." In his *Treatise*, Wigmore quoted this passage from Bentham to bolster his endorsement of a contemporary trend toward greater judicial discretion "in attempting to determine when this overbalance of disadvantages exists."[71]

Bentham also weighed external social policy considerations against the imperative of judicial inquiry, a stance that Wigmore emulated. For instance, Wigmore adopted—on policy grounds—Bentham's legitimation of the privilege for priests against divulging the substance of any confession. Bentham affirmed that in England, "the Catholic religion was meant to be tolerated. But with any idea of toleration, a coercion of this nature is altogether inconsistent and incompatible." Referring to that passage, Wigmore announced that even "Bentham, the greatest opponent of privileges" supported the privilege for confessions. "Does the penitential relation deserve recognition and countenance?" Wigmore asked. "In a State where toleration of religions exists by law, and where a substantial part of the community professes a religion practising a confessional system, this question must be answered in the affirmative." On this issue, Bentham and Wigmore both indicated their recognition that judicial inquiry was only one of several competing societal interests.[72]

Bentham preferred case-by-case decision-making to universal rules, which he criticized as overly mechanical and formalistic. Wigmore's opposition to numerical rules underscores Bentham's influence on this front. Numerical rules mandated that more than one witness testify against a defendant on select topics such as rape, treason, or perjury. Bentham derided such rules as capricious. "Nothing can be weaker," Bentham declared, "than the best security that can be derived from numbers." "In many cases, a single witness" can "stamp conviction on the most reluctant mind. In other instances, a cloud of witnesses, though all were to the same fact, will be found wanting in the balance." Wigmore followed Bentham's lead and cited him while maintaining that "our whole presumption should be against any specific rule requiring a number of witnesses" and "such arbitrary measurements are likely to be of little real efficacy." This example also illustrates Wigmore's tendency to resurrect calls for reform initially sounded by Bentham. Bentham in fact was more strident in his anti-universalism than Wigmore; the former categorically opposed fixed evidence rules of any kind and instead preferred guidelines only.[73]

Bentham saw the needs of the collective rather than the liberty of the individual as the proper dictate of legal doctrine, an approach that directed Wigmore's treatment of compulsory testimony. In his 1827 work *Draft for a Judicial Establishment*, Bentham asked, "Are men of the first rank and consideration . . .

to be forced to quit their business, their functions, or what is more than all, their pleasure, at the beck of every idle or malicious adversary, to dance attendance upon every petty cause? Yes, as far as it is necessary, they and everybody." Wigmore, for his part, cited the above passage in his *Treatise* and similarly upheld testimony as "a duty, not to be grudged or evaded. Whoever is impelled to evade or to resent it should retire from the society of organized and civilized communities, and become a hermit." Both jurists, then, saw cooperation with the justice system as a trade-off for living in society—a communal mentality made all the more salient in Wigmore's era of rapid modernization and attendant interdependence.[74]

Bentham also voiced a consequentialist outlook that shaped the tenor of Wigmore's thought. For example, Wigmore mirrored Bentham in emphasizing the *effects* of the public exhibition of trials. Bentham explained that "the publicity of the examination or deposition operate[d] as a check upon mendacity and incorrectness" because in the deponent's mind, every spectator was a potential witness poised to contradict any falsehood. Moreover, publicity alerted relevant witnesses unknown to the parties that a trial was underway. In Bentham's words, publicity "affords to justice" the opportunity "of receiving, from hands individually unknown, ulterior evidence, for the supply of any deficiency or confutation of any falsehood." Wigmore embraced these same two reasons. On the one hand, wrote Wigmore, exposure to public scrutiny "produces in the witness' mind a disinclination to falsify," and on the other, "it secures the presence of those who by possibility may be able to furnish testimony in chief or to contradict falsifiers." Not surprisingly, Wigmore quoted Bentham liberally on these points.[75]

While Wigmore self-consciously positioned his *Treatise* as an extension of Bentham's work on evidence, he distanced himself from Bentham on any number of evidentiary issues. In other words, Wigmore did not mindlessly parrot Bentham's agenda but selectively appropriated Bentham's ideas for his own purposes.[76]

Extrajudicial admissions constituted one area where Wigmore staked out a separate position from Bentham. "Admissions" in this sense referred to previous statements that a party had made off the witness stand that became admissible if they tended to support or refute the party's contention in court. One form of extrajudicial admissions was a pleading from a previous trial, in which each party had set forth allegations of fact and posed questions to its opponent in advance of the trial. In Bentham's day, the English court of equity (known as Chancery) operated by a set of rules that required the pleadings, known as "bills of chancery," to enumerate questions in statement form. As a result, what appeared to be affirmative declarations in the pleading were often not

true. Wigmore recognized that objections to such admissions were once credible "when the bill in chancery could be correctly said by [Anglican cleric]
John Wesley to be 'stuffed with stupid senseless improbable lies,' and by Jeremy
Bentham, a century later, still to be 'a volume of notorious lies.'" By contrast,
wrote Wigmore, "to-day, in the great majority of jurisdictions, the reforms in
pleading deprive this objection of all weight," and he supported extrajudicial
admissions of this character. Wigmore therefore departed from Bentham not
because of any fundamental disagreement but because they were operating in
different historical contexts.[77]

Wigmore further broke with Bentham in his terminology. For instance,
Wigmore used the term "autoptic proference" for evidence presented directly to
the senses of the tribunal. Bentham used the term "real evidence," which was less
precise than autoptic preference because (in Wigmore's words) Bentham "meant
by it any fact about a material or corporal object, *e. g.* a book or a human foot,
whether produced in court or not." The phrase "autoptic proference" therefore
drew a distinction that Bentham's use of "real evidence" glossed over—the difference between physical evidence itself and facts about that evidence.[78]

Other sources of division between Bentham and Wigmore suggest more
than just contextual or semantic disparities; for some rules of evidence, there
were substantive differences in their respective approaches. In general, Wigmore
wanted to reform the common law system while Bentham wanted to replace
it with statutory codes. In particular, they held markedly divergent views on
the oath. Bentham derided the oath as premised on the fallacious notion that
God obediently played his prescribed role in the earthly administration of justice. "The supposition of its efficiency is absurd in principle," he scoffed. "It
ascribes to man a power over his maker: it places the Almighty in the station
of a sheriff's officer; it places him under the command of every justice of the
peace." We would be better off, reasoned Bentham, to assume that God inflicts
punishment at his own discretion, not ours. Conversely, Wigmore saw the oath
as an effective instrument: "The class of persons whose belief makes them capable of being influenced by the prospect implied in an oath is decidedly the
immense mass of the community." If some witnesses feared God, then the legal
system should not hesitate to leverage that fear and induce credible testimony. Any atheist could appreciate this functional approach. Wigmore concluded,
"There seem to be no real disadvantages (in spite of Mr. Bentham's ingenious
suggestions) outweighing the gain in truthfulness produced by the oath." Here,
we see at once Wigmore's willingness to break with Bentham and his abiding
respect for Bentham's contributions to the field.[79]

Bentham and Wigmore also entertained opposed views on whether a document's contents could speak to its authenticity. Bentham argued in favor of a presumption that a letter with a given person's signature was actually from that person. "On what supposition can such a letter have emanated from any other hand than his?" asked Bentham. "On no other than that of forgery: a crime not to be presumed, or so much as suspected, without special ground, in any single instance." Wigmore proved more incredulous. While he conceded that "in the vast majority of transactions in everyday life, persons do act upon just such evidence of authenticity and no more; and it might be supposed that the law could well follow this practice," still, Wigmore pointed out that "frauds are constantly perpetrated in this very manner (as in obtaining goods by forging the name and letter-heads of reputable merchants)." Accordingly, he advised judges to subscribe to a higher threshold of authentication.[80]

Attorney-client privilege also prompted conflicting treatments. In Bentham's words, proponents of the privilege protested that a client could not divulge information to his lawyer "with safety" if "the facts confided to his advocate were to be disclosed" under legal coercion later on the witness stand. "Not with safety?" scoffed Bentham. "So much the better. To what object is the whole system of penal law directed; if it be not that no man shall have it in his power to flatter himself with the hope of safety" in the event that he was indeed guilty. Bentham's reasoning drew sharp criticism from Wigmore. First, Wigmore faulted Bentham for presupposing a world of clearly demarcated innocence and guilt: "There is in civil cases often no hard-and-fast line between guilt and innocence, which will justify us as stigmatizing one or the other party and banning him from our sympathy." He also pointed out that lawyers need not make themselves ex post facto accomplices to crimes that their clients had committed; attorneys could turn down cases or try to settle on terms agreeable to the opponent. Finally, Wigmore warned against forcing lawyers to serve as both "the solicitor and the revealer of the secrets of the cause. This double-minded attitude would create an unhealthy moral state in the practitioner." While Wigmore granted that "at first sight the Benthamic argument seems irresistible," he carefully marked his distance from his English predecessor on this issue.[81]

A final topic that divided Bentham and Wigmore was the privilege against self-incrimination. In Bentham's view, the privilege was the ill-advised product of "double-distilled and treble-refined sentimentality." With characteristic piquancy, Bentham delineated the logical fallacy of the privilege: "From his own mouth you will not receive the evidence of the culprit against him; but in his own hand, or from the mouth of another, you receive it without scruple: so that at bottom, all this sentimentality resolves itself into neither more nor less than a predilection—a confirmed and most extensive predilection, for bad evidence."[82]

Wigmore, however, found that "for the *ordinary witness*, Bentham's argument seems to fail." While true that "mere self-betrayal by the witness is of itself no evil" and warranted no special sympathy, still, Wigmore maintained, "there are other considerations. The witness-stand is to-day sufficiently a place of annoyance and dread. The reluctance to enter it must not be increased." In other words, although the privilege suppressed truth in some instances, its aggregate effect was to ease anxiety about testifying and facilitate judicial inquiry. Generally, Wigmore found Bentham's argument on this issue lacking. "For the *preliminary inquisition of one not yet charged* with an offence," posited Wigmore, "the claims of the privilege seem equally valid. This aspect of it seems to have been ignored by Bentham." Moreover, in the absence of such a privilege, the state's "inclination develops to rely mainly upon" the testimony of the defendant, "and to be satisfied with an incomplete investigation of the other sources. The exercise of the power to extract answers begets a forgetfulness of the just limitations of that power. The simple and peaceful process of questioning breeds a readiness to resort to bullying and to physical force and torture." From Wigmore's standpoint, this was "a problem to which Bentham's arguments did not do justice." That Wigmore felt compelled to acknowledge and engage with Bentham's reasoning rather than merely assert his own opinion betokens the centrality of Bentham's ideas to Wigmore's understanding of evidence law.[83]

Wigmore's *Treatise*

B<small>Y THE END</small> of the nineteenth century, the law of evidence had expanded into a disorienting litany of sundry, dated, and often contradictory rules. John Henry Wigmore began his scholarly intervention in evidence law as early as the 1880s with a series of law review articles. In 1904, he produced the first volumes of his enormously influential *Treatise*, a work that tamed the unwieldy field and subjected evidence doctrine to the tenets of legal modernism. Although Wigmore employed the traditional method of classifying rules and inducing general principles, he treated categories as constructed and principles as flexible. In short, Wigmore demonstrated that classification and induction were reconcilable with modernist values. His *Treatise* also bespeaks Wigmore's role as an optimistic pessimist; while he was dubious of juries, Wigmore possessed a steadfast faith in legal processes. The vitality of evidence law, he believed, lay in its conventions, such as cross-examination and the sequestration of witnesses.

The Law of Evidence Before Wigmore

The origins of evidence law remain murky. Individual rules of evidence developed at various times for different reasons. Moreover, much evidence doctrine antedates the conception of evidence as a distinct branch of law. That legal historians afford little attention to an already obscure subject renders it all the more difficult to recover the development of the field. It is possible, however, to offer some comment on the state of evidence law that Wigmore inherited.[1]

At the time that Wigmore entered law school, Simon Greenleaf's *A Treatise on the Law of Evidence* (hereafter *Greenleaf on Evidence*) had dominated the American market for over forty years and would for another twenty. Born in 1783, Greenleaf was reared in Maine and began to practice law in 1806. His stellar reputation in Maine legal circles earned him the coveted role of reporter of the state's supreme judicial court. He joined the Harvard Law School faculty in 1833 and there succeeded the famed Joseph Story as the Dane Professor of Law in 1846.[2]

Prior to the appearance of the first edition of *Greenleaf on Evidence* in 1842, practitioners had relied on American editions of two treatises by English authors—Samuel March Phillips and Thomas Starke. Greenleaf primarily wrote his own treatise as a textbook for his students, but he aimed to appeal to the practitioner as well. Since much English precedent was not applicable to US jurisdictions, Greenleaf tapped into a latent demand among American lawyers for a purely national reference work.[3]

Greenleaf on Evidence went through fifteen revisions over the next six decades. Greenleaf himself prepared the first seven iterations before his death in 1853. Subsequent editions were produced variously by Isaac F. Redfield, chief justice of the Supreme Court of Vermont; John Wilder May, chief justice of the Municipal Court of Boston; and Greenleaf's grandson, Simon Greenleaf Croswell. These editors added annotations for recent cases but did not substantively reshape evidence doctrine to address changing needs and conditions. As a result, *Greenleaf on Evidence* grew increasingly anachronistic.[4]

"Variance" was one instance of a Greenleaf doctrine that had grown out of touch with legal practice by the end of the nineteenth century. According to the rule, parties could not submit evidence that was at "variance" with "the essential elements of the legal proposition in the controversy." Greenleaf explained that evidence of intent was irrelevant in tort cases and therefore fell under the variance doctrine. "For removing earth from the defendant's land," Greenleaf offered by way of example, "whereby the foundation of the plaintiff's house was injured, the allegation of bad intent in the defendant is not necessary to be proved, for the cause of action is perfect, independent of the intention." In the decades after Greenleaf's death, rapid industrialization gave rise to novel kinds of torts that proved ill suited to inherited legal doctrine. Courts came to see intent as a germane aspect of tort law.[5]

Testimonial disqualification because of interest was another example of a Greenleaf doctrine inconsonant with modern legal practice. This rule held that a judge could bar from the stand a witness possessed of some vested interest in the outcome of the trial. Thanks to the efforts of David Dudley Field II, the state of New York repealed disqualification by interest in 1848, a move soon emulated by every other American jurisdiction. In his own *Treatise*, Wigmore suggested two reasons for this reversal: (1) the emergence of a dispassionate temperament in society at large, and (2) the legal fraternity's increased faith in cross-examination as a vehicle to expose the fallacies peddled by dishonest witnesses.[6]

Not only had much of Greenleaf's work proved obsolete by century's end, but also the legal fraternity now considered several of the topics in his treatise outside the ambit of the law of evidence. Consider, for instance, the Statute of Frauds, a seventeenth-century English law adopted in the United States that required parties to finalize certain kinds of agreements in writing. The Statute of Frauds had migrated from the procedural law of evidence to the substantive law of contracts.[7]

The gulf between modern times and Greenleaf's original framework purged evidence law of a governing principle, a system of order. In 1882, one commentator in the *American Law Review* observed dishearteningly, "Our present law of evidence—made up as it is of case law, modified by numerous statutory amendments made at different times, many of them based upon theories entirely inconsistent with each other, and some upon no theory at all—is a system of patch-work." At the twilight of the nineteenth century, James Bradley Thayer condemned the rules of evidence as "a great degree ill-apprehended, ill-stated, ill-digested," little more than a confused mass. Regarding those subjects mistakenly subsumed under the domain of evidence law, Thayer lamented, "It is discreditable to a learned profession to allow the subject to lie in the jumble that now characterizes it in this respect." From the vantage point of the twenty-first century, historian Tal Golan similarly concludes, "The law of evidence had turned . . . into a highly complicated and technical domain, sagging to the point of collapse under the burden of its own distinctions, exceptions, and exclusionary duties." The time had arrived for the Greenleaf of a new generation to fundamentally reshape the unruly mishmash of evidence rules.[8]

Wigmore's Early Evidence Scholarship

While the *Treatise* ensured Wigmore's place in the annals of great American jurists, it was not his first venture into the law of evidence. On December 12, 1888, he presented a paper to the Medico-Legal Society entitled, "Circumstantial Evidence in Poisoning Cases." (The society awarded the paper first prize, and Wigmore used the winnings to purchase an engagement ring for Emma.) Throughout the 1890s, Wigmore published a number of articles on evidence law in the pages of the *American Law Review*. An 1892 article argued in favor of the admission of scientific treatises, a stand that he would repeat in the *Treatise*. In 1896, Wigmore chronicled the history of proof for handwriting. A subsequent article, "Proof of Character by Personal Knowledge or Opinion: Its History," laid the historical groundwork for an argument that would surface in the *Treatise*: courts should admit evidence of personal knowledge as well as general reputation to establish the character of a party in question.[9]

These initial investigations into the law of evidence betokened Wigmore's early embrace of legal modernism. For instance, he voiced the common modernist complaint that legal reasoning fetishized abstract logic. "The judicial mind—one may say the legal mind in general—is apt to dwell apart in an atmosphere of its own creation," lamented Wigmore. He further chastised the law for "a disregard of practical experience and an adherence to dogmas and to the forms of things." Positing that the bench invented rationales to legitimate retroactively a priori positions, Wigmore observed, "As often happens in our law, the doubts which owed their source to a mere confusion of precedents began to have reasons supplied *ex post facto.*" Wigmore also subscribed to an anti-universalist approach that eschewed absolutes and countenanced contingencies: "No rule is a universal solvent; and a rule cannot be invoked where the conditions do not admit of its application." He understood law as perpetually in flux rather than immutable, insisting that "both doctrines and phrases have to be considered, not merely as fixed and at rest, but as moving." Finally, he displayed a preference for increased judicial discretion. Regarding the admission of scholarly texts, Wigmore declared, "the rejection of these books should lie in the discretion of the trial judge, and his decision should be final." He expressed his approval of "the tendency of the day . . . towards creating more competent trial judges and vesting in them a larger discretion."[10]

At the twilight of the 1890s, Wigmore finished his most ambitious endeavor yet in the realm of evidence—revisions for the sixteenth edition of the first volume of *Greenleaf.* He felt torn between his obligation "to leave the original text still available in its classical integrity" and his desire "to make the work as useful as possible to the profession and to the student of the present time." To fulfill the former, Wigmore reproduced, in an appendix, sections that he deleted from the original text. With respect to the latter, he incorporated three chapters entirely of his own authorship on physical evidence, circumstantial evidence, and exceptions to the hearsay rule. As an indication of the wide acclaim that met Wigmore's work on *Greenleaf,* the Harvard Law faculty awarded him the first-ever Ames Prize, bestowed every four years for the best English-language contribution to legal scholarship.[11]

The *Greenleaf* enterprise may have earned Wigmore high praise, but he was frustrated with the effort. His correspondence with Thayer reveals a scholar who felt hamstrung by his obligations to Greenleaf's original text. A revision was just that, and Wigmore hungered to produce a truly innovative work that would refashion evidence law to accord with the demands of modern legal practice. "The Greenleaf, of course, contained many statements (by me) which must have made you shake your head," Wigmore acknowledged to Thayer, "but I can only assure you that I believe myself to have authority for it all, and will some day defend it where space will allow ample opportunity." A few months later, the possibilities of a new, original, and comprehensive work remained at the forefront of Wigmore's thought. "As to Greenleaf," he told Thayer, "the condensation was such that I should not like to be judged by all I said there; some things had to be said roughly, and this perhaps without necessary qualification; other things could be better defended if space allowed."[12]

Fortunately for Wigmore, his publisher, Little, Brown, and Company, was as anxious as he for an entirely new treatise on evidence. Both Wigmore and the field were ripe for this project. Over the next several years, Wigmore poured himself into the enterprise and published a number of articles that anticipated his treatment of evidence doctrine in the *Treatise*. Finally, on November 1, 1904, the first two volumes of the *Treatise* debuted, followed by the third volume the following month and the fourth and final volume in February of 1905. In all, the *Treatise* spanned an arresting four thousand pages and included forty thousand judicial citations.[13]

Scope

Evidence law was an amalgam of judicial precedent, legislative statute, and scholarly commentary. The *Treatise* combined all three, serving both descriptive and prescriptive functions. On the one hand, Wigmore accounted for judicial decisions, statutes, and academic opinions pertaining to evidence; on the other, he weighed in with his own suggestions, variously endorsing a trend, rebuking a convention, or calling for full-fledged reform. In a typical section, he would provide a history of a given rule of evidence, explain its rationale, consider the arguments from its proponents and detractors, discriminate it from other rules, and enumerate any exceptions, all the while contributing his own opinion. When jurisdictions differed in their treatment of a rule, Wigmore's footnotes exhaustively listed the relevant precedents and statutes for every jurisdiction in the United States, Canada, and England. In an extreme case, his discussion on testimonial qualification featured nearly forty consecutive pages of a single, uninterrupted footnote. Sometimes his footnotes had footnotes.[14]

Judicial inquiry comprised several stages. First, parties collected and offered evidence; then judges admitted or rejected the evidence; next, the jury decided whether the aggregated evidence met the stipulated burden of proof; and finally, the judge determined the legal consequences of the jury's finding of fact. This was hardly a strict formula. A judge could potentially give testimony, and thereby offer and not merely admit evidence. The bench could afford judicial notice of a fact. Judges could also question witnesses at their leisure. Nevertheless, the phases of the trial and the roles of its participants generally operated in the manner described above.[15]

Wigmore's *Treatise* was concerned primarily with the second stage in which the bench admitted or excluded evidence submitted to the tribunal. There were five substages in the admission of evidence: "the Offer of Evidence, the Objection, the Ruling, the Exception, and the Judgment of Error." The proponent submitted evidence; then the opponent could object and state the relevant rule of evidence as grounds; the judge made a ruling on the objection; the losing party's position entered the "bill of exceptions"; and finally, a higher court could determine, on the basis of that bill, if a judgment of error warranted a new trial. The tribunal need not have proceeded through all five of these substages for every article of evidence. On the fifth point in particular, remarked Wigmore, "finality as to the findings of fact" was "by most Courts in theory, and by some Courts in practice, conceded to the trial judge."[16]

At times Wigmore drew a sharp separation between the function of judges and juries. A judge's domain was "admissibility," which "falls short of Proof or Demonstration." "The jury," Wigmore declared, "ultimately decide upon the total effect which we call Proof. . . . Weight, Proof, Demonstration, these terms have no application until the evidence is all introduced and the jury are [*sic*] ready to retire." In other words, the judge considered if an article of evidence was relevant, and the jury weighed the degree of relevance. "Indeed, it can be said," wrote Wigmore, "that there are no rules, in our system of evidence, prescribing for the jury the precise effect of any general or special class of evidence." It is not surprising, then, that he offered very little guidance in the realm of standards of proof, and noted only briefly that criminal cases required proof "beyond a reasonable doubt" and civil cases a "preponderance of evidence." Wigmore even derided as futile efforts to define sharply these standards.[17]

In reality, judges often involved themselves in matters of weight, proof, and demonstration, and of these instances the *Treatise* had much to say. To thwart "prejudice and hasty reasoning" by juries, the bench "has constantly seen fit to exclude matter which does not rise to a clearly sufficient degree of value. In other words, legal relevancy denotes . . . *something more than a minimum of probative value.*" A judge could bar otherwise relevant evidence if its weight was insufficient to counterbalance other considerations, such as the inconvenience of the evidence's production or its prejudicial nature. Still, this standard of "legal relevancy" was not impossibly high. Admission, according to Wigmore, was hardly limited to "strong, full, [and] superlative" evidence; its probative value needed merely to outweigh its potential detriments. In this way, the judge's function overlapped with the jury's because the bench had to consider both the pertinence *and* the relative importance of an article of evidence.[18]

Wigmore rarely drew distinctions between evidence rules for criminal and civil trials. Whether a proceeding was criminal or civil had no bearing on the judicial imperative to find the truth. "The relation between an Evidentiary Fact and a particular Proposition is always the same, without regard to the kind of litigation in which that proposition becomes material to be proved," he wrote. Nevertheless, there were sporadic instances where evidence law varied in its application to criminal and civil proceedings. For example, judges afforded the admissibility of confessions much greater scrutiny in criminal trials than in their civil counterparts because criminal defendants were, supposedly, more susceptible to false confessions. Evidence of habit or repute was usually sufficient to prove marriage in civil cases but insufficient in criminal cases involving multiple spouses or adultery, both of which required eyewitness testimony. Jurisdictions also frequently treated marital privilege—which allowed or even required spouses to abstain from testifying against each other—differently in the two types of trials, sometimes permitting the privilege in one while denying it in the other. Despite these occasional differences, the vast majority of evidence rules applied uniformly to criminal and civil proceedings.[19]

Wigmore sharply circumscribed the scope of the *Treatise*. His concern was limited to evidence in jury trials alone rather than evidence in other stages of legal proceedings. While prosecutors used evidence to persuade grand juries to bring a case to trial, and judges also considered evidence in sentencing, these topics lay outside the *Treatise*'s ambit. Wigmore also drew a definite separation between evidence law and substantive law; he contended that the former was subordinate to and in service of the latter. "We prefer to make the rules of evidence our tools rather than to become ourselves their helpless slaves," he declared. Like Thayer, Wigmore took pains to illuminate when substantive laws speciously posed as evidence rules and limited his considerations almost exclusively to evidence. He recognized the import of "rules and suggestions of tact and skill, which serve to guide the judgment of the examiner in obtaining the desired information," but labeled this a "dialectic art" distinct from evidence law. "The rules of law," Wigmore concluded, "and not the art of applying them, must here set the limits of investigation."[20]

Classification and Induction

Wigmore subjected the law of evidence to an industrious survey, created categories to organize the landscape of precedent and statute, and induced general principles that governed these various spheres of evidence law. Historians consider contemporary efforts to classify law and induce guiding principles as twin pillars of formal legal thought. James Herget specifically targets Wigmore's approach toward the classification of tort law as symptomatic of the formalist school's quest for "the holy grail of universals." For Wigmore, however, there was no tension between classification/induction on the one hand, and modernism on the other. He viewed principles not as universal and immutable but as provisional and flexible; moreover, Wigmore readily acknowledged that his classification schemes were constructed and convenient rather than natural and essential.[21]

Wigmore claimed to subsume all rules of evidence under a metaprinciple that was circular in its logic—a bit of sophistry that nominally paid homage to an organizing maxim while substantively affording Wigmore the flexibility he needed to accord evidence law with contingent circumstances. He appropriated his two-tiered metaprinciple, with due acknowledgement, from Thayer. The first component of the general principle was, "*None but facts having rational probative value are admissible,*" and the second, "*All facts having rational probative value are admissible, unless some specific rule forbids.*" The first directive simply proscribed irrelevant evidence, which, although sound, was far too broad to provide much practical guidance in shaping evidence doctrine. The second part was unequivocally circular; the rule was always in effect, unless it was not in effect.[22]

Wigmore's analysis of the "character-rule" throws into high relief the circular nature of his metaprinciple and the freedom it provided him. The character rule held that the prosecution could not submit evidence of the defendant's general bad character unless the defense first raised character as an issue. However, courts often admitted evidence relating to past crimes if relevant on grounds other than character. "Occasionally," Wigmore explained, "this principle is spoken of as though it involved an exception to" the character rule; instead, he framed it as consistent with the general principle of admitting evidence with probative value, "to which the character-rule is an exception."[23] In other words, evidence law embraced so many overlapping, often conflicting, principles that any given rule could find refuge under *some* principle. At the celebration of Wigmore's retirement as dean, attendees sang a chorus that included this telling verse about his *Treatise*:

> Although no one can read it and know what it's all about,
> It is a useful book to me and you,
> 'Cause when the other fellow opens volume one and starts to spout,
> You can find him over-ruled in volume two.[24]

Wigmore's contemporaries well understood the indeterminate nature of evidence law.

Contents of the *Treatise*

Wigmore's introduction outlined his metaprinciple, defined relevancy, and delimited the ambit of the *Treatise*. He also drew distinctions between law and fact, and distinguished evidence from argument. Wigmore then dedicated several chapters to circumstantial evidence, or evidence requiring an inference. For instance, a photograph of a man holding a bloody knife outside of a house where a murder was just committed was circumstantial rather than direct evidence of the man's guilt because the image merely implied culpability. Topics within circumstantial evidence covered by the *Treatise* included the party's character, physical ability to execute an alleged act, and emotional disposition before and after a crime.[25]

The next several chapters concerned testimonial evidence from witnesses. Wigmore reviewed rules that determined the qualifications of a witness to provide testimony. A judge's decision to allow a given witness on the stand could be influenced by the absence or presence of mental derangement, expertise, marital relationship to a party, and the opportunity to observe an event in question. The *Treatise* further outlined acceptable methods of interrogating witnesses. Wigmore also discussed the admissibility of confessions and rules relating to evidence of incentives for a party to confess to a crime he or she had not committed. This section additionally covered the discrediting of witnesses. Subtopics included witnesses' character, bias, corruption, and memory.[26]

The *Treatise* then turned to "autoptic proference," known popularly as "real evidence." This mode of evidence related to physical objects presented directly to the tribunal, such as a dagger or a document.[27]

For the next 1,575 pages, Wigmore devoted his attention to the rules of "auxiliary probative policy." This phrase referred to evidence that, although relevant, the judge could exclude because it might obscure rather than illuminate the truth. The core of auxiliary policy was the triad of confusion of issues, unfair surprise, and undue prejudice.

One of the most prominent topics under auxiliary policy was the hearsay rule, which prohibited the admission of evidence of statements made out of court. For instance, Andrew Johnson could not testify, "Stanton told me that Booth murdered Lincoln," to establish Booth's culpability. Stanton had to appear in court himself and subject his testimony to the rigors of cross-examination. Several chapters concerned exceptions to the hearsay rule, such as dying declarations and spontaneous exclamations.[28]

Wigmore developed an intricate classification for other rules of auxiliary policy. "Prophylactic rules" covered various mechanisms to ensure trustworthy evidence, including the oath and penalty for perjury. "Quantitative rules" required certain numbers of witnesses in particular scenarios. For instance, a charge of treason required more than one witness. The "opinion rule" also fell within the scope of auxiliary policy.[29]

The final volume of the *Treatise* began with an extended exploration of extrinsic policy (i.e., rules that prohibit evidence because of some consideration wholly external to the trial). Privileged communications between husband and wife, attorney and client, and physician and patient all fell within the province of external policy. Wigmore then offered a lengthy chapter on the parol evidence rule even though it was technically part of contract law rather than evidence law. The final chapters of the *Treatise* dealt with a litany of sundry issues. Topics included the burden of proof in civil and criminal cases, and judicial notice.[30]

Wigmore: An Optimistic Pessimist

Historian William Twining argues that "the Anglo-American heritage of writing about evidence" has been characterized by a "remarkably homogenous intellectual tradition," which he labels "optimistic rationalism." Indeed, Wigmore was an optimist, but he placed his faith primarily in legal procedures. If anything, he expressed a certain pessimism about jurors. Wigmore, for instance, supported the policy "that the prosecution may not initially attack the defendant's character," a practice designed to protect against "the deep tendency of human nature to punish, not because our victim is guilty this time, but because he is a bad man and may as well be condemned now that he is caught." In Wigmore's view, evidence law had to deprive the prosecutor of the opportunity to exploit the punitive instincts of jurors.[31]

The inherent bias of juries also prompted the evidence rule requiring parties to submit physical evidence only in tandem with witness testimony. Physical objects tended to project an automatic sense of legitimacy, so parties could include an object only when attached to otherwise relevant testimony. "A material object," Wigmore explained, "particularly a writing, when presented as purporting to be of a certain origin, always tends to impress the mind unconsciously, upon the bare sight of it, with the verity of its purport."[32]

If Wigmore entertained doubts about jurors, his misgivings were more than counterbalanced by an abiding faith in legal processes. According to Wigmore, the adversarial system, contingent on "partisan responsibility for the purveying of evidence," was "at least more successful in the thorough canvassing of all sources of evidence than any system of judicial responsibility could be in this country" and perhaps any other. Of the cross-examination, he boasted, "It is beyond any doubt the greatest legal engine ever invented for the discovery of truth" and "the great and permanent contribution of the Anglo-American system of law to improved methods of trial-procedure." Wigmore displayed similar confidence in "the expedient of sequestration" of witnesses, which was also "one of the greatest engines that the skill of man has ever invented for the detection of liars in a court of justice."[33]

That is not to say that Wigmore deferred entirely to processes rather than people. "A conscientious citizenship and a sound condition of politics" were, in his mind, "the only real safeguards of an innocent man." While these traits may have been necessary for justice, they were, for Wigmore, insufficient if not channeled by appropriate legal processes. He understood the fallibility of the jury not as a detriment to evidence law but indeed as its very rationale; the rules of evidence, in his view, had emerged to anticipate and account for the shortcomings of a lay-jury system.[34]

The extent to which the institution of the jury trial spawned the law of evidence is a matter of historical controversy. Medieval English juries were at one time self-informing (i.e., jurors had personal knowledge of an event in dispute and engaged in their own fact-finding). While historians disagree about when juries fully transitioned from investigators to spectators, the latter role was unquestionably in full force prior to American independence. A traditional view of evidence history—to which Wigmore, as well as Bentham and Thayer, subscribed—holds that the law of evidence developed as a filter to guard against the biases of jurors. Current proponents of this story point to a correlation between the waning use of jury trials in common law countries and the diminishing importance of evidence law. That civil law countries, largely without juries, never developed anything close to a full-fledged system of evidence rules underscores the merit of the traditionalist view.[35]

Wigmore's contemporary, and critic, Edmund M. Morgan acknowledged some causal links between the jury trial and the law of evidence but felt that the standard narrative overstated the case. In a 1937 contribution to the *University of Chicago Law Review*, Morgan noted that rules prohibiting testimony from witnesses of dubious trustworthiness bore no relation to the competencies of jurors. He also highlighted many features of evidence law—such as oaths and rules requiring original documents—that antedate the institution of the lay jury. Since courts permit but do not require cross-examination, reasoned Morgan, the practice of questioning an opponent's witnesses cannot logically be linked to concerns about the fallibility of jurors. It is hardly a radical proposition that a branch of law as multifaceted as evidence resists monocausal explanations for its historical development. Indeed, Wigmore's challenge was to bring a loose collection of rules—diverse in both origin and rationale—within the parameters of a unifying legal philosophy.[36]

Influence

It is difficult to overstate the hegemonic influence of Wigmore's *Treatise* on the rules of evidence. Perhaps no other work of scholarship in American history has exerted such plenary control over a branch of law. When the *Treatise* debuted in 1904, jurists immediately recognized it as a rare work destined to dominate its field. Some reviewers, to be sure, scrutinized Wigmore's complex system of categorization and his creation of new legal terms, but these were quibbles amid otherwise effusive praise. As the *Harvard Law Review* gushed, "It is hardly too much to say that this is the most complete and exhaustive treatise on a single branch of our law that has ever been written." According to the *American Law Review*, "No great topic of the law has ever received such a masterly and exhaustive treatment as Professor Wigmore has given to the law of Evidence." Judge Charles B. Elliott of the Minnesota Supreme Court similarly remarked, "Professor Wigmore has written one of the greatest law books ever produced in this country." Practicing lawyer and future Supreme Court justice Louis D. Brandeis offered an unequivocal assessment of the *Treatise* and its author: "Possessed of a keen legal mind, trained early by the masters of the Harvard Law School, and enriched by years of patient and devoted study, Professor Wigmore has produced a work which must prove of great value to the practitioner, the teacher, and the student of law." These appraisals were typical of the widespread acclaim that met the young dean's tome.[37]

Commentators realized that Wigmore had not merely organized the rules of evidence but offered a valuable addition to legal theory. E. A. Harriman, a practicing attorney who had previously taught at Northwestern Law, told the author of the *Treatise* that it was both of "great practical value" to "an active practitioner" and "a masterpiece of jurisprudence." The *Virginia Law Register* observed, "This is no ordinary production. It evidently comes from the mind of a man well versed in the philosophy of law." Meanwhile, Charles F. Amidon, a US District Court judge in North Dakota, credited Wigmore "as the most original and scholarly writer in the field of American jurisprudence" whose reference work "deal[t] with the law historically and philosophically."[38]

Jurists of all varieties predicted, accurately, that Wigmore's *Treatise* would monopolize the future of evidence law. David J. Brewer, US Supreme Court justice, said of the volumes that comprised the *Treatise*, "[I] believe that when they come to be known to the profession they will be recognized as the standard authority on questions of Evidence." In the same vein, Emlin McClain of the Iowa Supreme Court anticipated that "after this treatise appears no one will examine a difficult question of the law of Evidence without consulting its pages." Dean of Yale Law, Henry Wade Rogers, expressed "no hesitation in saying that Professor Wigmore has written what soon will be recognized as the authoritative American treatise on the Law of Evidence." These were no false prophets; Wigmore's encyclopedic survey of evidence law dictated legal practice for the better part of the twentieth century.[39]

In 1923, Wigmore issued his second edition of the *Treatise*. It was fundamentally the same treatise with some minor changes. He provided the most recent case law for established evidence rules by adding fifteen thousand citations to the preexisting forty thousand from the first edition, including relevant cases from US territories such as Alaska, Puerto Rico, and the Philippines. Much of the material from the footnotes of the 1904–1905 edition now appeared in the body of the text. This version also featured new topics such as interpreters for alien witnesses, exhumation of corpses, and illegal searches for liquor. Stylistically, Wigmore divided the long paragraphs from the first edition into shorter ones.[40]

If reviews of the first edition had predicted the hegemony of the *Treatise*, then reviews of Wigmore's second effort celebrated the dominance of his tome in the previous two decades. According to the *Cornell Law Quarterly*, "It is, unquestionably, the preeminent work on the law of Evidence in America, if not the English-speaking world." *Lawyer and Banker* referred to the *Treatise* as "the masterpiece of all textbooks" and "the last word on the subject." The *Yale Law Journal* recalled, "The publication of the first edition of this epoch-making work in 1904–5 put at the disposal of the legal profession the most exhaustive, scientific and scholarly treatise ever written upon the subject of evidence." "It is so far superior to any other treatise on the subject," the review added, "that comparison is impracticable. It is by all odds the best, if not the only real, authority on the law of Evidence."[41]

Commentators noted that Wigmore's *Treatise* had more than simply fashioned a comprehensive taxonomy of evidence doctrine; the text had actually reformed the rules of evidence. As the *California Law Review* acknowledged, "A tremendous change has come over the law of evidence in the last twenty years, almost a revolution, for which the author is principally responsible."

"Not only the *best* but the *only* authority."—*Harvard Law Review.*

WIGMORE ON EVIDENCE

1923 SECOND EDITION 1923

Revised and brought down to date
by the author

JOHN HENRY WIGMORE

A TREATISE ON THE SYSTEM OF EVIDENCE IN TRIALS AT
COMMON LAW, INCLUDING THE STATUTES AND JUDICIAL
DECISIONS OF ALL JURISDICTIONS OF THE UNITED
STATES, ENGLAND AND CANADA

By JOHN HENRY WIGMORE

Professor of the Law of Evidence in the Law School of Northwestern University

For eighteen years the previous edition of this treatise has stood unrivalled, and has been cited, quoted and relied upon in the courts of last resort in every state in the Union, as well as in all nations where the common law forms the basis of jurisprudence. No successful trial lawyer can dispense with the use of this treatise. (Ready April, 1923)

FIVE LARGE OCTAVO VOLUMES. LAW BUCKRAM. PRICE $50.00 DELIVERED

Boston   LITTLE, BROWN & CO.,   Publishers

Fig. 4: Box 228, Folder 6, Wigmore Papers.

Along similar lines, the *Harvard Law Review* reported, "When the first edition was published, it was only possible to judge of Mr. Wigmore's book as a statement of the law. During the intervening years it has become something more. It has created law." By all accounts, the supremacy of the *Treatise* was unchallenged.[42]

Sometimes, the sheer dominance of the *Treatise* was problematic. In his 1934 supplement to the second edition of the *Treatise*, Wigmore called on judges to be highly skeptical of rape charges. Based on a severe misrepresentation of the relevant psychiatric literature, he warned of "errant young girls and women coming before the courts" who fabricated "charges of sexual offences by men." According to Wigmore, many women were prone to "the narration of imaginary sex-incidents of which the narrator is the heroine or victim." They consequently garnered the "respect and sympathy felt by any tribunal for a wronged female" while "the real victim, however, too often in such cases is the innocent man." The influence of the *Treatise* all but assured a nationwide incredulity toward sexual assault victims. Leigh Bienen reported in 1983, "Wigmore's views are still given deference with the result that many female children sexually abused by adults have been told by courts or prosecutors that the state and the law did not believe them and would not protect them or punish the offenders." This tragic legacy must temper any depiction of Wigmore as progressive.[43]

Wigmore produced the third and final iteration of the *Treatise* in 1940. Assessing the state of the field in the preface, he was decidedly optimistic. Wigmore applauded what he viewed as a strengthening "'realist' attitude— ready to question any and every traditional rule or formula." Indeed, no one had done more to reorient evidence law along realist (i.e., modernist) lines than Wigmore. In updating the rules with the most recent judicial decisions, he now offered eighty-five thousand citations spanning ten volumes. The author lamented that "it is a pity that the book has had to be so large." Still, he defended the sheer mass of the treatise with an alliterative flourish: "If Legislatures will continue so copiously to legislate, and if Judges still refuse to justify with jejunity their judgments, shall not Authors continue assiduously to amass and to annotate these luciferous lucubrations for the benefit of the Bar?" In addition to this rhetorical indulgence, the third edition of the *Treatise* featured several new topics, including evidence produced from lie detectors, wiretapping, and truth serums. Wigmore also capitulated to a common request from users of the *Treatise*; he finally provided an "Index to Authors Quoted and Cited."[44]

Once again, commentators marveled at the preeminence of the *Treatise*. The *Minnesota Law Review* exclaimed, "Truly, there are few books in our legal literature that have had greater effect on the thinking and the action of the profession." The *University of Pennsylvania Law Review* observed that "in the thirty-six years since it appeared in first edition, Wigmore on Evidence has become a familiar masterpiece." Even Wigmore's staunchest critic, Edmund M. Morgan, praised the *Treatise*'s third edition in the pages of the *Boston University Law Review*. "Not only is this the best, by far the best, treatise on the Law of Evidence," conceded Morgan, "it is also the best work ever produced on any comparable division of Anglo-American law."[45]

Throughout his long career, Wigmore extended his influence on evidence law through a set of publications designed to complement the *Treatise*. In 1910, he published a *Pocket Code of the Rules of Evidence in Trials at Law*. Historians mistakenly characterize this work as an attempt to codify evidence doctrine. Michael Ariens writes, "In 1910, Wigmore wrote the first evidence code, which had little effect on evidence reform." Similarly, Eileen Scallen depicts the *Pocket Code* as "the earliest codification efforts of Wigmore." In fact, Wigmore explicitly disavowed any intent to codify in the introduction of the *Pocket Code*. "In its aspect as a Code," Wigmore set forth, "the present summary is not offered as a proposal for legislation." "Whether a legislative Code is ever desirable," continued Wigmore, "and if it is, whether it is now feasible, in the special conditions of our law and our legal profession—these are large questions, which it would be useless here to enter upon." His desire was to produce a relatively short reference work indexed to his *Treatise* for the convenience of practitioners. If the *Pocket Code* failed to engender reform in the mode of codification, it was because this was never Wigmore's goal. He also produced teaching materials geared to the *Treatise* such as *A Selection of Cases on Evidence* (1906) and *A Student's Textbook on the Law of Evidence* (1935).[46]

Although Wigmore dominated evidence law, certainly some of his contemporaries wrote about the subject. Experienced trial lawyer Francis L. Wellman wrote a book about cross-examination in 1903. Also, Charles C. Moore produced a *Treatise on Facts* in 1908 to assist the bar in the preparation and execution of factual arguments. In 1922, practicing attorney Charles S. Osborn published *The Problem of Proof*, a work that focused in particular on disputed documents and featured an introduction by Wigmore. Texts along these lines did not seek to replace Wigmore's *Treatise* so much as provide discussion on ancillary and specialized themes within the law of evidence. As Twining writes of evidence scholarship, "The first fifty years of the twentieth century represent a relatively fallow period, marked by much excellent and sophisticated work on particular topics, but more remarkable for the absence of attempts to develop general theories or to write systematic treatises as alternatives to Wigmore's."[47]

Law & Society

MODERN LEGAL THEORY embodied a set of coherent philosophical values that John Henry Wigmore translated into concrete evidence doctrine. More specifically, Wigmore's *Treatise* reflected a modernist conception of the relationship between law and society. He understood law as integral to rather than independent from society. As a corollary, his *Treatise* situated the individual in the context of the collective, and subjugated the rights of the former to the needs of the latter. Wigmore looked outside the law to modern science for a model of epistemic inquiry. He also conceived of legal rights, principles, and categories as socially constructed rather than natural and essential.

History

The *Treatise's* frequent excursions into the histories of various evidence rules betoken Wigmore's view of law as woven into the social fabric. While not every historical aside in the *Treatise* elaborated on the import of outside social forces on doctrinal development, still, Wigmore paid much greater attention to the interdependent relationship between law and society than did Holmes or Thayer.

Wigmore was particularly interested in the historical influence of the English class system on the law. He related, for instance, how the social hierarchy had favored patrician witnesses over their plebeian counterparts. In Elizabethan England, a statute mandated that parties compensate their witnesses for their appearances in court, including the cost of travel and lodging. "Under the statute," Wigmore explained, compensation "would vary according to the witness' 'countenance or calling,'—a distinction proper enough where the separation of ranks of life was so clear and fixed."[1] In other words, endemic social mores had demanded that genteel witnesses enjoy higher quality transport and accommodation. Courts of the seventeenth century also had permitted aristocratic witnesses to abstain from answering questions at their leisure because "the obligations of honor among gentlemen" had constituted "sufficient ground for maintaining silence."[2]

Wigmore further chronicled how class biases had engendered "excessive caution" by judges with respect to the admission of confessions. "In all countries having the social cleavages and the feudal survivals of England in the 1700s and early 1800s, the offenders against the criminal law come in the far greater proportion from what are known as the 'lower classes'" whose "petty forms of property-crime" were perhaps "the natural result of only hopeless poverty." This phenomenon combined perilously with "a submission, half-respectful and half-stupid, on the part of the 'lower classes' towards those in authority" and hence rendered commoners susceptible to false confessions if pressured by authority figures. As a result, many judges came to distrust confessions and excluded them from their tribunals. Wigmore considered the distinct political climate of his own day to warrant a reappraisal of such stringent restrictions on confessions. "The spirit of the community" was now marked by

> fearlessness of superior social and political power; of restiveness and struggling against bonds, not of orderly submission; of bold (if superficial) readiness to claim 'rights,' not of ignorant surrender to demands; and, in general, of keen appreciation of the possibilities of evading justice, rather than of cowed obedience to any authority however oppressive.

In response to this altered social milieu, Wigmore argued in favor of the admission of confessions.[3]

Just as Wigmore viewed class as a formative influence on legal norms, so too did his historical accounts point to culture as an external pressure on law. He recalled that courts had once barred persons with a vested stake in a given trial from providing testimony. He credited this doctrine to a transatlantic culture of "partisanship" in which "speech and action were ... passionate and violent" (in contrast to the "cooler and more rational motives of action" of his own day). In depicting this brand of impassioned partiality as a parallel to "the rise of Romanticism in literature and politics," Wigmore demonstrated his conception of the law as part and parcel of the broader social fabric.[4]

Wigmore's historiography also exhibited the imprint of economic life on the law. For cases involving business disputes, courts had once accepted "parties' shop-books or account-books" as valid evidence in part because "the conditions of mercantile and industrial life in the early days" of the American justice system had "left the party generally without other evidence than his own statements in the books." Wigmore also accounted for the rule concerning dying declarations with reference to the economic interests of the British crown. Such declarations had been admissible as exceptions to the hearsay rule in criminal cases only because of a historical "notion that a crime is more worthy [of] the attention of Courts than a civil wrong"—a "traditional relic of the days" when "criminal prosecutions in the king's name were zealously encouraged because of the fines which they added to the royal revenue."[5]

Along with class, culture, and economics, Wigmore's historical asides highlighted war as a factor in shaping legal norms. Referring to the legal reforms that Jeremy Bentham proposed, Wigmore recounted that "Bentham's causes" had resonated with "the radical readiness of the times. The French Revolution had acted in England; and as soon as the Napoleonic wars were over, the influence began to be felt." A minority of forward-thinking Englishmen argued for drastic change, while a majority of conservatives "felt assured that if the change did not come as reform, it would come as revolution; and so the reform was given, to prevent the revolution."[6]

Familial life was yet another social force that had, in Wigmore's view, left its mark on legal practice. He described the law's historical "repugnance" to "condemning a man by admitting to the witness-stand against him those who lived under his roof, shared the secrets of his domestic life, depended on him for sustenance, and were almost numbered among his chattels." Wigmore suggested that the evidentiary rule that a man could prevent his wife from testifying against him likely reflected this paternalistic orientation.[7]

The growth of literacy, reported Wigmore, also had profound implications for evidence doctrine. In the Middle Ages, "the chief varieties of transaction" were "practised with oral forms" because most people were "unfamiliar with writing." By the 1600s, however, English evidence law had come to accept fully the legitimacy of sealed documents for cases involving realty. "The community," Wigmore explained, "had become *more generally lettered*, and this in its turn had resulted from the spread of the printing process in the late 1400s. Reading and writing were no longer the mysterious arts of a few." As a result, it had become "natural to hold that a man was bound by his written version of the transaction."[8]

Wigmore's historical inquiries threw into high relief the impact of religion on the law. Courts had once widely assumed that the oath sworn on the Bible ensured the veracity of a witness. "When the community believed in the serious possibility of the manifestation of truth by the Divine hand in striking down the perjurer before the multitude, the oath's efficacy was at its highest," Wigmore related. Not surprisingly, the legal fraternity had used the oath to bar atheists from the witness stand. Wigmore noted that this prohibition against atheists had been swept away in the mid-nineteenth century, "an era marked, at the same time, by the indirectly related movements of literary romanticism, political liberalism, industrial invention, legal free speech, and theological free thought." Here, Wigmore displayed his understanding of the law as tied to literature, politics, industry, and religion.[9]

It is worthwhile to note that Wigmore did not shape history within a teleological narrative. In many cases, he found ill-advised evidence rules surviving in spite of their irrationality. For example, Wigmore renounced the rule that a party could not impeach its own witness. He described this practice as the "remnant of a primitive notion" that a party implicitly guaranteed the credibility of its own witnesses and was bound to their testimonies.[10] In other instances, Wigmore documented not only the survival of useless rules but also the abrogation of worthy ones. He endorsed the judicial tradition of writing "full notes of the testimony of the witnesses" so that judges could "aim themselves in commenting upon the testimony in the charge to the jury." "This practice," Wigmore lamented, "has naturally died out in the United States, under the misguided rule, now almost universal (a veritable mutilation of the common-law trial by jury), forbidding the trial judge to charge the jury upon the effect of the testimony." In acknowledging instances of degeneration and eschewing whiggish renditions of history, Wigmore broke from the conventions of many contemporary historians.[11]

If Wigmore's historical digressions described an interdependent relationship between law and society, then he prescribed a legal system in harmony with societal customs. For instance, Wigmore looked to business practices for guidance in shaping evidence rules that concerned the verification of written records. He offered a hypothetical scenario in which one person authored a memorandum and a second copied it. If the original document was lost, then the court should admit the duplicate, provided that the first person testified to "the accuracy of the original" and the second to "the correctness of the copy." "Since in commercial practice there is constantly such a separation of these functions among different persons," Wigmore posited, "there seems to be no reason why the law should not accept and sanction it." He was confident that an efficacious practice in industry could easily translate into law.[12]

Cultural Allusions

Wigmore frequently cited nonlegal sources in his *Treatise*, bespeaking his view of law as inexorably tied to the society at large; he appealed variously to novelists, playwrights, poets, and philosophers. Shakespeare was Wigmore's favorite cultural source of authority. He always kept a pocket edition of a Shakespeare play in his briefcase and found in the Bard's work many relevant applications to the rules of evidence. In advocating the rule that resemblance between a parent and child was admissible to establish paternity, Wigmore turned to a line from the "Bastard son" in Shakespeare's *King John:* "But that I am as well begot, my liege, Compare our faces and be judge yourself If old Sir Robert did beget us both And were our father and this son like him." Wigmore quoted part of another scene from *King John* in support of the doctrine that dying declarations were admissible as exceptions to the hearsay rule because approaching death ostensibly mitigated any reason to lie. On his deathbed, the French noble Melun asked, "What in the world should make me now deceive since I must lose the use of all deceit? Why should I then be false, if it is true that I must die here and live hence by truth?"[13]

Henry VI served as a further Shakespearean reference for Wigmore in his explanation of juror bias. As mentioned earlier, Wigmore warned that when a physical object was admitted in court, its very presence carried a misplaced authority that led jurors to believe readily allegations attached to it. To substantiate his point, Wigmore referenced a scene in *Henry VI* in which the leader of a mob attempted to convince a magistrate that he was the son of an earl, had been kidnapped, and eventually became a bricklayer. One of the leader's adherents, Smith the Weaver, added for effect, "Sir, he made a chimney in my father's house; and the bricks are alive at this day to testify it; therefore, deny it not!" As the existence of the bricks was wholly unrelated to the question of lineage, Shakespeare spoke to the specious legitimacy of physical objects that so alarmed Wigmore.[14]

If Shakespeare served as Wigmore's favorite literary reference, then Charles Dickens was a close second. For example, Wigmore drew from Dickens in highlighting the potential of aggressive cross-examination to elicit unintentionally spurious testimony. In *The Pickwick Papers*, Dickens created a scene in which a character named Nathaniel Winkle, under the strain of an antagonistic cross-examiner and a hostile judge, was "reduced to the requisite ebb of nervous perplexity" while two corroborating witnesses were similarly "driven to the verge of desperation by excessive badgering."[15]

Dickens's *Bleak House* also provided literary support for Wigmore's opposition to theological tests that assessed the capacity of a child witness to swear an oath. Dickens shared Wigmore's concern that a tribunal would needlessly ignore the valid testimony of a child merely because the youth lacked a mature understanding of religious conventions. A coroner in Dickens's novel dismissed the testimony of a youngster called "Little Jo" because he doubted the child's appreciation of divine punishment for perjury. "Can't exactly say what'll be done to him after he's dead if he tells a lie to the gentlemen here, but believes it'll be something very bad to punish him, and serve him right, and so he'll tell the truth," the coroner explained to the jurors. The coroner summarily rejected Little Jo's pretenses to truthfulness: "'Can't exactly say,' won't do, you know. We can't take that, in a court of justice, gentlemen! It's terrible depravity." Notably, Wigmore contributed to as well as borrowed from the fiction community; author Arthur Train maintained a close relationship with Wigmore and sought his advice for plots in legal novels.[16]

In crafting the rules of evidence, Wigmore also looked to the Bible as a source of cultural authority (next to the Shakespeare play that he kept in his briefcase was a copy of both the Old and New Testament). Wigmore asserted that a parent's conduct towards a child was admissible in proving lineage and recalled King Solomon's legendary resolution of a dispute between two mothers. In the First Book of Kings, two women gave birth within a few days and one of the babies passed away. Both mothers claimed parentage of the surviving infant, and King Solomon offered to divide the baby in two with a sword. While the imposter approved of Solomon's judgment, the true mother protested, "O my lord, give her the living child, and in no wise slay it." Solomon then ruled in favor of the real parent, whose maternal concern indicated the actual kinship.[17]

Wigmore again referenced the Bible in justifying the sequestration of witnesses to prevent collusion between them. In the "History of Susanna," from the Book of Daniel, the married Susanna rebuffed the advances of two men, who, in revenge, falsely accused her of infidelity. The slighted suitors both claimed that they had witnessed Susanna's illicit tryst take place under a tree in her husband's garden. Daniel separated the accusers and inquired what type of tree had sheltered the alleged adultery. When one answered "mastick" and the other "holm," Daniel exposed the inconsistency and exonerated Susanna. According to Wigmore, this episode catalyzed the time-honored practice of separating witnesses.[18]

While Shakespeare, Dickens, and the Bible were the Treatise's most popular nonlegal sources, Wigmore relied on a host of other figures of cultural import. On the efficacy of reputation as evidence of character, Wigmore cited both Confucius's warning, "How can a man conceal his character!" and Ralph Waldo Emerson's insight, "Human character evermore publishes itself." He referred to the Roman rhetorician Quintilian on the art of witness examination. To highlight the potential abuses of cross-examiners, Wigmore drew from the work of English novelist Anthony Trollope.[19]

Wigmore also made frequent allusions to extralegal authorities without citing them directly. His declaration, "To cross-examine, or not to cross-examine,—that is the fundamental question," echoed Shakespeare's *Hamlet*. Elaborating on an ancient, anonymous proverb, Wigmore remarked, "Whom the gods wish to destroy, they first make mad; which, for legal precedents, means that they must first be misunderstood." In a final example, he referenced characters in a Robert Southey poem in his description of the bench's mindless acceptance of the marital privilege doctrine. In the poem, the child Peterkin questioned his grandfather, Caspar, about the purpose of a fabled war, to which Caspar replied, "Why, that I cannot tell . . . But 'twas a famous victory!" Wigmore depicted an "inquisitive little Peterkin at the bar" who was "questioning too rashly the postulates and the platitudes of the Caspars of the profession" and "had to be satisfied with what was vouchsafed." Through these allusions—both explicit and implicit—to iconic cultural sources, Wigmore demonstrated a vision of the law as an integrated component of society.[20]

The Individual versus the Collective

Just as Wigmore understood law and society as an integrated whole, so too did he consider the individual in the context of the collective. More specifically, he joined other legal modernists in subjugating the individual to the whole. Wigmore articulated his general philosophy on the relationship between self and society in a discussion of a doctrine that legally compelled witnesses to testify in court. He acknowledged and dismissed two potential sacrifices demanded of the witness. While testifying in court often entailed "a sacrifice of time and labor, and thus of ease, of profits, of livelihood," nevertheless, "this contribution is not to be regarded as a gratuity, or a courtesy, or an ill-requited favor. . . . He who will live by society must let society live by him."[21]

A witness's second sacrifice was privacy. Wigmore recognized that testimony could foment "enmity or disgrace or ridicule or other disfavoring action of fellow-members of the community" against a witness. Still, Wigmore concluded that this too was "a contribution which he makes in payment of his dues to society." Denying any purely confidential domain, Wigmore contended that "when the course of justice requires the investigation of the truth, no man has any knowledge that is rightly private."[22]

For Wigmore, judicial inquiry appeared on its face to serve individual purposes, but in fact the community as a whole maintained a vested interest in the administration of justice. In legitimating compulsory testimony, he suggested,

> From the point of view of society's *right* to our testimony, it is to be remembered that the demand comes, not from any one person or set of persons, but from the community as a whole. . . . The dramatic features of the daily

court-room tend to obscure this; the matter seems to be between neighbor Doe and neighbor Roe. . . . But the right merely happens to be exemplified in the case of Doe *v.* Roe; that is all. The whole life of the community, the regularity and continuity of its relations, depend upon the coming of the witness. . . . The business of the particular cause is petty and personal; but the results that hang upon it are universal. All society, potentially, is involved in each individual case; because the process itself is one of vitality. Each verdict upon each cause, and each witness to that verdict, is a pulse of air in the breathing organs of the community.[23]

Wigmore's vision here was a deeply modernist one: individuals existed not as autonomous beings but only in reference to the broader society in which they lived. Seemingly personal disputes were, in reality, matters of the public welfare. Society, not self, constituted the organizing principle of law.

In Wigmore's analysis, the legal fraternity should not situate rules that facilitated fact-finding in the context of individual rights because judicial inquiry was a public good. He was keen, for instance, to emphasize that the auxiliary policy of "confusion of issues" was not rooted in any particular right. "It is not a question of rights," asserted Wigmore, "but of the discovery of truth." Similarly, he dismissed the argument that potential witnesses could abstain from depositions because of "personal inconvenience." "The notion that any citizen's private interests," Wigmore claimed, "should override his duty to the community is a false one. The principle that the whole community, and every member of it, should join in rendering all possible aid to the establishment of truth and justice is a fundamental one in civilized society."[24]

Wigmore systematically upheld or repudiated a given individual right based on its relationship to the commonweal. He approved of a privilege against disclosure of a witness's vote in an election because "the community's interest is that the citizen's vote" was "absolutely sincere," and only secrecy could guard against the "influences of oppression" that sought to "coerce the elector into an insincere vote." In a similar vein, Wigmore championed the privilege against self-incrimination. Regarding the defendant, such a privilege "does not require or condone his protection as an end good in itself or good under any circumstances. It is enough for justice and for the commonwealth that the privilege exists." Wigmore further characterized the privilege as "a particular harm which we suffer for the larger good."[25]

Just as Wigmore drew on communal concerns to support certain individual rights, so too did he reference the aggregate social welfare in renouncing others. For instance, he criticized "a privilege against the disclosure of political *opinion,* because it is not for the interest of the community that such beliefs should remain secret. The formation of a sound public opinion, by discussion and comparison, is essential in all representative government; and there is no good reason why any citizen should be encouraged to go through life with mute secrecy upon his political views." As the United States grew increasingly urban, industrial, and interdependent, society seemed to modernists such as Wigmore less a sum of autonomous individuals and more an organism whose constituent elements could not be disaggregated from one another.[26]

Science

Wigmore looked outside the law to modern scientific thought as a model for factual inquiry. For most of the nineteenth century, American scientists had subscribed to a "Baconian model" of investigation, named for the English thinker Francis Bacon (1561–1626). Baconians gathered facts empirically, created taxonomies that organized these facts, and induced general laws to explain these systems of truths. Baconianism, as it was practiced in the United States, bore little resemblance to Bacon's actual scientific philosophy. Whereas American Baconians emphasized the passive observation of nature and eschewed speculative theories, Bacon had actually championed experimentation and hypotheses. Historians have long commented on these discrepancies.[27]

The grip of Baconianism on American science began to loosen gradually in the 1830s and then more rapidly after the 1859 publication of Darwin's *Origins of Species*. By the close of the century, scientists had discarded the last vestiges of Baconianism. A "progressivist" mode of science came to embrace the utility of hypothesis, active experimentation as a vehicle for generating knowledge, and the contingency of scientific findings.[28]

Wigmore displayed his break from outdated scientific practice when he chastised the bench and bar for its reticence to allow experimentation as part of judicial inquiry. Blaming "juristic narrowmindedness," "an ignorance of precedents," and "a bigoted fear of everything not technical," Wigmore documented the "alarm at experimental evidence" among legal practitioners as well as their "disinclination to accept what does not come in the accustomed shapes of certified copies, sealed instruments, and sworn depositions." Wigmore applied his own faith in experimentation to a common inquiry in trials: "whether a certain machine, house, field, mine, or other thing" could accomplish an alleged act "under given conditions of time, strength, skill, or achievement." He concluded that "it is a crude error to suppose that the law of evidence here 'prefers speculation to experience, abhors actual experiment, and delights in guesswork.'" Far from evincing a Baconian preference for the mere collection of data, Wigmore strongly believed in experimentation to produce valid evidence.[29]

Wigmore's willingness to defer to scientific experts and their own professional standards further signals his embrace of modern science. He chastised judges who excluded the testimony of those persons recognized as scientific experts. Occasionally, a "Court assumes to intrude into the technical domain of the engineer, the physician, and other scientific professional men, and to deny the possibilities of knowledge therein." Noting the necessity of hyperspecialization in scientific pursuits, Wigmore understood the scientist's inevitable "reliance on the *reported data of fellow-scientists*, learned by perusing their reports in books and journals. The law must and does accept this kind of knowledge from scientific men." "To reject a professional physician or mathematician," he continued, "because the fact or some facts to which he testifies are known to him only upon the authority of others would be to ignore the accepted methods of professional work."[30]

Alongside his promotion of experimentation and respect for scientific standards, Wigmore adopted the modern scientific notion that agreement among experts was the litmus test for establishing truth. In a discussion of instruments, he indicated his appreciation of science as a process of approximating truth by means of professional consensus. To receive from a witness testimony premised on observations aided by an instrument (such as a microscope), the party had to establish the legitimacy of the instrument. According to Wigmore, "if the appropriate science or art has advanced to a certain degree of general recognition" among experts, then "this trustworthiness may be judicially noticed as too notorious to need evidence." As a corollary, Wigmore was hesitant to presume that which had not yet engendered scientific agreement. "A shock received by the mother during pregnancy may leave a mark upon the child has long been a popular belief," observed Wigmore. "Should it ever receive scientific sanction in any defined terms, the child's corporal mark after birth may be taken as evidential of the act which produced it."[31]

Wigmore also subscribed to the advanced scientific conception of "truth" as open to revision, in contrast to the Baconian ideal of absolute truth. His characterization of the law of evidence as embodying "the living principles of evidence" betokens his intention to frame the subject within the parameters of contingency. The *Treatise's* closing remarks underscore this interpretation: "There is still room for improvement and expansion. Here, as everywhere, the time has hardly come when the law can afford to consider as closed that great period of rational advance which owed its first marked impulse to the caustic preaching of Bentham." Wigmore's view of his own work as far from definitive, of law itself as dynamic rather than static, dovetailed with the scientific ethic of provisional knowledge.[32]

Wigmore's comfort with scientific discord further displays his departure from Baconian science. In the Baconian model, disagreement among scientists had appeared to undermine their pretenses to credible knowledge. Now, the scientific community viewed discord as a vital antecedent to consensus because science required rigorous investigators to test competing theories before they selected and refined the most compelling ones.[33] For Wigmore's part, he readily rejected arguments against the admission of "learned treatises" in court. "We are told," Wigmore recounted, "that science is shifting; that experiment and discovery are continually altering scientific theories and rendering them valueless; so that 'a medical book which was a standard last year becomes obsolete this year'; that there is no general agreement among scientists, and that testimony characterized by such instability and uncertainty is untrustworthy." Wigmore dismissed this claim as an "ignorant exaggeration" and noted that scientific experts called to the stand regularly disagreed and still their testimony was admissible. In his view, courtrooms were naturally conflict-laden arenas; that litigating parties exploited disputes in the scientific community did not obviate science's value to the law.[34]

While Wigmore certainly aspired to align evidence law with advanced scientific ideals, he also recognized that there were important differences between the laboratory and the courtroom. The limits of the legal system—such as the need for expediency and the lack of professional training for jurors—rendered judicial inquiry cruder than its scientific counterpart. "So far as the tribunal can attempt expressly to deal at all with logical questions," Wigmore conceded, "it can do so only roughly and loosely and in a general way." Another distinction was that a single scientist could consider all available evidence and draw conclusions, whereas "the legal tribunal is . . . divided in function; the judge passes first upon the evidence and sets aside the tidbits for the jury; that which is not worth considering, for one reason or another affecting its value, never reaches the auxiliary functionaries, the jurors." While the analogy between science and law was admittedly inexact, Wigmore still sought to ground the rules of evidence on a solid scientific foundation, and in so doing exhibited a patently forward-thinking conception of science.[35]

Social Constructs

Historian N. E. H. Hull, while acknowledging that Wigmore had some "progressive" tendencies, brands him "an advocate of nineteenth-century moralistic, natural law philosophy." To the contrary, Wigmore consistently championed the modernist view that legal principles, categories, and relations were socially constructed rather than natural and immutable. He held, for instance, that bright-line natural classification was a myth and openly acknowledged that he was creating legal taxonomies out of convenience. Consider the rule that when proving "a habit or cause of conduct," evidence of the "prior or subsequent existence" of any such conduct was admissible in court. Wigmore noted that this doctrine's "use is most frequent for facts which can at first sight hardly be ranked here in any natural classification." Similarly, he maintained that "in the classification of circumstantial evidence," "there can be, at certain points, no sharp distinction" between the various categories. "The propositions which come to be proved before tribunals of justice embrace every sort of fact in life, and no classification not purely arbitrary can divide them for practical purposes into classes always absolutely distinct." Wigmore readily accepted the capricious rather than innate character of legal classification.[36]

Wigmore also created rather than discovered categories for evidence pointing to a "tendency" of an entity that demonstrated the entity's "effects" (for instance, if a locomotive *tended* to emit sparks, this tendency may have indicated that the train *effected* a fire). In formulating a logical organization for subtopics within this general category, Wigmore offered: "*Material effects*," "*Corporal effects*," and "*Mental and Moral Effects.*" He was quick to acknowledge that "this classification is to some extent arbitrary, as all must be, in the sense that some cases might equally well go in one group or another." Still, he defended the scheme because "the grouping is the most useful" as "it enables us to compare the employment of analogous kinds of effects, and to see how far the uses of related kinds of effects throw evidential light on each other." For Wigmore, utility rather than some inherent essence of a category dictated classification.[37]

Expert witness qualification was yet another area where Wigmore recognized the constructed quality of legal categories. He delineated two general classes of experts. First, there was expertise based on "*special and peculiar experience*," such as that of an "advertising-agent" or "woodchopper," who could shed light on issues like fair prices in their respective industries. The second class comprised scientific experts, whose knowledge was rooted in "systematic training" in a "branch of some science or art." "Now the line," Wigmore remarked, "if any can be drawn, between these two" classes of experts "has no general legal significance. In truth no accurate line can be drawn. Each shades into the other imperceptibly."[38]

Various other kinds of evidence gave rise, in Wigmore's view, to artificial taxonomies. In determining which character traits were determinable by reputation, Wigmore concluded, "the line between those personal qualities which are properly provable by reputation and those which are not is a difficult one to draw; it cannot be definitely fixed by way of deduction from principle." He also identified three types of official documents—registers, returns, and certificates—and acknowledged that some documents fell under more than one category, while others, such as executive proclamations, resided in none. Moreover, in devising an organization for declarations of a mental condition, which were admissible as hearsay exceptions, Wigmore recognized that "the grouping must be somewhat arbitrary." Nevertheless, he strove to formulate "the most practicable" scheme, thereby underscoring his commitment to functionality as a guiding principle in classification.[39]

For some spheres of evidence law, Wigmore felt that any system of organization would be so capricious that he opted not to develop a classification at all. In discussing the futility of categorizing those circumstances likely to engender a particular emotion, Wigmore insisted that "it would be idle to attempt to catalogue the various facts of human life with reference to their potency in exciting a given emotion," and derided any such effort as "pedantic" and "useless." In the same vein, Wigmore determined that the numerous statutes allowing certain types of affidavits as hearsay exceptions were "too varied to admit of a systematic classification." Here again we see his preference to leave a mass of precedents in a confused state rather than impose a false sense of coherence.[40]

To qualify, Wigmore did not take the extreme view that all categories were arbitrary. He discriminated, for example, between various kinds of circumstantial evidence, and divided "Human Acts" from "Human Quality, Condition, or other attribute." Although the line separating these classes of evidence was "a rough and practical one," still, wrote Wigmore, the distinction was "in essence a real and unavoidable one."[41]

If classification was one subject that indicated Wigmore's conception of law as a social construct, then rationality was another. Rationality served as a key theme—arguably *the* central motif—of the *Treatise*. Wigmore's goal was to expose irrationality in evidence law wherever he could find it, and to ground the rules of evidence on a sober, enlightened foundation. As discussed in chapter 1, he viewed rationality as a product of transient societal definitions.[42]

Wigmore applied a constructivist conception of rationality to specific evidentiary issues. When the "insane millionaire" Horace Hawes ranked himself as the second greatest man in human history behind Jesus Christ, "it was easy to judge the irrationality of the latter statement." Conversely, "we do not regard Napoleon as irrational because he believed himself the greatest general in the world's history." In other words, context mattered. "The rationality of" one's "acts is to be ascertained only by comparing the results of his reasoning with the data that lay before him to be reasoned upon." In Wigmore's view, rationality was defined not by any internal logic but by the milieu; particular circumstances could imbue a statement or action with rationality.[43]

Although Wigmore depicted rationality as a social construct rather than an essential standard, he found the concept coherent enough to be useful. In determining whether a testator possessed the requisite mental capacity to make decisions about the inheritance of his estate after death, Wigmore suggested the court look to the will itself as evidence. If the will featured "such terms as a rational man would presumably have sanctioned," then the tribunal could infer mental capacity. Wigmore's application of rationality presumed it to be a commonly understood and basically uncontested subject. In light of the centrality of rationality to the *Treatise*, anything less would prove fatal to the whole enterprise.[44]

In addition to classification and rationality, Wigmore perceived knowledge as the product of social processes. For example, he believed that truth itself was a historically contingent concept. In reviewing an obsolete rule that had disqualified witnesses with some stake in a given trial, Wigmore recalled that the legal system formerly considered "total exclusion" as the only "proper safeguard" against potentially biased witnesses, and anyone with a "pecuniary interest" in the proceeding automatically fell into the class of proscribed witnesses. Both of these premises, "though they may now seem fallacious enough, were in the 1700s accepted as axioms of truth." Truth changed over time; it was not an immutable ideal.[45]

Wigmore viewed truth as historically contingent because it was through communal processes that society created knowledge. He contended, for instance, that one's reputation was admissible for proving character if "there is likely to be such a constant, active, and intelligent discussion and comparison that the resulting opinion, if a definite opinion does result, is likely to be fairly trustworthy." In Wigmore's estimation, knowledge was produced by the community, not uncovered by the individual.[46]

While property was a sacrosanct concept in the formalist model, Wigmore readily depicted property as a transient social construct. "The money which others are willing to lay out in purchasing" an article was the only measure of its value, not its "nature or quality." Wigmore preferred the precision of market value to the hazy notion of property's essential nature. "Their offers of money not merely indicate the value," he insisted; "they *are* the value." Wigmore applied this reasoning to cases involving the establishment of a property's value. A witness's "knowledge of the various qualities and uses of an article" was inadmissible as testimony "if it stops short of including the exchangeable rate which these qualities actually give it."[47]

Risk was also a social construct, according to Wigmore. He discussed cases in which an insured party failed to disclose information that may have allowed an insurer to charge a higher rate for the insurance policy, an omission that potentially voided the policy because its terms were not genuine. This became an evidentiary issue when a tribunal relied on an expert witness to testify as to whether the undisclosed information would have changed the risk *as defined by industry standards.* "The word 'risk' does not mean 'actual danger,'" Wigmore explained, "but 'danger as determined by the insurer's classification of the various circumstances affecting the rate of premium.' Our main inquiry, then, is as to the insurer's schedule of classified 'risks.'" For the purposes of the justice system, "risk" was an industrial-legal construct rather than an "objective reality." This was the position of only a few courts before the publication of the *Treatise*, suggesting that Wigmore's view of law as socially constructed was among the more advanced elements of his modernist agenda.[48]

Wigmore also saw indecency not as an essential abstraction but as a concept contingent on social settings. He acknowledged that courts hesitated to admit an indecency as evidence because it could "excite prurient attention" among spectators and cause "shame and embarrassment" for the party possessed of the indecent evidence. Wigmore then challenged the idea of an inherent sense of indecency. Noting that it "is often regarded as though it were an absolute quality of words and actions," he insisted, "in truth, it is merely a relative term." Wigmore offered the example of "indecent exposure" of one's body, which would have been entirely appropriate in a doctor's office. Accordingly, he saw fit to defer to the discretion of the trial judge, who could best respond to the particularities of the given case, for only a specific context rendered an act indecent.[49]

Criminality was a final concept that Wigmore recast as a social construct. In a review of the privilege against self-incrimination, Wigmore asserted that a party could not invoke the privilege for an activity that had been decriminalized. "Criminality is the creation of the law," he maintained, "not an inherent element in the act itself. It may therefore be taken away by the law." Here Wigmore articulated a central component of legal modernism: if the core concepts of law were merely constructs rather than immutable principles, then they were susceptible to government regulation.[50]

Relationalism

Just as modernists broke from essentialist thought by treating core legal concepts as socially constructed, so too did they militate against essentialism by emphasizing the relations between things rather than some intrinsic quality of each. In an integrated world where law was only understood with reference

to society, and the individual in connection to the collective, essentialist approaches gave way to relational treatments. Wigmore adopted relationalism and
applied to it diverse areas of evidence law.

Wigmore repeatedly highlighted the connection between evidence and the
fact to be proved because it was this relation—not some property inherent to
the evidence—that determined which rule governed admissibility. Hearsay was
one area where he stressed this relational aspect. To use Wigmore's example,
consider a man on trial for the murder of a woman whom he had allegedly
seduced. The hypothetical defendant claimed that the victim discovered that
she was pregnant and this knowledge caused her to commit suicide. A witness's
testimony that he had heard the woman mention her pregnancy was admissible,
explained Wigmore, if the defense used the testimony to establish the deceased's
belief in her own pregnancy. It was, however, inadmissible as hearsay if intended
to show that she was actually pregnant. In other words, the testimony could
speak to the existence of the woman's statement but not to the truth of that
statement. Similarly, Wigmore suggested that testimony from a witness who
claimed that he heard a man declare an absurdity such as, "I am the King of
Dahomey," was admissible if meant to demonstrate the man's insanity rather
than his royal station.[51]

If hearsay was one branch of evidence law where Wigmore focused on the
relation between evidence and the fact to be proved, then the authentication of
documents was a second. He noted that courts typically required parties to produce the original version of a contested document. "But," pleaded Wigmore,
"'original' is a relative term only." He considered the instance of an original
libelous document retained in a desk and a copy made public. Technically, the
original had to be produced in court although the copy, in reality, was the article in question. Wigmore concluded, "The terms 'copy' and 'original,' being
purely relative to each other, have no inherent relation to the present rule"
requiring documentary originals.[52]

In addition to hearsay and documents, reputation was another realm where
Wigmore emphasized the connection between evidence and an alleged fact.
He explained that a party could submit reputation as circumstantial evidence
intended to speak to one's actual character (i.e., the jury could infer that one's
reputation accurately reflected his or her character). In a wholly distinct scenario,
a party could offer evidence of a maligned reputation to prove defamation. Here,
"reputation is the fact to be proved, irrespective of the actual character reputed,"
so the evidence in this instance is not circumstantial. According to Wigmore, the
relation between reputation evidence and the fact to be proved, not some internal essence of the evidence, determined which rules of admissibility applied.[53]

Just as Wigmore illuminated the links between evidence and the fact to be proved, so too did he consider the association between different articles of evidence. Rules regarding documents figured prominently in this strand of relational thinking. For a so-called "ancient document [i.e., a document at least thirty years old] whose age renders testimonial corroboration of its authenticity impossible," Wigmore recommended viewing the document in light of other relevant evidence. The document's location, appearance, and "other circumstances, suffice, in combination, as evidence to be submitted to the jury."[54]

He also employed this holistic approach in his treatment of crime. According to Wigmore, a series of acts, none inherently criminal, could aggregate into criminal behavior. He cited embezzlement, arson, and forgery as crimes involving many steps, where "no one of the component facts constitutes of itself the crime, and yet every one of them must be established in order to establish the crime." Wigmore treated fraudulent transfers of property in the same vein, maintaining that the tribunal had to review, in tandem, "the *quantity* of property," "the *persons* to whom the transfers are made," "the *time* of other transfers," and "the *consideration*" (i.e., was the transfer voluntary). "On the whole," Wigmore surmised, "while several sorts of circumstances are significant, their weight may vary in each case, and no one of them is essential." His aversion here to essentializing crime dovetailed with his characterization of crime as a social construct.[55]

Wigmore's interest in the relations between articles of evidence further informed his treatment of the identification of a person or object. Proper identification, he believed, turned on no one essential feature. "The process of constructing an inference of identification," observed Wigmore, "consists usually in adding together a number of circumstances, each of which by itself might be a feature of many objects, but all of which together can conceivably coexist in a single object only." To use Wigmore's example, a will left an estate to a son named John Smith. Many men shared the name, and the court had to determine whether a particular John Smith, alleging to be the rightful heir, was indeed the son of the deceased parent. Assume that it was known that the actual son had the middle name "Barebones Bonaparte," resided at a particular address, and fathered a specific number of children. If the alleged son could prove that he himself was described by this peculiar set of facts, then it was likely that he was the heir in question. Wigmore advised that courts not consider each element of identity individually; only "the total combination of circumstances" could determine admissibility.[56]

Wigmore's relational framework encompassed yet another sphere of evidence law—witness qualification. For instance, derangement only disqualified a witness if that impairment had a connection to the topic of questioning. "The inquiry is always as to the relation of the derangement to the subject to be testified about. If on this subject no derangement appears," Wigmore concluded, "the person is acceptable, however untrustworthy on other subjects." Regarding expert witnesses, Wigmore wrote that "the capacity is *in every case a relative one, i. e.* relative *to the topic about which the person is asked to make his statement.*"[57]

The relations between evidentiary admissions influenced a range of other rules in the *Treatise*. In determining what constituted a self-contradiction, Wigmore stated that any "inconsistency is to be determined, not by individual words or phrases alone, but by the whole impression or effect of what has been said or done." Similarly, when trying to prove a verbal utterance, the tribunal had to examine "the utterance as a whole" by "comparing the successive elements and their mutual relations. To look at a part alone would be to obtain a false notion." Wigmore also maintained that counsel had to demonstrate the relation between a physical object submitted as evidence and the party in question. For instance, a knife could not simply be admitted under the assumption that it belonged to the defendant; the party offering the knife had to prove its connection. "A chain binds no prisoner if any link is missing," he announced in a particularly apropos metaphor for his holistic method. Wigmore's was an approach typical of an increasingly interdependent world that found essentialist views barren.[58]

Sociological Jurisprudence

Wigmore was not entirely modernist in the *Treatise*; indeed, he demonstrated little interest in a major component of legal modernism: sociological jurisprudence. Content to defer to his own sense of "experience" or "human nature," Wigmore crafted evidence doctrine with little reliance on social scientific data. For example, he maintained that while there had "been no careful collection of statistics of untrue confessions," still, "in a rough and indefinite way, experience" formed the "ground of distrust of confessions," which, he warned, were sometimes colored by "a promise of certain pardon" or "a threat of instant hanging by a mob."[59]

While sociological jurisprudence was absent from the *Treatise*, it would be unfair to suggest that Wigmore failed to anticipate this vital pillar of modern legal thought. In reality, he carefully considered social scientific findings but was incredulous of their applicability to evidence law. A dispute between Harvard psychologist Hugo Münsterberg and Wigmore offers the best indication that Wigmore's views in this area were not antiquated but prescient; Wigmore understood before other modernists did the difficulty in building a meaningful bridge between social science and law.

In 1908, Münsterberg published *On the Witness Stand*. In this text, the author sharply criticized the legal fraternity for failing to implement the findings of psychology. Whereas other spheres of society had reaped the benefits of his field, Münsterberg lamented that "the lawyer alone is obdurate." "The lawyer and the judge and the juryman," Münsterberg continued, "are sure that they do not need the experimental psychologist. They do not wish to see that in this field preeminently applied psychology has made long strides." He targeted his book to a popular audience in the hopes that public opinion would force legal practice to reconcile itself to psychological research.[60]

In the *Illinois Law Review*, Wigmore delivered a devastating blow to *On the Witness Stand*. He argued that the application of psychology to legal practice was premature because psychologists themselves had reached no consensus on how to establish credible testimony. "Judges are quite likely to admit new psychological instruments," Wigmore assured his readers, "as soon only as these are guaranteed beyond question of trustworthiness, by the psychological profession." It was hardly surprising that little consensus emerged from this corner of academe; the psychological study of witness testimony was, as Wigmore pointed out, a novel field. Psychologists engaged in the subject "confess that thousands of experiments and years of research will be required before they will be practicable, if ever." He cited several relevant academics who openly doubted the usefulness of their findings to legal practitioners. Wigmore was skeptical that psychology would ever benefit the law. "The individual variety of personality," he declared, "defy [*sic*] applied psychology." Wigmore further noted that even in the very countries where this research occurred, courts had not adopted any of these psychological methods.[61]

Wigmore also outlined several specific criticisms of the psychological research that Münsterberg lauded. According to Wigmore, the suggestion in the literature that witness testimony was not reliable was hardly groundbreaking. Wigmore quoted several judges who had already offered the very conclusions from the bench that scholars were now publishing in journals. Another source of concern was that psychological studies focused on testimonial reliability among witnesses who strived for honesty, but, as Wigmore related, many witnesses in court deliberately obscured the truth. Even if psychologists made substantial progress in this area of inquiry, he predicted, the privilege against self-incrimination would allow defendants to nullify these scientific gains. So comprehensive was Wigmore's treatment of the relevant scholarship that his article became a useful survey for many psychologists.[62]

It is worthwhile to distinguish between Wigmore's hesitance to apply psychology to trials and his respect for Münsterberg as a scholar. Indeed, Wigmore asked Münsterberg in 1913 for permission to publish a portion of *On the Witness Stand* in his forthcoming *Principles of Judicial Proof*. Münsterberg acceded to the request, and Wigmore wrote to "thank you heartily for your kind consent to my use of the passage from your book." The Northwestern dean also sought to allay any residual concerns that Münsterberg might have entertained given Wigmore's earlier reproach. "You need not fear that I should attempt to take advantage of the occasion to continue the sarcastic controversy of three years ago," Wigmore assured the psychologist. "I am anxious, in this book, to see your views expounded fully to law students." That Wigmore incorporated Münsterberg's ideas into *Principles* but not the *Treatise* is telling; Wigmore was willing to engage psychology in a work of theory, but this did not mean he was ready to translate psychological findings into evidence doctrine.[63]

In the decades that followed, many modernists grew increasingly drawn to the promise of social science only to see their efforts repeatedly fail. In the most thoroughgoing historical study of unsuccessful bids to recast law as a social science, John Henry Schlegel targets "the professional identity of the law professor" as the ultimate detriment to a social scientific agenda. Legal rules were central to legal scholarship; by discounting the primacy of rules, "science was too threatening" to the "special preserve of the law professor." Stated another way, the professional predilection to "teach law" proved inconsonant with the social scientific imperative to "teach about law." Considering that reformers never molded the discipline of law into an empirical science, Wigmore's caution in this arena is better understood as farsighted rather than reactionary because he carefully considered the possibilities and foresaw their pitfalls.[64]

Judging

I N CRAFTING THE rules of evidence, John Henry Wigmore consistently directed the bench to adhere to a modernist conception of judging. He called on the judiciary to eschew universal principles and instead treat cases on individual bases. As a corollary, Wigmore championed increased judicial discretion, deriding the notion of judge-as-umpire. The *Treatise* advocated balancing tests wherein the judge would weigh competing principles, stakeholders, and interests. Wigmore also exhorted the bench to focus on actual outcomes, draw wisdom from lived experience, and reject hollow abstractions. His ideal judge was a consummate functionalist who prized practicality and expedience.

Anti-Universalism

Modernists rejected the quixotic search for universal principles and absolute truths. Instead, they sought a flexible legal system that could both accommodate the contingencies of individual cases and acknowledge uncertainties. To this end, Wigmore's *Treatise* was deeply modernist, conspicuous in its embrace of an anti-universalist ethic. He may have nominally subsumed evidence law under one unifying (albeit circular) principle, but in the substance of the *Treatise*, Wigmore admonished judges to oppose axiomatic thinking as inherently inconsistent with the demands of legal practice. In his view, evidence law generally "does not result in abstract rules; each ruling stands by itself, and can form no precedent." He often spurned even suggestive guidelines and preferred courts to make case-by-case decisions.[1]

Wigmore frequently applied his anti-universalist mindset to documentary issues. Courts sometimes allowed a party's failure to respond to a document to constitute an admission of the document's legitimacy (because an erroneous document would have prompted a response). Refusing to issue a mandate, Wigmore wrote that "any definite rule" would "seem impracticable; and the precedents indicate that each case must stand on its own facts." The judiciary also struggled to determine if one document explicitly referring or implicitly relating to another triggered the admission of the second document. The decision, stated Wigmore, "will depend upon the circumstances of each case and the character of each document, and no fixed rule can fairly be laid down." The courts also entertained controversy over the authentication of ancient wills and deeds. Some judges contended that possession of a given tract of land was a necessary antecedent to proving the authenticity of the will or deed for that land, but Wigmore disagreed. "It would seem better to lay down no fixed rule," he declared, "but to let the circumstances of each case indicate whether there is any additional corroboration of genuineness." In other cases, when parties claimed that a document was lost and could not be produced in court, the bench had futilely tried to develop tests to determine whether the search for the document had been exhaustive and the document deemed irretrievable. According to Wigmore, "*There is not and cannot be any universal or fixed rule to test the sufficiency of the search* for a document alleged to be lost. The inquiry must depend entirely on the circumstances of the case." For Wigmore, a lack of rules was not a limitation for the bench to concede but a solution to champion.[2]

In addition to documents, hearsay exceptions presented a number of dilemmas that Wigmore refused to counter with guiding principles. Courts reasoned that imminent death removed worldly motives to distort the truth, and therefore admitted dying declarations as hearsay exceptions. It was unclear, however, when a person truly possessed "a knowledge of approaching death." Wigmore declared, "No rule can here be laid down. The circumstances of each case will show whether the requisite consciousness existed." Evidence law further exempted from the hearsay rule entries in a company's books because they were fairly credible if made in the course of ordinary business. While an "entry should have been made at or near the time of the transaction recorded," still, Wigmore insisted that "the rule fixes no precise time; each case must depend on its own circumstances." Elsewhere, Wigmore considered the admissibility of a previous trial's bill of exceptions as an official statement and therefore a hearsay exception. He reviewed the arguments in favor of and opposed to the policy and concluded, "The question is a difficult one to settle by a general rule, and must depend much on the local professional methods." Moreover, courts generally considered spontaneous exclamations sincere and therefore exempt from the hearsay rule. Wigmore chastised the various supreme courts for "unnecessary and unprofitable quibbles" in determining how long after an event an exclamation was no longer deemed spontaneous. "Instead of struggling weakly for the impossible," he averred, "they should decisively insist that every case be treated upon its own circumstances." In Wigmore's mind, the search for universals was a fool's errand.[3]

If documents and hearsay exceptions were two topics where Wigmore applied an anti-universalist ethic, then questions for witnesses constituted a third. He reviewed the admissibility of hypothetical questions to experts based on premises unlikely to be accepted by the jury. On the one hand, it was difficult for the judge to predict what premises the jury would probably believe, so erring on the side of admission seemed preferable; on the other, the jury might accept the answer to a hypothetical question while forgetting its misleading premises. Although Wigmore endorsed efforts to "repress the abuses of the hypothetical question at the hands of unscrupulous tricksters," nevertheless, he affirmed, "it is improper and unnecessary to lay down any general rule." Similarly, Wigmore avoided issuing directives about questions premised on the veracity of other witnesses' testimony. The admissibility of such questions "must depend on the circumstances of the case. There should be no fixed rule excluding such a question." Furthermore, evidence law prohibited leading questions during direct examination for fear that they "may be misused" by counsel "to supply a false memory for the witness." On the futility of strictly defining a "leading question," Wigmore informed his judicial readership, "there can be no invariable test for the impropriety, merely so far as the form is concerned. Any question may be or may not be suggestive."[4]

Along with documents, hearsay exceptions, and witness examination, Wigmore treated witness impeachment from an anti-universalist perspective. He explained that a party could use both extrinsic testimony and cross-examination to impeach the credibility of witnesses on the specific topics of their testimony, but only cross-examination to impeach their general character. Evidence relating to an expert witness's "defect of skill" straddled this line and therefore raised difficult questions for judges about the propriety of extrinsic testimony. Ultimately, Wigmore concluded, "The line of distinction is so indefinite that no settled rule or definition can anywhere be surely predicated." In a discussion of a witness who improperly received advance notice of counsel's questions, Wigmore noted that this practice "is a difficult problem, which has been solved by declining to lay down any rules." He took a similar tack regarding the admissibility of evidence of external circumstances that likely induced bias in a witness, contending, "Accurate concrete rules are almost impossible to formulate, and where possible are usually undesirable." Wigmore therefore not only rebuked futile attempts to formulate rules but at times also opposed their creation even when feasible.[5]

Wigmore's distrust of categorical axioms extended to testimonial recollection as well. He considered the dilemma of allowing a witness to review a document in court to refresh his memory before providing testimony. The danger, Wigmore recognized, was that "these expedients for stimulating recollection may be so misused that the witness puts before the Court what purports to be but is not in fact his recollection and knowledge." Wigmore resolved that "no hard-and-fast rules can be laid down for invariable application. That which is suspicious and reprehensible in one instance may be entirely trustworthy in the next." In another recollection matter, courts differed in their approaches to past recollection. (Past recollection was something that a witness had recalled earlier and recorded in some form but could not recollect during the trial, in contrast to present recollection, which was something that a witness recalled on the stand.) Some judges required only that past recollection "when recorded, should have been *fairly fresh*" to warrant admission; others dictated a more stringent rule that past recollection must have been "recorded *at or near the time* of the events" to be admissible. Wigmore preferred the first alternative because it afforded greater leeway and thus "exemplifie[d] the excellent policy of leaving the law flexible and rational and not chilling it into rules more or less arbitrary." In conflating flexibility with rationality, Wigmore implied that universalism was irrational.[6]

Mental condition was yet another arena of evidence law where Wigmore called for an ad hoc approach from the bench. For example, he considered the admissibility of evidence of one's disposition upon arrest as evidence of guilt: "No fixed relations of inferences can be predicated for the same conduct in different persons," and therefore "no fixed rules should be laid down." Concerning insanity, courts held that evidence of "prior and subsequent mental condition" was admissible to prove insanity, but there was "no agreed definition of the limit of time within which such prior or subsequent condition is to be considered." According to Wigmore, "in the nature of things no definition is possible. The circumstances of each case must furnish the varying criterion." Another insanity matter involved the capacity of a lay witness to comment on whether she had witnessed symptoms of insanity in someone else. The courts agreed that, in principle, the layperson qualified, but disagreed on a test for determining what constituted a sufficient opportunity to observe insanity. "A precise definition," wrote Wigmore, "which shall be at once both flexible enough to meet various situations and exact enough to be a rule at all, is difficult, if not impossible." He concluded, "The attempt to invent an all-sufficient form of words is as inexpedient as it is vain." In his view, absolutists were hubristic in their neglect of contingency.[7]

Wigmore situated the completeness rule within an anti-universalist para-digm. This doctrine held that parties could not admit verbal utterances, either written or spoken, in atomized parts that distorted the meaning of the words. If evidence law demanded the whole of the utterance to color fully the meaning of the part, then, asked Wigmore, what exactly constituted "*the whole* of the utterance?" "The possibilities are infinite and the boundaries indefinite in this search for entirety of utterance [*sic*]," he conceded. "It will be difficult for the law, in applying the principle, to employ any fixed test." In particular, he refused to apply a strict completeness test to public records. "The various sorts of pub-lic records," Wigmore explained, "differ so widely in tenor and constitution of parts that no fixed rule is possible."[8]

Secret communication was another topic in the *Treatise* that betokened Wigmore's anti-universalist approach. He noted that the attorney-client priv-ilege applied only when the client believed that the communications were confidential. In discerning when such an assumption existed, Wigmore con-tended, "These circumstances will of course vary in individual cases, and the ruling must therefore depend much on the case in hand." In another example, a witness could invoke a privilege against testifying about a secret divulged by his or her spouse. Secrecy need have been only implied rather than expressed, but certain circumstances, such as the presence of a third person, could have negated the "implication of secrecy" and therefore invalidated the privilege. Wigmore maintained that "fixed rules are scarcely possible" in determining which circumstances undermined the claim of secrecy.[9]

Wigmore conceded that general rules were, at times, useful to judges, but he also insisted that any rule should stand as a suggestion rather than a dictate. To legitimate this position, he turned to the nation's founders. Wigmore argued that they had designed federal and state constitutions not to be followed blindly to the letter but to be employed as general propositions that could bend to the needs of individual circumstances. He pointed to the "brief constitutional sanc-tion for trial by jury," which, "though absolute in form, did not attempt to enu-merate the excepted cases to which that form of trial was appropriate nor to describe the precise procedure involved in it." Similarly, "the brief prohibition against 'abridging the freedom of speech' was not intended to ignore the excep-tion for defamatory statements." According to Wigmore, the Constitution's role was to establish an accommodating framework, and so his malleable approach to evidence doctrine was simply an extension of the vision that the architects of American government set forth.[10]

Wigmore applied this ethic of flexibility to inconsistent statements from a witness. He explored a controversy involving alleged inconsistencies between a witness's testimony and another statement that the same witness made out of court. Judges often required cross-examiners to offer a "preliminary question" in which witnesses were asked if they indeed had made the inconsistent statement, thereby providing them with an opportunity to explain the inconsistency and warning that their opponent would use the out-of-court statement against them. Wigmore endorsed the rule, but insisted, "this requirement, instead of being rigid and invariable, should be open to exceptions." In another example, logic would seem to dictate that if a witness made a statement about an event out of court but later was unable to recall the same occurrence on the stand, then the initial statement should be admissible as evidence of inconsistent testimony. Courts, however, rejected this kind of evidence because the content of the initial statement tended to exert a greater impact on the jury than the statement's "aspect as a mere contradiction." Wigmore accepted this common judicial practice while warning, "An absolute rule of prohibition would do more harm than good."[11]

Wigmore's belief in pliant evidence doctrine further informed his rules of "auxiliary probative policy." In proving an injury at the hands of a "Machine, Highway, Railroad, or Building," a party often sought to demonstrate that others had endured harm from the same entity in question. Wigmore acknowledged that the auxiliary policy of "confusion of issues" potentially applied because "the introduction of many new controversial points" could distract the jury from the material issue in the case and produce "an expense of time disproportionate to the usefulness of the evidence." He supported the judicial prerogative to bar this kind of evidence, but derided the custom of "excluding such evidence absolutely and invariably" as "unnecessary and finical." Regarding the subset of auxiliary rules known as "simplicative rules," Wigmore affirmed, "It is a cardinal doctrine, applicable generally to all of the ensuing rules, that they are not invariable, that they are directory rather than mandatory." He went on to belittle those "inflexible dictates of absolute justice" that would hold otherwise. Universalism was Wigmore's anathema.[12]

A number of procedural issues covered in the *Treatise* reflected Wigmore's contention that any doctrine was at most a suggestion. Regarding a rule that prescribed public access to trials, he felt that "it is an excess of sentimental fastidiousness to deny the propriety of allowing exceptions," especially in instances where the crowd could erupt in violence. Typically, judges could not offer testimony in those trials over which they also presided. Wigmore, however, opposed any categorical prohibition on this dual role. In a rare use of an analogy, he proclaimed, "Military commanders do not train cannon on a garden-gate; and the law of evidence need not employ the cumbrous weapon of an invariable rule of exclusion to destroy an entire class of useful and unobjectionable evidence." To take another procedural example, courts usually banned the admission of evidence after closing arguments had begun. Wigmore chastised judges who ossified this rule into "a fixed and deadened formula" and thereby fomented "actual and frequent the possibilities of practical harm which were otherwise only latent" in the rule. In his mind, absolutism was inevitably detrimental to the administration of justice.[13]

Wigmore's comfort with contradiction also signaled his embrace of an anti-universalist ethic. He accepted the murky and conflict-laden character of the law, and preferred to acknowledge contradiction rather than impose a false sense of coherence. For example, Wigmore applied this approach to rules regarding a testator's beliefs about his own will. If a testator believed he had a will, then he likely did. Courts, however, grappled with the admissibility of evidence that demonstrated such belief but violated the hearsay rule. Given the mixed condition of judicial precedents, Wigmore declared "it impracticable to examine at this point the general state of the law." He drew similar conclusions regarding the admissibility of evidence of similar acts to demonstrate the increased likelihood of an alleged act: "It is hopeless to attempt to reconcile the precedents under the various heads." Wigmore further noted the ambiguity of statutes in various jurisdictions that dictated the admissibility of entries made in a business's book by a deceased person, reasoning, "It is perhaps vain to attempt to construe statutes whose framers themselves seem not to have understood precisely the bearing of their enactments." To qualify, he did not celebrate incoherence in the law—Wigmore very much deplored "leaving the law in a state of desperate uncertainty"—but he refused to project the illusion of harmony onto an unavoidably disputatious sphere of civic life.[14]

In general, Wigmore felt that probabilities, not quixotic aspirations to certainty, should govern the rules of evidence. If a party sought to establish, for instance, that person X's footprint in a given location indicated X's presence, Wigmore declared, "no one would contend" that "complete proof is necessary." Therefore, "when the fact of X's presence elsewhere is offered in disproof of his participation any evidence rendering this fact *probable* is receivable" [emphasis added]. Wigmore also framed causality within a probabilistic context: "Stated in its broadest form, the notion of cause and effect is merely that of invariable sequence. It is only rarely, however, if at all, that such an abstract assertion can be made in universal terms that will stand examination. . . . In short, instead of an absolute certainty or invariability of sequence, the assertion will be only of a very high probability of sequence."[15]

Furthermore, Wigmore considered witness testimony an inherently probabilistic enterprise. "If the law received as absolute knowledge what" a witness
"had to offer," considered Wigmore, "then only one witness would be needed
on any one matter; for the fact asserted would be demonstrated." Of course,
few if any trials concluded after a single person took the stand. In Wigmore's
view, the law must have reasonable expectations of witnesses and account for
the probabilistic nature of their testimonies. "The result of the witness' observation," he assured, "need not be positive or absolute knowledge. Such a degree
of certainty cannot be demanded, even in theory." The final three words are
telling; if epistemic certainty was illusory in practice, then for Wigmore it was
illegitimate in theory.[16]

Judicial Discretion

Whereas the formalist model envisioned the judge as a passive vehicle for
the application of legal doctrine to individual cases, Wigmore consistently
advocated increased judicial discretion throughout the *Treatise*. This tendency marched hand in hand with his anti-universalist ethic; in the absence of
binding rules, the judge necessarily had to take a more active role in the
courtroom.

In several key passages, Wigmore elaborated on his general philosophy of
judicial discretion. For example, he sought to revive the bench's prerogative to
question witnesses, a convention whose demise he blamed on "the sporting
theory of the common law." Under this theory, "litigation was a game of skill,
to be conducted according to specific rules," with "the judge primarily in the
position of the umpire of a game, whose duty it was to interfere only so far as
needed to decide whether the rules of the game had been violated." Wigmore
derided this mode of judicial passivity as a "degenerate tendency" and called
on judges to "maintain and vindicate" their right to question witnesses. He
further blamed this "spirit of gentlemanly sportsmanship," passed down to the
Americans from the English, for the loathsome Exchequer rule, which automatically granted a new trial for even a minor error in the admission or exclusion of evidence. Wigmore exclaimed, "The judge must cease to be merely an
umpire at the game of litigation."[17]

Wigmore found the umpire metaphor instructive in his condemnation of
the judiciary for allowing abusive cross-examinations. "The typical tendency
of the modern American judiciary," he lamented, "is to abdicate that power
of control over the trial which tradition and the due course of justice demand
that they shall have, and to become more and more mere umpires, who rule
upon errors and make no attempt otherwise to check the misconduct of

counsel." Here, Wigmore definitively eschewed the formalist vision of the judge as night watchman.[18]

Wigmore's discussion of the bench's relationship to the jury also captures his deeply modernist conception of judging. He endorsed the defunct practice that "the judge was entitled and bound to assist the jury, before their retirement, with an expression of his opinion (in no way binding them to follow it) upon the weight of the evidence." In most American jurisdictions, this "orthodox function of the judge to assist the jury on matters of fact" was "eradicated from our system" in a "misguided moment." He also bemoaned that American judges, unlike their English counterparts, typically failed to question jurors about their verdict before it became final to ensure that they had not "proceeded on a palpable mistake of law." According to Wigmore, in the "system in the United States, in which the judges tend to degenerate into mere umpires," this safeguard was regrettably rare.[19]

In many areas of evidence law, Wigmore found applications for this general philosophy of judicial discretion. Issues surrounding witness testimony in particular triggered Wigmore's deference to the ad hoc instructions of the bench. In the realm of testimonial qualification, Wigmore stated his position in unequivocal terms: "Emphatically, the *trial Court must be left to determine*, absolutely and without review, the fact of possession of the required qualification by a particular witness." For instance, if a witness suffered from "mental derangement" or was a child who might not possess "sufficient intelligence" to testify, then "the trial Court must be the one to determine" the witness's ability to take the stand.[20]

Within the domain of testimonial qualification, the role of expert witnesses posed a number of controversies that Wigmore felt were best left to the bench to decide. The legal community entertained doubts regarding the admissibility of expert testimony from recent medical school graduates because of their lack of experience. Wigmore conceded that contemporary medical education did involve practical experience, but nevertheless concluded that "the matter should rest in the trial judge's discretion." He also confronted the issue of expert witnesses who sought to provide testimony about a foreign legal system in which they were well versed but did not practice. While Wigmore recommended that the degree of similarity between a witness's domestic law and the system in question should determine the witness's qualification, still he insisted on "much being left to the discretion of the trial judge." Similarly, in discussing the legitimacy of handwriting experts, Wigmore asserted that "the determination of this skill must of course depend on the discretion of the trial Court as applied to the circumstances of each case." Amid a quickly professionalizing society marked by a rapid increase in self-declared experts, Wigmore was ready to afford judges leeway in regulating supposed experts' access to the witness box.[21]

Just as Wigmore was inclined toward judicial discretion in the scrutiny of the qualifications of expert witnesses, so too did he support judicial discretion in regulating the content of expert testimony. Wigmore noted that it was "improper" to ask an expert witness to draw an ultimate inference on the material question of the case based on his or her consideration of "*all the testimony*" because conflicting testimony would force the witness to decide what evidence to ignore in order to draw an inference. However, if there were no conflicting testimony, then, reasoned Wigmore, such inferences could be allowable at the "discretion of the trial Court." He further advocated "the discretion of the trial judge" in determining the propriety of hypothetical questions posed to experts, such as, "Assuming the truth of the testimony for the plaintiff (or the defendant), what is your opinion?" Moreover, if a question was premised on "the truth of a *single witness' testimony*," then its admissibility "should rest in the discretion of the trial judge." Along the same lines, Wigmore maintained that "the discretion of the trial judge ought to be absolute" in allowing or refusing a question "which by its length tends to confuse or mislead the jury without being of appreciable service."[22]

In addition to the qualifications of expert witnesses and the substance of their testimonies, attesting witnesses (i.e., witnesses who certified documents by signing them) presented yet another set of testimonial issues that Wigmore referred to the trial judge. Evidence law typically required the testimony of an attesting witness to verify the authenticity of a deed in question. Wigmore advised that a judge offer an exemption if counsel could prove that the attesting witness resided outside the jurisdiction of the court. "The sufficiency of the *proof of absence* at the time of trial has been the subject of many rulings which cannot profitably be treated as precedents," Wigmore acknowledged. "The matter should be left entirely to the discretion of the trial Court." If the whereabouts of the attesting witness were unknown, then "it must be shown that [an] *honest and diligent search* for the attester has been made" before other corroborating evidence became admissible. Regarding the "sufficiency of this search," again, "the matter should be left entirely to the determination of the trial Court." In the event that an attesting witness planned to claim a privilege against testifying, Wigmore called on the judge to decide if the witness needed to arrive in court to invoke the privilege.[23]

The process of questioning witnesses raised further testimonial concerns that Wigmore held were best settled by the judge at his discretion. While courts typically considered questions that required "*a simple 'yes' or 'no'*" response to be "leading and improper" during direct examination, ultimately, Wigmore concluded that "the tone of the voice" rather than "the form of the words" dictated whether a question was leading. "This is peculiarly a case for the principle that the trial Court's determination controls," he concluded. Wigmore noted that counsel's repetition of a question that the court had already allowed and a witness had already answered on direct examination was "ordinarily superfluous and therefore improper." Nevertheless, he conceded the possibility that "circumstances may arise which make it desirable to emphasize certain facts anew; and the trial Court's discretion should control." While typically only one examiner at a time could question a witness, this doctrine was, in Wigmore's words, "of course subject to reasonable exceptions allowable in the trial Court's discretion." Moreover, he suggested that "the *largest possible scope* shall be given to evidence attempted to be procured" by cross-examination, and left it to the judge to determine "the scope in a given instance." "The discretion of the trial court" further regulated the recall of witnesses, just as "the general principle of the trial Court's discretion" governed the order of cross-examination.[24]

If testimony was one broad sphere within evidence law where Wigmore consistently advocated judicial discretion, then controversies surrounding evidentiary procedures constituted a second. Documents in particular posed difficult procedural issues. Wigmore deferred to judicial discretion when so-called "collateral" facts about a document were in dispute. Although normally a party need not have produced an original document in that event, "collateral" had proved "an unfortunate and elusive word, which is almost impossible of consistent application in practice." Nevertheless, Wigmore remained optimistic that "the misfortune of inconsistent precedents and the disadvantage of an obscure definition can be obviated by applying strictly that salutary doctrine of judicial discretion." The word "salutary" bespeaks Wigmore's belief that judicial discretion was not a last resort in the absence of clear guidelines but the mark of an advanced legal system attuned to contingent needs.[25]

Various other procedural concerns within the rules of evidence prompted Wigmore to support the ad hoc judgment of the bench. The "trial Court's discretion," he contended, ought to determine whether to sequester a witness and whether a witness who was in violation of a sequestration order could still testify. Not infrequently, counsel would submit evidence not obviously germane to its case while promising its relevance would later become clear. On the admissibility of such evidence, wrote Wigmore, "the *trial Court's discretion* ought to have free play." A party usually could not submit evidence after it rested its case. However, this policy sometimes proved "unnecessary and unjust." As

Wigmore explained, "in the trial Court's discretion, evidence may nonetheless be subsequently admitted." He also approved of "the trial Court's discretion" in deciding the rectitude of additional rounds of rebuttals.[26]

Along with testimony and procedure, Wigmore applied his philosophy of judicial discretion to matters involving time. He determined that the judge should fix "a limit of time for the range of the evidence" of "any physical condition" or of a "habit or cause of conduct." When a party sought to prove an "emotion of hostility" with evidence pointing to "the existence in the same person of the same emotion at another time," the time span from which evidence was admissible was "always to be left to the discretion of the trial Court." For cases involving "Sexual Passion," the "*limits of time* over which the evidence may range" in demonstrating lust hinged "largely on the circumstances of each case, and should be left to the discretion of the trial Court." Concerning the requisite recency of evidence that spoke to a witness's character, Wigmore maintained, "the character must not be so distant in time as to be void of real probative value in showing present character; this limitation to be applied in the discretion of the trial Court." Sometimes subsequent acts of forgery or counterfeiting shed light on a previous act in question. Wigmore resolved that "the length of time over which we may range in search of evidential instances is obviously determinable by no fixed rule" and thus "the discretion of the trial Court should here control." Regarding the time period from which evidence was admissible to prove a prior or subsequent condition, he concluded, "the matter should be left entirely to the trial Court's discretion."[27]

Wigmore's deference to the bench on hearsay issues further betokens his commitment to the principle of judicial discretion. Declarations of family history made prior to a legal dispute were generally admissible as exceptions to the hearsay rule because courts considered them fairly credible, while those made after the dispute began were typically inadmissible. Wigmore argued that this doctrine should only exclude the latter type of declarations if the nature of the dispute would have engendered biased statements of family history. "There is opportunity for much latitude in applying this limitation," Wigmore recognized, and "it should be a matter for the trial Court's discretion whether under the circumstances of each case bias can be supposed to have existed." He also discussed a parallel dilemma regarding the admissibility of statements, as hearsay exceptions, of physical pain made after a suit had been filed. On the one hand, Wigmore warned against the automatic disqualification of potentially legitimate declarations of suffering. On the other, he feared creating an incentive for people to feign afflictions. The exclusion of such declarations, he concluded, "ought to depend on the circumstances of each case, and to be left to the trial Court's discretion."[28]

Counsel's argument raised further hearsay dilemmas, which Wigmore also referred to the judge's ad hoc consideration. Evidence law dictated that a litigator could put forward arguments based only on facts presented in court and not on any new information. Still, Wigmore appreciated that "in the strain and fervor of argument honest errors of memory may easily occur, [and] improper assertions may come to be made unwittingly." The bench had to strike a balance between "judicial charity" for the minor infraction and "judicial caution" against the egregious error. "The occasions for interfering," Wigmore resolved, "may best be left, as all agree, to the discretion of the trial judge."[29]

Reputation was yet another realm of evidence law where Wigmore championed judicial discretion. Under the "overt act" doctrine, active in some jurisdictions at the time, a killer pleading self-defense could point to an "overt act" of hostility on the part of the deceased. Such an act "might be otherwise colorless, but when interpreted by his known character becomes apparently an act of aggression" and therefore a justification for the murder. Wigmore endorsed the practice of accepting evidence of an aggressive reputation only after the defense offered compelling evidence of an "overt act." Determining when "an overt act is sufficiently evidenced to lay the foundation for reputation-evidence" was best *"left entirely* in the hands of the *trial Court."* Otherwise, warned Wigmore, "our law is to become a mass of quibbles which no practitioner can master and every murderer will welcome." He applied similar reasoning to evidence of one's neighborhood reputation. "There are certain classes of facts for which it is entirely appropriate," while "there are others for which it may not be. The matter is one in which it should be left to the discretion of the trial Court."[30]

As discussed in chapter 2, there was one key area in which Wigmore did *not* advocate judicial discretion: judicial review. Lockstep with modernist jurists, he argued for greater deference to the legislature from the bench. Modernists embraced a balanced ideal of the judge who used his discretion on a case-by-case basis to achieve social justice while respecting the efforts of legislative bodies to do the same. It was this very equilibrium between judicial discretion and restraint that Wigmore championed.

Balancing Tests

In the formalist model, a judge determined the essence of a case, situated the case within the proper category, and then applied that category's governing principle. Modernist jurists derided as myth this notion of the judge as a nondiscretionary arbiter of the law. In turn, they argued for balancing tests in which the bench weighed competing concerns, doctrines, and interested parties. Wigmore embraced balancing tests, a position that dovetailed with his preference for increased judicial discretion.

The three core tenets of auxiliary policy comprised "confusion of issues," "unfair surprise," and "undue prejudice"; a judge, explained Wigmore, had to perpetually balance these concerns against the probative value of any given article of evidence. For instance, the bench could reject circumstantial evidence when its "probative usefulness" was "more than counterbalanced by its disadvantageous effects in complicating and confusing the issues before the jury, or in creating an unfair prejudice in excess of its legitimate probative weight." Similarly, in the realm of testimony, the admission of a litany of witnesses who added little qualitatively to the mass of evidence could outweigh their cumulative probative value. "It is obvious," insisted Wigmore, "that each additional witness increases, in almost geometrical ratio, the possibilities of confusing the issues and of thus diverting the jury from a clear and concentrated consideration of the precise issue in dispute." The judge was left "to determine when this overbalance of disadvantages exists."[31]

Expert testimony raised additional issues of auxiliary policy, and Wigmore supported the judge's prerogative to apply balancing tests in these circumstances. When a party sought to undermine the credibility of an expert witness, courts usually allowed cross-examination to unearth inconsistencies in the witness's testimony but barred other witnesses from testifying about the expert's errors. Wigmore argued that the admission of this latter mode of "extrinsic testimony" could engender "confusion of issues, by the introduction of numerous subordinate controversies involving comparatively trivial matters," as well as "unfair surprise, by leaving the impeached witness unable to surmise the tenor or the time of supposed conduct which might be attributed to him by false testimony." However, Wigmore believed that in some instances the probative value of extrinsic testimony could compensate for these concerns, and endorsed the trial judge's discretion in determining the balance.[32]

Even when Wigmore displayed a clear preference in a matter of auxiliary policy, he still urged that the court could apply a balancing test on a case-by-case basis. In criminal trials, counsel often objected to the presentation of "deadly weapons" or "cruel injuries" because their sight "tends to overwhelm reason and to associate the accused with the atrocity without sufficient evidence." Wigmore affirmed the judicial tendency to overrule these objections because they were often "frivolous," but he still insisted that "the trial Court has a discretion" to weigh the prejudicial nature of such provocative evidence against its probative value.[33]

In addition to auxiliary policy, the imperative of timely justice created a further need for balancing tests. According to Wigmore, if the admission of physical evidence occasioned "inconvenience, by obstruction of the court-room or by too great expense of time, to bring the desired object before the tribunal," then "its production may be forbidden in the trial Court's discretion." In the event that a jury had to travel to a given site to view evidence that counsel could not present in court, the judge had to decide if "the inconvenience of adjourning court until a view can be had, or of postponing the trial for the purpose" would "overcome the advantages of a view." In each of these instances, Wigmore advocated a balancing test between the probative value of evidence and its hindrance to the efficient administration of justice.[34]

Documents raised another set of dilemmas that required an appraisal of competing interests. For example, parties typically had to produce the author of a document to verify its authenticity. A business's books, however, may have had its entries dictated or recorded by many people. Wigmore explained that a judge could admit the company books as hearsay exceptions *provided the practical inconvenience of producing on the stand the numerous persons thus concerned would in the particular case outweigh the probable utility of doing so.*" Furthermore, if a document disclosed "the private affairs of the witness" or "would in his opinion inconvenience him," then the judge had to weigh "the document's utility in evidence" against "the detriment to the witness."[35]

Wigmore also promoted balancing tests during the examination of witnesses. The rules of evidence prohibited counsel from posing leading questions to their own witnesses so as not to suggest the desired answers. However, noted Wigmore, "there arise situations in which these dangerous questions become a necessity," and he left it to the trial judge to measure "the risk of losing useful testimony" against "the risk of false suggestion." Wigmore also noted the potential for a direct examination to be so broad that it left the cross-examiner unprepared to interrogate the witness on the full range of testimony. The judge had to determine whether the sweep of the questioning created a "substantial injustice" that overbalanced the probative value of the testimony.[36]

The desirability of newspaper coverage of trials was yet another issue where Wigmore advocated a balancing test. He considered the benefits and costs of allowing journalists into the courtroom. Publicity helped "to improve the quality of testimony" and allowed more citizens not present in the tribunal to follow the proceedings. However, newspapers often proved "neglectful of the civic duties of their occupation;" the "exploitation of the news of crime" had little appreciable value to the justice system. Wigmore also recounted that the jury trial had successfully functioned as a transparent institution long before the advent of the daily paper. "There are thus balancing considerations" for the bench.[37]

Wigmore further explored the balance of interests in the disclosure of trade secrets. He recognized the potential for witness testimony that divulged company secrets to "become by indirection the means of ruining an honest and profitable enterprise." While patents and copyrights often preempted this scenario, Wigmore contended that when it did arise, the bench had to weigh the probative value of the evidence against the harm to a witness's commercial venture. If the disclosure was "but a subordinate means of proof," then the witness could invoke a privilege against testifying, but when "the rights of possibly innocent persons depend essentially or chiefly" upon the testimony in question, then the business interests became secondary.[38]

Various other evidentiary doctrines in the *Treatise* called for balancing tests. At times, a threat of harm or promise of reward tempted an innocent party to offer a spurious confession. Regarding the admission of potentially false confessions, Wigmore exhorted judges to balance the likely "benefit [to the confessor] of realizing the promise or the benefit of escaping from the threat, against the drawbacks moral and legal." Wigmore also found balancing considerations in the admissibility of a corporal injury as evidence. A party may have been reluctant to bear his or her body before the tribunal, either in person or through the proxy of court-appointed medical experts. Wigmore deferred to the trial court to weigh the probative value of the evidence against the "inconvenience, shame, or risk to health that may be involved." Finally, Wigmore considered the credibility of testimony in which a witness had conflicting motives—one to lie and the other to speak the truth. He encouraged courts to "attempt to strike a balance between the two opposing interests and admit the statement only if on the whole the disserving interest preponderates in probable influence." To conclude, Wigmore perceived evidence law as a contested arena where the bench often had to balance conflicting doctrines, interested parties, and social concerns.[39]

Consequentialism

Modernists valued the actual consequences of a rule rather than its logical integrity or harmony with abstract principle. In the *Treatise*, Wigmore called on judges to apply a consequentialist perspective to rules of evidence that either (1) facilitated the tribunal's search for truth or (2) upheld some external social policy concern at the expense of fact-finding. It would be inaccurate, however, to suggest that matters of admissibility hinged on a balance between tribunal fact-finding on the one hand and social policy on the other. Judicial inquiry was itself a social policy objective, so the balance was only between the social policy imperative of the administration of justice and external policy considerations. In drawing on social utility as a guiding force in evidence law, Wigmore marched lockstep with modernists who wanted the bench to reform law on the basis of social policy outcomes.

Regarding concerns internal to trial proceedings, Wigmore exhorted judges to apply a consequentialist approach to the treatment of witnesses. In a discussion of whether a lawyer could impeach a witness's character, he warned that an impeached witness "may be condemned by public opinion and disgraced before the community." As a result, Wigmore advised against permitting the impeachment of a witness's character, not out of concern for "the mere feelings of the witness," but because "the prospect of this ordeal of public disgrace threatens to make the witness-box a place of dread to its innocent occupant, and to deprive justice of the fullest opportunity to obtain useful testimony." Efficacy, not sympathy, dictated the doctrine.[40]

Other times, Wigmore's results-oriented perspective afforded less protection to the witness. His discussion of the so-called "Queen's Case rule" illustrates this effect. Originating in England, the doctrine was adopted by American courts even though Parliament was swift to repudiate it. The Queen's Case rule had mandated that counsel hand a witness a given document before asking questions about its contents, a policy that courts thought accorded with the doctrine that documents had to be produced in court when their contents were in issue. In modernist fashion, Wigmore was more concerned with the results engendered by the rule rather than its harmony with cognate doctrine. He criticized the rule because "it abolished a most effective mode of discrediting a witness on cross-examination." He preferred that a judge give counsel the opportunity to illuminate discrepancies between a witness's testimony and documents the witness allegedly had authored or handled prior to the trial—an impossible task if the witness was first offered the document in question while on the stand.[41]

In considering the validity of exceptions to the hearsay rule, Wigmore asked the judiciary to look to the outcome of the exceptions. He supported an exception that admitted the hearsay statements of witnesses that violated their own material interests; people tended not to spread lies that hurt them, the courts reasoned, so the statements were likely credible. However, Wigmore noted with dismay that the bench had settled on the doctrine that "the interest prejudiced by the facts stated must be *either a pecuniary or a proprietary interest*, and not a *penal interest*." This created the absurd result that a court would exclude a hearsay confession, "however well authenticated," of someone who explicitly "has avowed himself to be the true culprit" of a crime merely because he had a penal interest in the case.[42]

Wigmore further dismissed thorny epistemic issues that, if countenanced, would have resulted in an inoperable legal system. In voicing his support for the admission of official statements at face value (i.e., as exceptions to the hearsay rule), Wigmore argued, "Even if the traditional assumption of the potency of official duty and honor be in some regions or for some classes of incumbents more a fiction than a fact, it is at least a fiction which we can hardly afford in our law openly to repudiate." In other words, he accepted a workable fiction rather than an unworkable fact. Similarly, Wigmore renounced efforts of judges to define sharply the standard of proof in criminal trials—beyond a reasonable doubt—because those efforts had proved futile. "When anything more than a simple caution and a brief definition is given," he observed, "the matter tends to become one of mere words, and the actual effect upon the jury, instead of being enlightenment, is rather confusion, or, at the least, a continued incomprehension." In the same vein, Wigmore conceded that juries were often wrong but insisted that little would be gained from dwelling on their shortcomings. "A jury's verdict in theory establishes facts, and the law could never admit any other supposition; but the truth often remains untouched by a verdict," he acknowledged. Nevertheless, this unfortunate reality "cannot deter a sane and practical justice from exercising its functions."[43]

In a strident rejection of epistemic relativism, Wigmore issued this pronouncement on the validity of physical evidence: "The law does not need and does not attempt to consider theories of metaphysics as to the subjectivity of knowledge or the mediateness of perception. It assumes the objectivity of external nature; and, for the purposes of judicial investigation, a thing perceived by the tribunal as existing does exist."[44] It would be easy to conclude from a pedestrian reading of the *Treatise* that Wigmore simply evaded difficult epistemic matters, but that would be an overly simplistic reading of his position. He openly acknowledged the existence of insoluble epistemic dilemmas and insisted that the bench reject epistemic commitments that failed to materially benefit the administration of justice.

Two other rules point to Wigmore's interest in evaluating legal doctrine according to its effect on fact-finding. He endorsed secrecy for grand juries because only jurors "immune from apprehensions of injury from the persons charged by them" could faithfully decide whether or not to indict a defendant. Wigmore also maintained that if a "client is compellable to give up possession" of a document, such as a deed, then the judge must bar the client from turning the deed over to his or her attorney, who, in turn, could withhold the deed under the doctrine of attorney-client privilege. Otherwise, Wigmore deduced, "the client's obligation to produce could always be evaded in a very simple fashion by placing the deed with the attorney; and such a quibble could not be tolerated."[45]

Just as Wigmore applied a consequentialist perspective to evidence doctrine that enhanced the tribunal's search for truth, so too did he implement an outcome-based approach to rules that privileged external social policy concerns over judicial inquiry. For instance, Wigmore called on judges to prohibit evidence, however relevant, that would hinder the smooth functioning of government. He contended that one court should not admit a record from another tribunal. Any other policy would render it "impossible for the time being for others to use the records; there would be a serious risk of loss; and there would be a constant additional wear and tear upon the document." The same reasoning proscribed removal of any "official records from their usual place of custody" and of "private documents" of "such general and constant use and importance that their liability to removal for production as evidence would cause not merely individual but general inconvenience." Wigmore's concern for the efficient operation of the state further led him to advocate the acceptance of hearsay statements from government officers. Since judicial inquiry often encompassed many standard activities of state officials, "the work of administration of government and the needs of the public having business with officials would alike suffer" if agents of the state were required to perpetually provide testimony in person to verify previous statements.[46]

While Wigmore believed that the rules of evidence had to account for the effectual performance of civic institutions, he distinguished sharply between foreign and domestic affairs. Wigmore voiced his support for the testimonial privilege of government officials against revealing "secrets of State" whose "disclosure would endanger the nation's relations of friendship and profit with other nations" or would hinder "*military precautions against foreign enemies.*" However, he found that there were no "matters of fact, in the possession of officials, concerning *solely the internal affairs* of public business, civil or military, which ought to be privileged from disclosure." In Wigmore's view, "the responsibility of officials to explain and to justify their acts is the chief safeguard against oppression and corruption." Thus, in supporting the admission of this latter type of evidence, he relied on a social policy consideration as his guiding rationale.[47]

Alongside the capable management of the public sphere, the prevention of crime was another extrinsic policy interest that Wigmore brought to bear on evidence law. In the event that a defendant charged with murder claimed that he had acted in self-defense, Wigmore wanted courts to reject evidence of a victim's threats if there were "clear evidence that the *defendant was the aggressor.*" Otherwise a murderer could "use the threats" of another person "as a mere pretext for justifying the killing of one who was making no actual attempt to injure him." Wigmore's interest in thwarting crime also influenced his treatment of the character rule. Under this doctrine, someone with a criminal background could, in theory, block evidence relating to previous crimes because it impugned his character. Ironically, "the greater the criminal brought to bar, the more closely the traces of his crimes were involved in other misdeeds, the more stupendous his scheme of crime culminating in the act charged, so much the more safe and invulnerable would he have rendered himself." So as not to encourage criminal behavior, Wigmore strongly objected to the application of the character rule in trials that featured defendants who had long histories of prior crimes.[48]

In addition to government administration and crime prevention, Wigmore highlighted the maintenance of transportation routes and machines as additional social policy concerns affecting the rules of evidence. If someone had been injured using "machines, bridges, sidewalks, and other objects," the owner may have feared that fixing the tortious property could unwittingly "indicate a belief on his part that the injury was caused by his negligence." Wigmore advocated judges prohibit evidence of these otherwise relevant acts so as to promote repairs.[49]

Wigmore also embraced the public consciousness as a legitimate external policy consideration. In expressing his general approval of publicity for trials, Wigmore alluded to the "educative effect of public attendance." "Respect for the law," "acquaintance with the methods of government," and "confidence in judicial remedies" were all positive outcomes flowing from a transparent system of justice. In Wigmore's view, the legal fraternity should capitalize on the normative effects of its practices.[50]

Other social policy factors influenced Wigmore's *Treatise*. He affirmed the marital privilege against testifying about confidential spousal communications. In his view, judges should consider "the relation" between a husband and wife to be "a proper object of encouragement by the law." Wigmore feared that "the injury that would inure to it by disclosure is probably greater than the benefit that would result in the judicial investigation of truth." He then cited with approval judicial decisions that discussed the importance of mutual trust in a marriage as essential to happiness.[51] In another example, Wigmore recommended that courts disregard their usual preference for an attesting witness to authenticate a document "when the attester is at the time of trial so ill, or so infirm from age, that it is impracticable, without danger to his life or health, to compel his attendance in Court." According to Wigmore, marriage and health were valid affairs of broad social concern for which the bench had to account.[52]

A consequentialist orientation was also evident in Wigmore's willingness to discount an apparent social policy consideration if it had, in reality, no negative outcomes. For instance, he argued against the privilege of confidentiality between a physician and patient, in part because "people would not be deterred from seeking medical help" due to "the possibility of disclosure in court." For Wigmore, judicial inquiry took precedent over a seemingly compelling but actually negligible extrinsic social policy factor.[53]

Logic & Experience

In 1881, when Holmes wrote his famous aphorism on the first page of *The Common Law*—"The life of the law has not been logic; it has been experience"— he signaled a modernist repulsion to abstract reasoning and an embrace of lived experience as the ultimate legal lodestar. Wigmore internalized this tenet of modernism, translated it into substantive evidence doctrine, and called on trial judges to do the same. Indeed, the preface to the 1915 supplement to his tome featured Holmes's canonical adage about logic and experience. It is perhaps not without irony that Wigmore, an ivory tower theorist, prized "experience" as the organizing principle of law more so than some practitioners did.[54]

Wigmore frequently cast light on sound logic that resulted in pernicious practice. Some courts required that expert witnesses who had personally observed a given phenomenon state the premises upon which they drew their inferences about that phenomenon. Of the expert, Wigmore asked, "Is it here necessary that he should first state in detail the facts of his personal observation, as premises, before he can give his opinion? In academic nicety, yes; practically, no." Wigmore explained that this rule created the absurd scenario in which an expert with personal observation would have less credibility than one drawing conclusions based merely on provided data because only the former would have to justify his premises and therefore be subject to greater scrutiny in cross-examination. In a telling phrase, Wigmore derided this "fallacy of being too logical" and endorsed the many courts that had rejected the doctrine.[55]

In a similar rebuke of the apparent dictates of logic, Wigmore considered the common scenario in which a defendant on trial for murder claimed self-defense. He conceded that "the reputation of the deceased for a violent, dangerous, or turbulent disposition" would, on its face, seem highly relevant and warrant admission as evidence by the judge. While the "abstract validity of this reasoning cannot be doubted," Wigmore insisted that "the unconditional and indiscriminate admission of such evidence is dangerous" because it would prejudice the jury against the deceased and provide undue protection for the truly guilty.[56]

Testimonial impeachment was another area where Wigmore contrasted a rule's sensible form with its suspect function. Courts disagreed on whether counsel could impeach the general character or only the credibility of a witness. Wigmore recognized that a witness's general flaws, in theory, could suggest a particular "degeneration of the truth-telling capacity" and therefore "bad general character" should become admissible. In practice, however, a party could use the threat of character impeachment to exact revenge on a witness or scare a witness into silence. "In spite of logic's demands," Wigmore concluded, "policy requires that the line be drawn at bad general character, and that no specific quality other than that of veracity be considered." He wanted judges to see that the abstract coherence of a rule often had little bearing on its real-world value.[57]

In addition to highlighting how sound logic could unwittingly engender adverse consequences, Wigmore repudiated the judiciary's tendency to invoke logic as a hollow façade. He roundly condemned the Exchequer rule, which readily declared a mistrial in response to even a trivial error in trial procedure. According to Wigmore, the bench's obsession with technicality on this point had "done more than any other one rule of law to increase the delay and expense of litigation" and "to encourage defiant criminality and oppression." Still, judges vigorously defended the Exchequer rule on two grounds: (1) "a party has a legal right to the judicial observance of the rules of evidence *per se*," and (2) "the judicial consideration of the weight of all the evidence, as a motive for refusing a new trial, would be a usurpation of the jury's function." Wigmore concluded that "there must at least be some ostensible reason; and these two have served in that capacity." In other words, logic served as a retroactive rationalization for the rule. He echoed this sentiment in a discussion of a doctrine that prohibited a wife from testifying against her husband. "The variety of ingenuity displayed, in the invention of reasons *ex post facto*, for a rule so simple and so long accepted, could hardly have been believed, but for the recorded utterances," exclaimed Wigmore. It was a common contention among legal modernists that judges first arrived at conclusions and then conjured up legitimating reasons.[58]

Wigmore simply did not believe in the promise of formalism—that dispassionate judges, wielding a common set of principles, could secure uniform application of the law. Consider the admissibility of evidence to prove malice in defamation suits. Wigmore reported that the bench often excluded certain types of evidence on the basis of auxiliary policy. However, the ban was never absolute, and judges varied widely in marking the limits of exclusion. "The amusing yet confusing feature of their application" of auxiliary policy, Wigmore noted, "has been that exactly opposite conclusions have been occasionally deduced from the same reason, so that if all the deductions were sound, the law would be in a paradoxical and unmanageable state." In the same vein, judges futilely strove for universal application of auxiliary policy relating to evidence of "a tendency, capacity, or quality." Wigmore relayed that "the evidence has more often been either rejected or accepted as if by a fixed rule, although the natural result has been a lack of uniformity in the rulings of such Courts." In his view, formalism served to create an arbitrary rather than a consistent administration of justice.[59]

Wigmore further maintained that much judicial logic was patent fiction. He derided the bench's contention that "the demeanor of an accused person in court during the trial is too elusive to be justifiably considered as any indication whatever of his guilty consciousness." From Wigmore's standpoint, courts were powerless to prohibit jurors from observing the disposition of a defendant and were best off conceding this point. "It is as unwise to attempt the impossible as it is impolitic to conduct trials upon a fiction," he asserted, "and the attempt to force a jury to become mentally blind to the behavior of the accused sitting before them involves both an impossibility in practice and a fiction in theory." Wigmore drew similar conclusions about a rule proscribing the impeachment of one's own witness. Premised upon the notion that each party vouches for the credibility of its witnesses, the rule created situations where a party cross-examined and impeached the opponent's witness, only later to recall that same witness and thereafter be expected to affirm the integrity of the testimony. "If we are building a rule upon fiction," wrote Wigmore, "there is nothing else to be done but to carry out the assumed requirements of the fiction. It is all a ridiculous structure in the air of legal fancy." Here, Wigmore's frustration was a consummate expression of modernist impatience with the bench's abstract logic.[60]

The *Treatise* was peppered with jabs at the logical gymnastics that enamored the judiciary. Wigmore denounced "the subtle power of cant over reason, and of the solemn absurdity of explanations which do not explain and of justifications which do not justify." His declaration that "metaphysical quibbling will not command the support of healthy minds" bespoke his belief in the dearth of healthy minds in the legal fraternity. When Wigmore lamented that "the law, in its endeavor to maintain abstract fundamentals, is already sufficiently callous to concrete failures of justice," he spoke to an abiding modernist concern for the divorce of judicial logic from the demands of real life.[61]

If Wigmore subscribed to the first half of Holmes's aphorism by faulting logical abstraction, he embraced the second clause by championing experience as the proper guide for judges. Testimonial recollection was one domain of evidence law where Wigmore looked to experience for direction. While every witness's ability to recollect was potentially a point of contention, Wigmore maintained that "experience has carved out certain rough rules of convenience which, if applied at the outset, may save the necessity of a detailed investigation." He provided the example of a blind man preemptively disqualified from testifying about the color of a horse. Wigmore also suggested that "judicial experience" taught "that testimony most glibly delivered and most positively affirmed is not always the most trustworthy," and courts should countenance "the honest witness who will not exaggerate the strength of his recollection."[62]

Just as experience informed Wigmore's views on testimonial recollection, so too did he draw on observations of actual legal practice to craft rules for cross-examination. In general, he observed that a faith among practitioners in cross-examination as the ultimate "safeguard for testing the value of human statements" had "found increasing strength in lengthening experience." Turning to more specific examples, Wigmore recognized that when a judge permitted a cross-examiner to repeat a question that a witness initially had deflected, this practice "not only savors of intimidation and browbeating, but also tends to waste time." Accordingly, he supported judicial discretion in disallowing such questions. Wigmore, however, felt that experience testified to the efficacy of this convention's limited use. "Simple as this expedient seems," he wrote, "it rests on a deep moral basis; and the annals of our trials demonstrate its power" for "over three centuries."[63]

In Wigmore's view, experience could belie the putative utility of a rule. He asserted that a generation of legal practice had exposed the defects of an evidence doctrine limiting cross-examiners to questions on only those topics already raised by the opposing counsel. "Since the test of experience has passed," Wigmore reported, "few have been found to defend it; nor can it be successfully defended." He exhorted judges to look to experience as an arbiter of a rule's value.[64]

In addition to testimonial recollection and cross-examination, Wigmore applied an experiential approach to matters of auxiliary policy. He explained that the purpose of "*prophylactic* rules" (which sought to ensure trustworthiness through means including the perjury penalty and oath) was "to remove, before the evidence is introduced, such sources of danger and distrust as experience may have shown to lurk within it." Regarding "simplicative rules" (which prohibited evidence that would impair rather than enhance fact-finding), Wigmore suggested that "one might *a priori* specify various sorts of such evil effects" proscribed by this set of rules, but "we are here concerned only with the standards and the experience of the judges and of the legislators, as embodied in the rules actually laid down by them and found in operation in trial by jury." Wigmore's concern here for actual legal practice over a priori assumptions typified modern legal thought.[65]

Hearsay exceptions constituted yet another sphere of evidence law shaped by experience. Wigmore endorsed the judiciary's admission of "spontaneous exclamations" as hearsay exceptions, "based on the experience that, under certain external circumstances of physical shock, a stress of nervous excitement may be produced which stills the reflective faculties and removes their control, so that the utterance which then occurs is a spontaneous and sincere response." As mentioned earlier, he also supported the exemption of dying declarations from the hearsay rule. Wigmore stipulated that death had to be *imminent* because "an expectation of ultimate but distant death is obviously, in experience, not calculated to produce that sincerity of statement which is desired."[66]

Wigmore often drew direct links between experience and his probabilistic epistemology. He relayed that "the doctrine of chances and the experience of conduct tell us that accident and inadvertence are rare and casual; so that the recurrence of a similar act tends to persuade us that it is not to be explained as inadvertent or accidental." For this reason, Wigmore advocated the bench admit evidence of "*other similar acts*" that pointed to criminal intent. He also deferred to experience in recounting the likelihood that a person lied to potential heirs about the substance of his will. "The probability of his feigning this conduct," Wigmore advanced, "in order to deceive designing relatives and to obtain peace and quiet, is in general experience not a small one." Furthermore, Wigmore contended that agents frequently committed fraudulent acts at the behest of their employers. While "no mere technical theory of agency will suffice to charge" an employer, neither should "mere technical deficiencies of proof be allowed to exonerate him; due regard to the common probabilities of experience should be paid."[67]

In the *Treatise*, Wigmore also used experience to highlight elements of human nature. For instance, he maintained that "as a matter of human nature in daily experience," a defendant's character was relevant to proving his or her guilt. Regarding the ability to infer a person's mental state from his conduct, Wigmore declared that the foundation of this inference "is our experience of the operation of human nature." He also insisted that entries in a business's books were typically accurate sources of evidence. According to Wigmore, "experience of human nature indicates" several "motives which operate to secure in the long run a sufficient degree of probable trustworthiness" such as the likely discovery of any error and reprimand from a supervisor.[68]

Wigmore asked judges to have faith that, in some circumstances, the common experience of the lay juror qualified him to make rational choices in weighing evidence. For instance, Wigmore suggested that, in most cases, courts should trust the jury to account for witness bias rather than preemptively bar prejudiced witnesses: "To attempt to measure judicially the weight of a circumstance which the jury can equally well estimate by the unwritten and unconscious canons of experience is to encumber the law with needless rules." In another instance, he argued that a tribunal should not discount the entire testimony of a witness who lied. Wigmore was doubtful that the judge should remind the jury that it "*may* disregard the testimony" in light of the witness's error, "for it merely informs the jury of a truth of character which common experience has taught all of them long before they became jurymen." In Wigmore's view, experience was a tool for judge and juror alike.[69]

While true that Wigmore denounced abstract logic and looked to experience in shaping evidence doctrine, it does not follow that he saw no place for logic in the law. Indeed, Wigmore viewed logic as a vital component of a rational system of evidence and enumerated several important principles of logic to guide causal attribution in jury trials. The "*Method of Agreement*" test attempted to determine if *a* caused *b* by seeing if, in other similar situations, *a* previously caused *b*. If so, explained Wigmore, the tribunal could dismiss other factors as noncausal. The "*Method of Disagreement*" principle stated that if *a*, *b*, and *c* together caused *x*; and *a*, *b*, and *d* together caused *y*; then there was a causal link between *d* and *y*. In "*Explanation by Inconsistent Instances*," if *x* was followed by *y* in situations *a*, *b*, and *c*, but not *d*, then *x* did not cause *y*. "*Explanation by Cumulative Instances*" intended to prove that *x* did not cause *y* by showing *y* in the absence of *x*. According to Wigmore, the legal system had to reject abstract reasoning and instead ground itself on these conventions of "applied logic."[70]

Wigmore, then, did not seek to privilege experience over legitimate logic but rather hoped to reconcile the two. "The conclusions and tests of everyday experience," he insisted, "must constantly control the standards of legal logic." In an ideal form, the judiciary "is asked to lay down the rule of law as a proposition reached inductively on the basis of experience." The application of the rule may then take on a "deductive form," but the entire enterprise, affirmed Wigmore, should be one of logic rooted in experience.[71]

Practicality

Wigmore championed a "whatever works" pragmatist ethic. He idealized functionality and boasted that the Anglo-American law of evidence constituted an "eminently practical legal system." His insistence that the bench legitimate an evidence rule on the sole grounds that it was convenient aligned with a modernist outlook that prized solving problems without concern for theoretical hairsplitting.[72]

He exalted practicality in the realm of witness qualification when he condemned a judicial convention that disallowed nonphysicians from testifying about a person's exhibition of illness, injury, or insanity. While only physicians could serve as *expert* witnesses on medical science, Wigmore found the bench's prohibition on the credible observations of lay witnesses to be "a pedantic enforcement of legal nicety inconsistent with the needs of practical life."[73]

His appreciation of the necessities of industry indicates Wigmore's premium on utility. Concerning the verification of a business's books, he noted that some jurisdictions had come to acknowledge the "practical impossibility, on the grounds of *mercantile inconvenience*," of unconditionally calling for testimony of "all the clerks, salesmen, teamsters," and others who had issued entries in a given company's records. Throwing his support behind this trend, Wigmore exhorted the judiciary to "cease to be pedantic and endeavor to be practical."[74]

Classification was a key area where Wigmore championed practicality. Parties submitted evidence of circumstances that would have offered a person in question a particular impression (e.g., person A lived in neighborhood B so likely would have learned of commonly known fact C). Jurists typically divided such evidence into four classes: direct exposure, express communication, reputation, and quality of the occurrence. Wigmore, however, found this classification less than comprehensive and maintained that "practically," it was "more convenient to group the cases, not according to the above modes of operation, but according to the various ultimate facts the knowledge or belief of which is to be shown."[75]

Function rather than form directed Wigmore's classification of hearsay and circumstantial evidence. Hearsay evidence, typically excluded, was inferential because the juror inferred from a statement *about* a fact that the fact itself was true. Circumstantial evidence, usually admissible when relevant, was by definition inferential. As a result, a judge could confront evidence that was at once excluded by the former doctrine and admitted by the latter. Wigmore's solution was, for convenience's sake, to carve out a special class of evidence that the bench could admit because the "circumstantial nature of the inference strongly dominates the testimonial aspect" and therefore the circumstantial rules would apply. "The distinction thus reached," he acknowledged, "is a fairly practical one."[76]

Practicality also informed the *Treatise*'s rules toward witnesses. Wigmore noted that a court assumed an adult's mental capacity to testify, unless and until otherwise proven, because most people were sane. A professed expert, however, needed to demonstrate his "Experiential Capacity" to the judge since most people were not experts. "These differences," he explained, "are based on practical convenience." Wigmore also repudiated a rule, suggested by some, "requiring an eye-witness to the fact of loss or injury." He derided the proposed rule as "impracticable, because such testimony may often be unattainable" and would provide protection for criminal conduct in the absence of witnesses. In a discussion of the privilege against self-incrimination, Wigmore dismissed the argument that a judge should inform a witness of the privilege before the witness answered a potentially damaging question. Wigmore did so, in part, because "in practical convenience, there is no demand for such a rule."[77]

Documents posed additional evidentiary issues that Wigmore felt were best resolved with reference to utility. If a fact to be proved required an intensive review of many detailed records, "it is obvious that it would often be practically out of the question" for the judge to demand "the production of the entire mass of documents." "The convenience of trials" allowed the testimony of "a competent witness who has perused the entire mass and will state summarily the net result." Wigmore further approved of the "statutory innovation" that abrogated an evidence rule concerning certified copies of originals. Formerly, evidence law had dictated that "the whole of a document be shown forth, in proving any part of it," but "decidedly this was too strict a rule for practical convenience." Wigmore also endorsed a shift in the rules of evidence relating to official state documents. Such documents were "to be assumed genuine" in light of the "intolerable inconvenience of having to prove" their authenticity.[78]

Official statements from government agents comprised yet another sphere of evidence law where Wigmore applied his practical ethic. While judges admitted official statements as hearsay exceptions to prevent officials from constantly appearing in court, often an official did not "have personal knowledge of the thing recorded, certified, or returned" because the subordinates handled much of his paperwork. This raised the question of whether a judge should exempt from the hearsay rule an official statement that a given officer had not personally formulated. Wigmore felt that "good sense and practical convenience" required "exceptions" for statements from officials with many people working underneath them. He also urged the bench to admit a stenographic report of "a statement made under an official duty" that had been previously admitted in a different tribunal, and emphasized that "practical convenience would certainly be advantaged."[79]

Wigmore championed a functionalist approach to many other rules of evidence. He advised judges against requiring the production of evidence that featured written letters "on something so firmly fixed to the realty that its removal for production would be impracticable under the circumstances." In the realm of reputation, Wigmore reviewed the discrepancy between one doctrine that excluded testimony about character from the intimates of the party in question and another that accepted reputation in the community as evidence. The result of these rules was that a judge would bar a witness with firsthand knowledge of the party in question while affording another witness with only cursory familiarity access to the stand. "So far as *practical* policy and *utility* is concerned," Wigmore contended, "there ought to be no hesitation" from the bench in admitting testimony based on "personal knowledge and belief" and not just reputation [emphasis added]. Finally, Wigmore asserted that the legal fraternity could not reasonably expect one jurisdiction to enforce the laws of another. Aside from any issue of principle, "practical considerations also deter. The Court of one State knows nothing of the policies and rules of other systems; and it risks error and adds great burdens in attempting to master them." It was this abiding belief in the practical that lay at the heart of Wigmore's jurisprudence.[80]

Contemporary Recognition

AMONG THE STRONGEST indications of the centrality of evidence law to modern legal thought is the litany of leading modernists who embraced Wigmore's *Treatise* as a contribution to their new mode of jurisprudence. Preeminent professors, deans of elite law schools, and Supreme Court justices included the *Treatise* in modernism's canon of foundational texts. Many modernist jurists not only recognized Wigmore's work as central to their endeavor but also relied on his treatment of evidence doctrine in the development of their own ideas.[1]

Roscoe Pound

If Oliver Wendell Holmes Jr. was the high priest of modern legal thought on the bench, then Roscoe Pound (1870–1964) was his counterpart in academia. In a career that lifted Pound from an adjunct position at the University of Nebraska to the deanship of Harvard Law School, he produced books and articles that proved tremendously influential in shaping the tenor of modernist jurisprudence. Pound reiterated Holmes's critique of the law while adding a sociological dimension; he championed social scientific research as the proper dictate of legal practice. Pound derived core elements of his legal philosophy directly from Wigmore's *Treatise*.[2]

Pound was born in Lincoln, Nebraska, on October 27, 1870, to a well-regarded lawyer and judge. The precocious Pound enrolled at the age of fourteen in the University of Nebraska, where he studied classics before turning to botany. Like his pragmatist contemporaries William James and Charles S. Pierce, Pound's interest in science preceded his study of philosophy. Two years after Wigmore finished graduate work in Cambridge, Pound left for Harvard Law School, where he studied under Thayer, although Pound returned to Nebraska before completing his degree to aid his ailing father with his law practice. Back home, Pound soon scored his first victory in a jury trial over future populist firebrand William Jennings Bryan.[3]

Throughout the 1890s, Pound gained a formidable reputation in the local legal community. In 1900, the thirty-year-old Pound became an appellate judge and soon ascended to deanship of the University of Nebraska's College of Law. From this office, he advocated many of the same reforms that Wigmore concurrently pursued at Northwestern—higher admission standards, a three-year law degree, and more full-time faculty members. Pound often lunched in Lincoln with the renowned sociologist Edward A. Ross at a local haunt called Jimmie's. It was during these meals that Pound first cultivated an interest in sociological approaches to law.[4]

Pound emerged on the national scene in 1906 when he delivered a damning critique of the law at the annual meeting of the American Bar Association (ABA). Over the next four years, he joined the faculty at Northwestern Law and then the University of Chicago before returning to Harvard, where Pound remained for the rest of his long career. Pound quickly established himself as the most distinguished member of Harvard's already prestigious law faculty, and, in 1916, he became dean. His most important scholarship appeared during his years in Illinois and the first decade of his tenure at Harvard.[5]

It is difficult to overstate the centrality of Pound's work to the modernist enterprise, as his contemporaries attested. Louis Brandeis remarked to Wigmore in 1912 that "Roscoe Pound will be a potent influence at Harvard in" reversing the "waning respect for the law, the Courts and the profession." The father of modern free speech theory, Zechariah Chafee, reported that during his student days at Harvard Law, Pound's class on jurisprudence "entirely changed my views of law and I believe the results of it will stay with me through life." In 1916, Learned Hand, a prominent modernist judge, informed the new dean of Harvard Law, "Many of us look to you as the natural leader of legal education in the country today." Another modernist judge, and future Supreme Court justice, Benjamin Cardozo reflected in a 1920 letter to Pound, "Thoughts that seem fairly obvious today have become part of the common stock of ideas for American lawyers and judges as a result, in large measure, of your efforts." Pound's reputation was instrumental in luring to the Harvard Law faculty Felix Frankfurter, the modernist leader who would replace Cardozo on the Supreme Court.[6]

Several historians note that later in life Pound disavowed some of his earlier ideas and broke publicly with younger modernists in the 1930s. Conversely, N. E. H. Hull suggests that these disagreements were of little philosophical import. Even if there were a substantive jurisprudential breach, the fact remains that

Pound's earlier writings, informed by Wigmore's treatment of evidence doctrine, laid the groundwork for the modernist enterprise of the interwar years.[7]

Pound first caught Wigmore's attention in 1905 when the former published, "Do We Need a Philosophy of Law?" in the *Columbia Law Review*. Although this article did not cite Wigmore directly, its central message had much in common with Wigmore's *Treatise*. Lockstep with Wigmore, Pound argued that the individualistic orientation of the common law was increasingly inconsonant with modern life. He described the "isolated individual" as "an abstraction" that "has never had a concrete existence." "We look instead," wrote Pound, "for liberty through society. We no longer hold that society exists entirely for the sake of the individual." His comment that the law mistakenly "tries questions of the highest social import as mere private controversies between John Doe and Richard Roe" had strong echoes of Wigmore's own contention that "the matter seems to be between neighbor Doe and neighbor Roe," but, in reality, the "results that hang upon it are universal. All society, potentially, is involved in each individual case." Wigmore wrote Pound to express his approval of the article, and the young Nebraskan was grateful for the kind word. Years later, after Wigmore's death, Pound recalled that

> many a young man who had diffidently published his first paper in a law review was encouraged to enter a fruitful career of law writing by an appreciative letter from the author of the Treatise on Evidence. I well remember how when I published my first paper in an important law review it brought me at once a letter from Dean Wigmore, who I had never met and knew only from his book.[8]

While Pound's article implicitly shared much in common with Wigmore's *Treatise*, Pound's incendiary address to the ABA the following year explicitly drew from Wigmore's tome on evidence. On August 29, 1906, the leaders of the profession gathered in the capitol building in St. Paul for the annual ABA meeting. Instead of offering a traditional and uncontroversial speech, Pound issued a strident censure of the law along modernist lines entitled, "Causes for Popular Dissatisfaction with the Administration of Justice." He characterized the American legal system as "inefficient," "defective," "antiquated," "obsolete," and "archaic." In the *Treatise*, Wigmore consistently advocated increased judicial discretion and rebuked the image of a judge as a passive umpire, what he termed "the sporting theory." Pound, too, derided "the sporting theory of justice, the 'instinct of giving the game fair play,' as Professor Wigmore has put it." Pound then interspersed language from Wigmore's *Treatise* with his own as he lamented the "sensational cross-examinations 'to affect credit,' which have made the witness stand 'the slaughter house of reputations.'" Pound later acknowledged in a letter to Wigmore that "a great deal of the actual material of the paper was derived from a somewhat careful reading of your work on Evidence. Our judges ought to be made in some way to read the critical portions of that book." Indeed, Pound would refer to Wigmore's criticism of the "sporting theory of justice" time and again.[9]

Immediately following Pound's speech, the reform-minded Everett P. Wheeler suggested that the ABA send copies of the address to each of its members and to the judiciary committees in Congress. The conservative leaders of the bar were outraged at the prospect of the ABA's dissemination of such heresies. While Wheeler's motion was tabled—a temporary victory for the bar's reactionaries—Wigmore was moved by Pound's words. Feeling "a thrill of interest" as he listened in the audience, Wigmore then joined like-minded jurists on the steps of the capitol to discuss how they could bring Pound's ideas to bear on legal practice. Soon after, Wigmore remarked to Holmes, "If you haven't read [Pound's] 'Causes for Popular Dissatisfaction with the Administration of Justice,' . . . pray do so. Under a modest guise he conceals the most erudite and clear seeing mind aged 37 now in this country." Three decades later, Wigmore recalled that "for many ensuing years the St. Paul speech was the catechism for all progressive-minded lawyers and judges." "That speech," Wigmore declared, "made history."[10]

After the ABA meeting, Wigmore cultivated his budding relationship with Pound. In 1907, Wigmore brought Pound to dinner with Holmes in Washington, and in so doing, united two giants of modern legal thought. Charmed to have met the author of the *Lochner* dissent, Pound wrote to Wigmore, "It would not be possible to express my indebtedness to you for the opportunity of meeting him which you gave me." Holmes, for his part, had corresponded with Wigmore previously about Pound's scholarship, and related after the meal, "I wish I could have seen more of you and your pal." The justice later commented to Sir Frederick Pollock, "The two best men that I know of, of the generation or half generation after us, in this country are Wigmore and Roscoe Pound."[11]

A few weeks after the dinner in Washington, Wigmore began an aggressive campaign to bring Pound to Northwestern Law. In a letter soliciting the approval of university president A. W. Harris, Wigmore gushed effusively over Pound. According to Wigmore, Pound "has not only read every book that I have read" but also "almost every book that I have known of." Wigmore further praised Pound's "clear and rational judgment" and credited him with "the keenest and most judicious understanding of all of a lawyer's and educator's problems." "As I look over the field at this crucial moment of selecting" a new faculty member, "there is no one (known to me) who could for a *moment* be compared to him." Wigmore relayed that he would "regard it as an extraordinary find if we could attach him to our School." Harris acquiesced, and Pound seized the opportunity to join a law faculty of national stature.[12]

Known for writing funny legal verses, Wigmore penned a poem for Pound that aptly illustrates Wigmore's enthusiasm for the recent addition to his law school:

All hail the newest star,
now fixed amidst our constellation!
A brilliant varied spectrum
marks your lofty stellar station.
As a sociologic jurist,
may the message of your pen
Widely spread a mighty influence,
from your editorial den!
When Pharoah set the Israelites
to make bricks without straw,
He didn't know how harder
'twould be to reform the law;
But Pharoah had his Moses:
you're the Moses by whose hand
Our common law will pass from bondage
to the promised land.[13]

Thirty years later, Wigmore boasted, "I was the far-seeing jurist who discovered Roscoe." In Wigmore's rendition, Pound "was scintillating in the (then) faraway Nebraska plains. I detected his talent, kidnapped him to Chicago, and there set him upon an eminence."[14]

With Pound now in close proximity to Wigmore, the *Treatise* continued to exert its influence on Northwestern Law's newest faculty member. The most illustrative example comes from Pound's influential article, "Mechanical Jurisprudence," which reflected Wigmore's consequentialist perspective. This 1908 piece in the *Columbia Law Review* criticized the bench for fetishizing legal rules while neglecting the ends of law. In his *Treatise*, Wigmore delineated how judges excluded scientific treatises because their admission constituted a violation of the hearsay rule if the author could not be cross-examined in court. This doctrine created the absurd outcome that a scientific treatise was inadmissible, while expert testimony drawn from the same treatise faced no opposition from the bench. It was this kind of fixation on technicality without concern for illogical consequences that Pound sought to repudiate in his article. Referencing the *Treatise*, Pound spotlighted scientific treatises to instantiate the misguided "conception of the competency of evidence at the expense of the end of evidence."[15]

The following year, the University of Chicago tried to lure Pound to its law faculty and a bidding war ensued. In April of 1909, Pound informed Wigmore that Chicago had offered him an initial salary of $5,500 that would soon rise to $7,500 (the latter sum is equivalent to $195,000 in today's dollars). Wigmore quickly organized meetings with President Harris, members of the board of trustees, and Northwestern's business manager; Northwestern was now prepared to provide Pound $6,500 for the subsequent academic year with a rapid escalation to $7,500 annually. If necessary, Wigmore would resign as dean and instate Pound in his place. Although the terms of the Northwestern proposal exceeded Chicago's, Pound relayed to Wigmore that "upon careful and painful consideration, I feel convinced that I must avail myself of the offer made by Chicago." Federal district judge Charles F. Amidon was pleased with Pound's decision. "To have both you and Professor Wigmore in one law school in Chicago," the judge wrote to Pound, "was perhaps an unlawful monopoly of talent."[16]

Pound continued, at the University of Chicago, to produce scholarship that bore the consequentialist mark of Wigmore's *Treatise*. In a 1910 article published in Northwestern's law review, Pound mined the *Treatise* to support his argument that the legal system fixated on technicalities while losing sight of the end goals of litigation. Quoting directly from the *Treatise*, Pound explained that "a chief factor in developing" this infatuation with rules "has been, to use the language of Professor Wigmore, 'the spirit of strenuous struggle and unrestrained persistence which drives the bar of our country to wage their contests to the extreme of technicality.'" Pound then scorned the judiciary for "the lavish granting of new trials," a practice that "Professor Wigmore has called 'the monstrous penalty of a new trial.'" His footnote for this section referred readers to Wigmore's "Evidence, sec. 21, p. 79. The whole of this section should be read and pondered by every student of American procedure."[17]

Pound's article also saw in Wigmore's *Treatise* a rejection of abstraction. "The trial judge," Pound directed, "should be allowed to explain the principles by which evidence should be weighed, not in the abstract, but concretely. Professor Wigmore's arguments on this matter are extremely weighty." Pound further seized on Wigmore's embrace of contingency; the former praised the latter's analysis for highlighting how "artificial rules for weighing evidence" ultimately "ignore the varying circumstances of concrete cases."[18]

In an article entitled "A Practical Program for Procedural Reform," published in 1910 in the *Green Bag*, Pound persisted in emphasizing the value of Wigmore's consequentialist approach. With a focus on ends rather than means, Pound declared that "the point, then, is to make the rules of procedure rules to help litigants, rules to assist them in getting through the courts, not, as Professor Wigmore has put it, 'instruments of stratagem for the bar and of logical exercitation for the judiciary.'" Pound then delineated his major principles for procedural reform and lifted from Wigmore's *Pocket Code of Evidence* the rule that a court should only grant a new trial if an error of procedure is so egregious that it has a substantive effect on the outcome of the trial.[19]

Pound soon left the University of Chicago to assume the Story Professorship at Harvard—a post that he secured with Wigmore's assistance. In a letter to Wigmore, Harvard president A. Lawrence Lowell expressed both enthusiasm and hesitation at the prospect of bringing Pound back to Harvard. "His ability," Lowell acknowledged, "is generally admitted to be great, but somebody has suggested that he is not always perfectly frank, so I write confidentially to ask you about him." If Wigmore felt any bitterness toward Pound because of Pound's abrupt departure from Northwestern two years prior, there was no evidence of it in his response to Lowell. Wigmore described Pound as "the most eligible man in the United States for the appointment" and informed Lowell that "Harvard Law School could not find any one who would be of greater utility to it." In 1921, Pound would have the opportunity to return this favor. Columbia University School of Law dean (and future chief justice of the US Supreme Court) Harlan F. Stone solicited Pound's advice on a new hire, and Pound replied in unequivocal terms: "The man of all men is Wigmore." Wigmore, of course, remained at Northwestern for the duration of his career.[20]

From his new position at Harvard, Pound built upon another central element of Wigmore's *Treatise*—the notion that law was integral to rather than independent from society. In his 1911 article in the *Harvard Law Review*, "The Scope and Purpose of Sociological Jurisprudence," Pound called for "a legal history which shall not deal with rules and doctrines apart from the economic and social history of their time" but rather "show[s] us how the law of the past grew out of social, economic, and psychological conditions." Pound identified as an exemplar of this method the *Treatise*'s explanation of the history of confessions, which showed how the deferential nature of the English class system encouraged false assertions of guilt from the accused. When Pound revised a second edition of his *Readings on the History and System of the Common Law*, he announced that "every one who has to do with either the history or the system of our law is under a debt to Professor Wigmore" and referred readers to Wigmore's history of the development of the jury in volume 1 of the *Treatise* for its depiction of "certain external circumstances on the rules [of evidence] at large." In a letter to Wigmore, Pound explained his desire to draw from this section: "I can find nothing at all to compare with this for the purpose I have in view." Apparently, Pound thought Wigmore unique in the extent of his efforts to situate legal development within the context of broader social forces. When Pound published *Interpretations of Legal History* in 1923, he dedicated it to Wigmore "in token both of personal regard and of the debt which" jurists concerned "with the science of law in the last twenty years owe to you."[21]

In these early years at Harvard, Pound also championed Wigmore's anti-universalist ethic. As president of the Association of American Law Schools, Pound called, in his 1912 address, for a rejection of the illusion of universalism in the law. "It is obvious," Pound observed, "that this fundamental unity of law is coming to be more formal than substantial, more theoretical than actual." Quoting from the preface of the *Treatise*, Pound continued, "Professor Wigmore says truly: 'The fact that there are half a hundred practically independent jurisdictions must be conceded and faced. What is the law? is a question which cannot be answered, except as with fifty tongues speaking at once. . . . It is time for the profession to discard the amiable pretense that precedents can be cited interchangeably.'" Here, Pound fully endorsed Wigmore's inclination to rebuke the fiction of uniformity and face the reality of contingency.[22]

At the close of his first decade at Harvard, Pound, now dean of the Law School, reflected on the profound impact of Wigmore's evidence treatise on his own jurisprudence. In a letter to Wigmore in 1919, Pound waxed sentimental: "Indeed you cannot hope to appreciate what your volumes on Evidence and later association with you at Northwestern meant to a half-trained practitioner in the rough-and-tumble of the Nebraska courts, searching for a legal science he could but feel must exist somewhere." He further relayed his "hope that another generation may have the benefit of your leadership in legal thought and that, as a better-trained generation—largely through your efforts—it may be able to profit thereby even more than we have done."[23]

This last comment was more than just a nicety; Pound's scholarship increasingly exhorted other jurists to use Wigmore's *Treatise* as a model for their own work. In a 1927 article entitled, "What Can Law Schools Do for Criminal Justice?," Pound lamented the absence of a treatise on criminal law comparable to "the monumental creative treatise of Wigmore." "It is imperative," asserted Pound, "somewhere to develop . . . the Wigmore who shall give shape to the received materials of our criminal law that they may be of the greatest service to justice and the legal order." Seven years later, in the *West Virginia Law Quarterly and the Bar*, Pound again upheld the *Treatise* as a lodestar: "We need thoroughgoing historical-economic doctrinal studies, such as Wigmore's interpretation of the English and American law as to confessions, in every field of the legal order." Pound's 1938 book, *The Formative Era of American Law*, counted "Wigmore on Evidence" among the "permanent contributions to our law" and "necessary forerunners, under the conditions of today, of the great treatises that must come presently from the law schools." In Pound's view, the need for reform was urgent, and Wigmore's work on evidence was the paragon for jurists to emulate.[24]

Pound's consistent advocacy of Wigmore's *Treatise* emerged in the context of a cordial and long-standing friendship marked by mutual praise and support. At ABA meetings, Pound and Wigmore would entertain their colleagues, with Pound singing "Dives and Lazarus" and Wigmore on the piano. When Wigmore won the prestigious ABA medal in 1932, Pound wrote a letter of congratulations and assured his old friend, "No one could have deserved it so much. Indeed the things you have done for American law in more than a generation of fruitful writing are exactly what such a medal was, or ought to have been, intended to recognize." Wigmore, who often addressed Pound as "my dear Roscoe," offered a self-deprecating response: "That medal—judging by the age of the recipients—seems to be obtained by a sort of survivorship. A fellow has to last quite a while to get it. Judging by my date, you have some seven years yet to wait." Wigmore was not far off; eight years later, the ABA, at Wigmore's insistence, finally awarded Pound its medal.[25]

Wigmore also spearheaded the fundraising effort for the Roscoe Pound Professorship at Harvard Law in 1937. When the University of Pittsburgh Press collated a lecture series from Pound into a book, E. A. Gilmore, the dean of the Pittsburgh School of Law, turned to Wigmore to author the foreword. Wigmore's contribution was exceedingly laudatory as he celebrated "Roscoe Pound's genius." Pound was equally generous. He brought Wigmore to Harvard in 1935 to give a lecture series on evidence law, and Wigmore returned to Harvard at Pound's request the following year to deliver a talk as part of Harvard's tercentenary celebration. "As the first legal scholar of America," Pound wrote to Wigmore, "I feel deeply that you ought to have a conspicuous place in the Conference, and should like to have you the first speaker on the *first* afternoon."[26]

At the twilight of Wigmore's life, more than thirty-five years after the debut of the *Treatise*, Pound continued to tease out its lessons. In 1940, Pound relayed to Wigmore that he had consulted "the ten volumes of the third edition of Wigmore on Evidence." "It is," Pound declared, "a magnificent performance." According to Pound, no "one else could possibly have put out a book so complete, so scholarly, so scientific, so thoroughly satisfactory." He continued, "I have been turning to Wigmore on Evidence for light on problems of jurisprudence in all sorts of connections ever since the first edition appeared." "Your very kind words," shared Wigmore, "are absolutely the most cheering that I have received." His comment to Pound that "no one else's testimonial could be so authoritative" suggests that Wigmore would have been pleased with this final assessment from Pound, written shortly after Wigmore's death:

> Dean Wigmore will be longest and most generally remembered for his monumental work on the law of evidence which has been more than an authoritative exposition for bench and bar. It has its place with the creative law books of the formative era of American law and for a generation has been a quarry for those who have been urging a more effective administration of justice.[27]

Benjamin Cardozo

Benjamin Nathan Cardozo was arguably the nation's foremost modernist judge after Holmes and Brandeis. His signal contribution to modern legal thought was his candid acceptance of judicial discretion. Cardozo is also renowned for helping to reorient tort law along relational rather than essentialist lines. In these respects, and as well as in his anti-universalism and embrace of balancing tests, Cardozo drew from evidence law.

Cardozo was born into a prominent Jewish family in New York City in 1870. He showed academic promise early in life and enrolled in Columbia University for his bachelor's degree when he was only fifteen years old. After two additional years at Columbia Law, Cardozo joined the law firm where his father—a lawyer and judge—had practiced. Thanks to his sharp intellect and affable disposition, Cardozo earned a stellar reputation in New York's legal circles, in contrast to his father, who had resigned as a judge due to ties with the Tweed political machine. In 1913, the forty-three-year-old Cardozo was elected to the New York Supreme Court and almost immediately ascended to the state's court of appeals (in New York, the supreme court is a trial court and the court of appeals is the highest court). Cardozo became the chief judge of the court of appeals in 1927 before succeeding Holmes on the federal Supreme Court in 1932. Cardozo's tenure on the Court was relatively brief; after suffering a heart attack and a stroke, he died in the summer of 1938 at the age of sixty-eight.[28]

Cardozo's most significant contribution to modern legal thought was his book *The Nature of the Judicial Process*, which forthrightly acknowledged the reality of judicial discretion. To be sure, Cardozo stressed that he decided most cases in the conventional manner; through analogical reasoning, he compared a given case to relevant precedents and decided similar cases accordingly. However, this method of "logic" did not always suffice, and Cardozo explained that he often turned to history, communal customs, and sociology as alternative means of rendering a decision. Initially delivered as the Storrs lectures at Yale Law School to capacity crowds, *The Nature of the Judicial Process* made Cardozo famous nationwide and endures as one of the classic legal texts of the era. Some of Cardozo's predecessors had already conceded that the bench did more than merely discover law, but his monograph marked the first time that a sitting judge offered a systematic exposition of his decision-making process.[29]

The Nature of the Judicial Process drew directly from Wigmore's work on evidence to highlight the inevitable role of judicial discretion in litigation. Cardozo's commentary was largely an extension of an argument that Wigmore had long made and Pound then championed: the "sporting theory of justice," which exalted the judge as a passive umpire, denied the ineluctable and desirable role for discretion from the bench. Cardozo celebrated the increasing disavowal of "the conception of a lawsuit either as a mathematical problem or a sportsman's game." Referencing the *Treatise* and affording full credit to its author, Cardozo continued, "Our own Wigmore has done much to make that conception out of date." The most influential book of its generation on judicial discretion extolled Wigmore's treatise on evidence as vital to the reorientation of legal thought on the subject.[30]

In addition to his views on the judicial role, Cardozo is also noteworthy for his outspoken embrace of relational analyses. Cardozo's classic statement of relational thought came in what is perhaps the most famous tort case in American history, *Palsgraf v. Long Island Railroad* (1928). Writing for the majority, Cardozo's *Palsgraf* decision argued for a conception of "negligence, not at large or in the abstract, but in relation to the plaintiff." In other words, negligence was not a universal concept but a contingent one that hinged on the relationship between the parties in any given circumstance.[31]

While evidence law did not feature in *Palsgraf*, several of Cardozo's other decisions from his tenure on the New York Court of Appeals demonstrate how he derived a relational method from Wigmore's *Treatise*. In *Matter of Fowles* (1918), for example, Cardozo held that the court must consider a will in light of its relation to external circumstances. The parol evidence rule generally forbade such inquiry, but Cardozo insisted that "some reference to matters extrinsic is inevitable. Words are symbols, and we must compare them with things and persons and events." To substantiate this contention, Cardozo cited a section from the *Treatise* in which Wigmore rejected "the stiff formalism of earlier interpretation" of wills that dictated "the meaning must be found in the document itself." Instead, Wigmore endorsed the modern conception of "the purely relative nature of words—their necessary association with external objects." In a similar ruling from 1930, Cardozo simply lifted an excerpt from the *Treatise* to explain his relational stance: "It has been said by Professor Wigmore: 'The truth had finally to be recognized that words always need interpretation; that the process of interpretation inherently and invariably means the ascertainment of the association between words and external objects; and that this makes inevitable a free resort to extrinsic matters for applying and enforcing the document.'" This citation of Wigmore was typical of Cardozo, who referenced treatises three times more often than his peers on the court of appeals.[32]

In addition to the interpretation of wills, Cardozo found Wigmore's relational orientation instructive in determining the existence of fraudulent intent. The *Treatise* asserted that in such cases, it was increasingly likely with each additional instance of misrepresentation that a defendant's behavior was systematic and deliberate rather than sporadic and unintentional. "There must be shown a connection of features," declared Wigmore, "in all the instances, so strong as to indicate a system throughout them." That is, the tribunal should admit evidence that allowed the jury to view instances of misrepresentation in relation to each other rather than as discrete events. Cardozo cited this analysis from the *Treatise* in *People v. Gerks* (1926), where he ruled that "fraudulent intent in the earlier transaction does not precede the consideration of its significance in relation to the second. The two are to be viewed conjunctively, with all the sidelights cast by one upon the other." Drawing the same conclusion as Wigmore, Cardozo lamented, "We miss the evidence of system when we ignore the succession, and concentrate our gaze upon the isolated acts." The judge who popularized relational reasoning in tort law gleaned much from the rules of evidence.[33]

Another jurisprudential value that Cardozo drew from Wigmore's *Treatise* was its anti-universalism. Consider Cardozo's defense of the American Law Institute (ALI), dedicated to the publication of "restatements" that promised to simplify the unwieldy common law. A founding member and vice president of ALI, Cardozo gave an address at the organization's second meeting in which he sought to disabuse the ALI's opponents of the fear that the restatements would assume the form of legally binding codes. According to Cardozo, the organization had no such intention. "They fancy that we shall impose shackles," he said of the ALI critics, "when we seek to loose and free. They fancy that we are building a new labyrinth in which justice will be imprisoned, when we are seeking to give a key to the ancient labyrinth from which she has long cried to us for outlet and escape." He conceded that the restatements would occasionally prove "fallible" and even "erroneous," so the institute intended its work to serve as nothing more than "considered counsel and advice." Cardozo upheld Wigmore's *Treatise* as an ideal instantiation of the kind of legal scholarship that sought not rigid universality but accommodating flexibility. According to Cardozo, the Northwestern dean had not "turned his readers into blind worshippers of authority" but rather "was lashing them into thought, breaking the graven images and setting up the cult of reason."[34]

Cardozo applied Wigmore's anti-universalist bearing to his work on the bench as well. In *People v. Miller* (1931), the defendant, accused of murder, asked to inspect the proceedings of the grand jury because the prosecution cited testimony from that tribunal during the jury trial. The prosecution protested by invoking, in Cardozo's words, "the rule whereby the secrecy of the proceedings before the grand jury must be preserved inviolate." Cardozo, however, denied that this rule constituted any categorical mandate: "It is a rule not without exceptions." He referenced a section of the *Treatise* where Wigmore held that a grand jury's secrecy was "only *temporary* and provisional." "Permanent secrecy," maintained Wigmore, "would be more than is necessary" and "would go too far." As a caveat, Cardozo ultimately ruled in favor of the prosecution on consequentialist grounds; inspection of the grand jury testimony would not have altered the outcome of the trial and so warranted no exception to the general rule proscribing such a review. Nevertheless, Cardozo and Wigmore shared an aversion to uniform edicts that failed to provide allowances.[35]

Within modernist jurisprudence, the embrace of balancing tests was a corollary to increased judicial discretion—and another principle that Cardozo borrowed from the law of evidence. In the *Treatise*, Wigmore stipulated that "in apportioning the burden of proof in a specific case," any given factor "merely takes its place among other considerations of fairness and experience as a most important one to be kept in mind." He insisted that there existed "no one principle, or set of harmonious principles, which afford a sure and universal test for the solution of a given case," and instead judges must weigh all relevant exigencies. In *Morrison v. California*, Cardozo, now on the US Supreme Court, relied on Wigmore's exposition. Referring readers to the aforementioned section of the *Treatise*, Cardozo stated that the burden of proof rested "upon a balancing of convenience or of the opportunities for knowledge" between the two parties.[36]

Like Pound, Cardozo called on jurists to fashion their work after Wigmore's tome. In his book *The Growth of the Law*, based on another lecture series at Yale

Law in December 1923, Cardozo envisioned Wigmore's *Treatise* as an example of the kind of progress possible in restatements. "We know how much can be done by one man, acting and speaking only for himself, to build up a common law." Referencing four of the most influential treatise writers of American law to date, Cardozo continued, "Kent and Story did it in their day. Williston and Wigmore are doing it in ours." Thanks to "the guidance of these masters," otherwise "sane and sound judgments" and "useful members of society" would "have been brought into the world defective and deformed."[37]

While Cardozo shared Pound's appreciation for the *Treatise*, only the latter could claim a close friendship with its author. Nevertheless, Cardozo's correspondence with Wigmore does reveal a cordial and professional relationship. Through the 1930s, Cardozo frequently expressed gratitude to Wigmore for his encouragement. In 1932, Cardozo informed Wigmore that he had just opened "your book, 'The Principles of Judicial Proof,' with an inscription which I shall always treasure." A few weeks later, the recent Supreme Court nominee remarked to Wigmore, "I know it isn't easy to satisfy your exacting taste and scholarship, and the knowledge adds another cubit to my pride in your approval." From the high court, Cardozo assured Wigmore that his supportive comments "will serve as an antidote to opprobrious communications, some anonymous and others not, which I receive from day to day." Cardozo, the most influential modernist judge after Holmes and Brandeis, appreciated the value of Wigmore's *Treatise*, extended its agenda, and exhorted others to do the same.[38]

Oliver Wendell Holmes Jr.

Not surprisingly, Oliver Wendell Holmes Jr. embraced the *Treatise* that so conspicuously reflected his influence on its author. After the appearance of Wigmore's exhaustive exposition on evidence, the mentor-protégé relationship between the Supreme Court justice and Northwestern dean began to mature into a friendship between equals. In 1905, Holmes relayed to Wigmore, "I wish I could talk with you sometimes. There is a good deal of loneliness in the midst of much society here" in Washington. When Wigmore sent a birthday message to Holmes in 1911, the seventy-six-year-old justice responded, "I purr like a cat at the kind things you say but inwardly glow at the kind feeling that I know lies behind. My living friends grow fewer." Referring then to Wigmore and his wife, Holmes continued, "I trust that the two in Evanston may last until I come up to the last post, as I suppose I have turned the last corner." Holmes would live for another twenty-four years.[39]

A subsequent birthday letter from Wigmore prompted Holmes to inform his old friend that there was "no pleasure that is not made keener by your taking part in it," and "such messages give one courage on the home stretch." The following year, Wigmore published an article in the *Harvard Law Review* that described Holmes as the only justice in the history of the Supreme Court "who has framed for himself a system of legal ideas and general truths of life, and composed his opinions in harmony with the system already framed." Holmes soon shared with Wigmore, "The Law Review has come—and all that I can say is that your kindness brought tears to my eyes. I never expected such a reward and you have given me unmixed joy." In 1916, Holmes related to Wigmore "what a constant joy your friendship has been to me and with what pleasure I follow each of your achievements. It has made life happier and easier to me to know you." For a man who would survive his wife, bore no children, and had witnessed his friends bleed to death on the battlefields of Ball's Bluff and Antietam, Wigmore was the rare intimate whom Holmes did not outlive.[40]

In these decades after the premiere of the *Treatise*, Holmes frequently acknowledged Wigmore's enduring contribution to legal theory and practice. Holmes viewed Wigmore's work as an extension of his own. Crowning Wigmore "the first law writer in the country," Holmes observed in 1911, "No one seems to twig my effort as you do." As Holmes entered his fifth decade on the bench, he reflected in a letter to Wigmore, "While a man really lives he can't

Fig. 5: A postcard from Wigmore and his wife to Holmes, recalling Holmes's visit to Northwestern. It reads, "In token of our remembrance of the choice occasion of 1902 and in hopes of another meeting some day." Box 65, Folder 25, Wigmore Papers.

repose on his past, but when he has behind him what you have he has a right to do things by a self regarding serenity." In 1925, Holmes marveled at "the ever growing appreciation of your work, which assures you that your efforts have not been in vain." Never slowing in scholarly production, Wigmore "amaze[d]" Holmes with his "fertile activity" in 1929. "You have done a wonderful lot for the law," the justice added.[41]

While Holmes was interested in more than just Wigmore's work on evidence—they shared a mutual approach to tort law, for instance—there was much in Wigmore's development of evidence law that intrigued the father of modern legal thought. Holmes was particularly impressed with Wigmore's use of history in the refinement of evidence doctrine. Consider Holmes's warm reception to Wigmore's history of the privilege against self-incrimination in the fourth volume of the *Treatise*. Wigmore's treatment of the subject embodied the view that law was deeply woven into the fabric of society. Wigmore noted that the "long story" of the privilege "is woven across a tangled warp" of "the political and religious issues of that convulsive period in English history, the days of the dictatorial Stuarts." Some months after the appearance of this volume, Holmes reported to its author, "I just have been thinking of you as I had been reading in connection with a case your admirable history of the privilege for self criminatory facts." Holmes wished "to show that I read with a certain care, as with very certain delights." Wigmore responded predictably: "I was thrilled to hear that *you* were reading my History-chapter." The jurist that had famously declared in *The Common Law* that "the law embodies the story of a nation's development through many centuries" recognized that Wigmore was bringing his vision to fruition. Holmes's introduction to Wigmore's *Continental Legal History* series—in which the justice commented that "the law might be regarded as a great anthropological document"—stands as a further indication of their common conception of the law as an integral component of society.[42]

Holmes's judicial decisions underscore his endorsement of Wigmore's *Treatise*. For instance, the justice's dissent in *Donnelly v. United States* (1913) exemplifies how Holmes and Wigmore both privileged real-world outcomes and impugned universal rules. In this case, Charles Donnelly was tried for a murder to which another man, Joe Dick, had confessed out of court. A lower court had excluded Dick's confession because he had passed away and therefore any testimony establishing his confession would constitute hearsay. The Supreme Court refused to ease the prohibition against hearsay because, in the words of Justice Pitney, any such "relaxation of the ordinary safeguards must very greatly multiply the probabilities of error" and prove "an unsafe reliance in a court of justice." In the *Treatise*, Wigmore derided the English precedents for Pitney's ruling as "barbarous." "The practical consequences of this unreasoning limitation," he seethed, "are shocking to the sense of justice" because "it requires, in a criminal trial, the rejection of a confession, however well authenticated, of a person" who "has avowed himself to be the true culprit. The absurdity and wrong of rejecting indiscriminately all such evidence is patent." This emphasis on actual consequences and rebuke of unbending doctrine found favor with Holmes. In his dissent for *Donnelly*, Holmes offered curtly, "The history of the law and the arguments against the English doctrine are so well and fully stated by Mr. Wigmore that there is no need to set them forth at greater length" and he referred readers to the relevant sections of the *Treatise*.[43]

To qualify, Wigmore's *Treatise* was more a reflection of Holmes's thought than an agent that shaped the justice's jurisprudence. That Wigmore dedicated his *Pocket Code* of evidence to Holmes bespeaks the heavy debt that the dean felt toward his mentor in reforming evidence doctrine. In the course of Wigmore's preparation for the code, he told Holmes, "I want to have on the motto-page: 'The law has got to be stated over again,' which I will remind you is your own remark." Indeed, Holmes had issued this challenge at an address at Harvard Law School in 1886 when Wigmore was a student there. After Holmes received a copy of the *Pocket Code*, complete with a dedication praising his "lofty ideals" and "tokens of kindness," he relayed to the author that he was "much touched and moved by the dedication and...proud that you should feel able to use such kind words." The passage of time brought only increased interest in Holmes's work from Wigmore with respect to the rules of evidence. In 1930, as Wigmore was coming "down to date on 'Evidence,'" he informed Holmes, "I expect lots of entertainment in catching up with your opinions,—which I read (but no others/*regardless* of their subject!)." Although Holmes was much more of a formative influence on Wigmore than the reverse, still, Holmes's enthusiastic embrace of Wigmore's *Treatise* underscores the consonance of evidence law with modern legal thought. As Holmes once remarked to Wigmore, "If I cited you as often as I appreciate you I should put you in every case."[44]

Other Modernists

In Pound, Cardozo, and Holmes, Wigmore's *Treatise* had found a receptive audience among the pioneers of modern legal thought. There was also a number of other modernists, influential but not quite as prominent, who saw in Wigmore's treatment of evidence doctrine a set of tools with which to refashion the law.

Morris Cohen was a modernist philosopher at the City College of New York with a particular interest in law and a keen estimation of Wigmore's contribution to jurisprudence. Cohen conducted research on legal philosophy at

Northwestern, and his subsequent correspondence with Wigmore reveals a shared theory of law. For example, in a 1920 letter to Cohen, Wigmore offered a rebuke of metaphysical rights. "You and I do not carry around rights in our pockets, nor hung on like watch chains," Wigmore told Cohen. "When the law attributes rights of legal personality to you or to me, it merely creates a conventional abstraction." Cohen placed a high premium on Wigmore's opinion. After Cohen delivered a lecture at Northwestern Law in 1933, Wigmore wrote to thank him and Cohen responded, "A letter such as yours from one whose intellectual achievements and integrity I respect so highly, strengthens my faith in the function of philosophy."[45]

Within the context of this professional relationship, Cohen borrowed from Wigmore's *Treatise* for his own philosophical expositions. In a discussion of legal acts in the *Treatise*, Wigmore called on courts to apply a relational framework that considered the meaning of acts through their associations with surrounding circumstances. Wigmore characterized "the process of Interpretation" as "part of the procedure of *realizing a person's act in the external world.*" He suggested further that "the process of interpretation, then, though it is commonly simple and often unobserved, is always present, being inherently indispensable." In a 1914 *American Law Review* article, Cohen expanded on Wigmore's idea to undermine the neat dichotomy that ascribed lawmaking to the legislature and law-interpretation to the judiciary. If, as Wigmore argued, the process of interpretation was inherent to all legal actors, then the tidy formalist division between the legislative production of law and judicial interpretation of law was a myth. In Cohen's words, "Interpretation, as Wigmore has pointed out, is essentially a process of realization, i.e., a process of translating maxims into actual human arrangements; and it is necessary not only to all who take part in the administration of law but to the legislature as well." This example highlights Cohen's ability to extrapolate lessons from the *Treatise* beyond the ambit of Wigmore's immediate concern.[46]

In a 1916 piece in the *Harvard Law Review*, Cohen advanced a moderate modernism, upholding Wigmore's *Treatise* as a model. He repudiated any notion of law based on "self-evident truths, and eternal principles of justice and reason," and instead applauded legal ideas geared toward "social welfare" and "the real or practical need of the times." Still, Cohen opposed those critics of the law who were "inclined to deny all value to logic and general principles." To infuse logic into the law without slipping into sophistry, he advocated a "rational deductive system" in which "we try to reduce the law to the smallest number of general principles from which all possible cases can be reached." In Cohen's view, the *Treatise* was the archetype of this favored method. "In our own day," he commented, "Thayer's general views on evidence and Wigmore's classical treatise on the subject have transformed a conglomeration of disconnected rules into something like a system." Cohen joined the long list of renowned jurisprudents who lauded Wigmore's tome as a blueprint for legal reformers.[47]

Jerome Frank was another major intellectual presence who placed Wigmore's work on evidence law in the canon of modern legal thought. Frank initially worked in private practice, then served in Franklin Roosevelt's administration in several capacities, and later sat on the Second Circuit Court of Appeals from 1941 to 1957. Frank is perhaps best remembered for his 1930 book, *Law and the Modern Mind*, in which he coined the phrase "Legal Realism." This monograph, informed by Frank's treatment in psychotherapy, argued that society looked to the law as a father figure that absolved people from the choice between right and wrong by providing a false sense of moral absolutism. Frank is also noteworthy among modernists for his exceptional interest in legal fact-finding.[48]

Frank countered criticism of Wigmore from Morris Cohen's son, Felix, who was a legal philosopher in his own right. In his well-known article "Transcendental Nonsense and the Functional Approach" (1935), Felix S. Cohen argued that "the really creative legal thinkers of the future will not devote themselves, in the manner of Williston, Wigmore, and their fellow masters, to the taxonomy of legal concepts and to the systematic explication of principles of 'justice' and 'reason,' buttressed by 'correct' cases." Instead, "creative legal thought will more and more look behind the pretty array of 'correct' cases to the actual facts of judicial behavior" and "seek to map the hidden springs of judicial decision and to weigh the social forces which are represented on the bench." According to the younger Cohen, Wigmore merely surveyed the superficial layer of the law and took decisions at face value.[49]

In fact, Wigmore's *Treatise* was explicit in its efforts to penetrate the façade of judicial rhetoric and recover the core of actual judicial behavior. "We must shape our treatment of the law of evidence by what the Courts do," advised Wigmore, "and not by what they say." Jerome Frank recognized that Felix Cohen's characterization of Wigmore was inaccurate. In the *N.Y.U. Law Review*, Frank insisted, "The reference to Wigmore is most unfair." Referring readers to Wigmore's *Principles*, which provided an epistemic elaboration of the *Treatise*, Frank continued, "Wigmore had a much livelier interest than does Cohen in the 'unruly,' unsystematic, phases of judicial activities."[50]

Frank not only defended Wigmore from attack but also used Wigmore's ideas about evidence in the development of his own scholarship. In the *Notre Dame Lawyer*, for instance, Frank referenced the *Treatise* to highlight the idiosyncratic rather than universal nature of judicial inquiry. "Wigmore has said repeatedly," Frank observed, "that there are no rules available to aid juries in giving proba- tive value to the testimony or any part of it." As a result, "the facts 'found,' after listening to witnesses, by one trial judge or jury may be quite different from those which would be 'found' by another trial judge or jury, hearing the same witnesses." Later in the article, Frank credited Wigmore's *Principles* for its candid concession that judicial proof hinged on a "trial judge's or jury's reaction to the witnesses' fallible reports of their fallible recollections of their fallible observa- tions of the actual facts." Both Frank and Wigmore preferred to acknowledge difficult legal realities than indulge in the false comfort of legal fictions.[51]

In his book *Courts on Trial* (1949), Frank continued to elaborate on Wigmore's anti-universalist ethic. Frank valued Wigmore's emphasis on contingency, stat- ing, "I agree with Wigmore that some legal rules are excessively inflexible, and that there is need frequently to individualize cases." When Frank asked, "Is there any standard of belief a trial court can employ when trying to determine the facts?" he again deferred to Wigmore's *Principles* for the answer. In Frank's words, Wigmore "demonstrates that there are no principles of that kind, and probably never will be." Frank saw in Wigmore's approach to evidence a rejec- tion of certainty that dovetailed with his own legal theory.[52]

Harlan F. Stone also perused Wigmore's body of work for modernist lessons. The former Columbia Law School dean (to whom Pound had recommended Wigmore) served on the US Supreme Court from 1925 to 1946, the final five years as chief justice. Together with Brandeis and Cardozo, Stone was a member of the liberal "Three Musketeer" faction on the Court. That Stone asked Wigmore in 1922 to speak about evidence at a series of conferences on jurisprudence bespeaks Stone's understanding of Wigmore's *Treatise* as not just a collection of rules but a contribution to legal theory.[53]

The justice's ruling in *United States v. Trenton Potteries Company* (1927) illus- trates his use of a modernist dimension of evidence law—experience. Recall that the opinion rule limited a witness to a description of facts and forbade the witness from offering inferences that the jury could draw for itself. Still, Stone held that "a certain latitude may rightly be given the court in permitting a witness on direct examination to testify as to his conclusions, based on com- mon knowledge or experience." This deference to experience was a common theme in the *Treatise*, and Stone's *Trenton Potteries* decision cited a passage where Wigmore called for experience to trump convention: "An inference or opinion may always be stated to the tribunal by a witness experientially qualified to form it." Although this position on the opinion rule was, to use Wigmore's term, "rad- ical" when the *Treatise* debuted, it resonated with the progressive Stone.[54]

The primacy of experience in the *Treatise* also proved instructive to Stone in *District of Columbia v. Clawans* (1937). Here, the justice was incredulous of testimony from private investigators, whose pecuniary interests often undermined their fidelity to the truth. "Common experience teaches us," Stone remarked, "that the testimony of such witnesses, especially when uncorroborated, is open to the suspicion of bias." Stone referred to a section of the *Treatise* in which Wigmore argued that the "experience of human nature" was a guide to those circumstances "from which bias may be inferred."[55]

One of the last letters that Wigmore received before his death was from another Supreme Court justice and renowned modernist, Felix Frankfurter, who reflected on the influence of the *Treatise* early in his career. "Ever since my days as a cub Assistant Attorney," he recalled, "I have drawn on your learning regarding the privilege of self-crimination." The historical record confirms that the forward-thinking Frankfurter had been turning to Wigmore and his work on evidence for decades. Frankfurter's 1915 piece in the *American Bar Association Journal* commented on "the steady, wholesome influence of Dean Wigmore upon the law of evidence." In 1923, Frankfurter told Wigmore that he had "browsed through the vast fields" of the second edition of the *Treatise* and wished to express his "great admiration." Frankfurter well understood that Wigmore was centrally concerned with the adaption of law to the exigencies of a new century. He once referred to Wigmore as "one of the profoundest leaders in the task of shaping the law to meet the needs of the modern state." Like Holmes, Frankfurter recognized Wigmore as an evidence scholar *and* a jurisprudent; indeed, the two roles were inseparable. As he relayed to Wigmore in 1912, "I have the good fortune down here [i.e., Washington, DC] of seeing Justice Holmes from time to time, and when talking of our profession and legal thinking in this country you are a never failing subject of our enthusiasm."[56]

Yet another legal modernist influenced by Wigmore's *Treatise* was Max Radin (1880–1950), a longtime law professor at Berkeley. In a 1928 contribution to the *California Law Review*, Radin criticized the attorney-client privilege in modernist fashion. He exhorted the legal community to consider the privilege not in the abstract but in the concrete world of expedient application. Referring readers to relevant sections of the *Treatise*, Radin wrote of the privilege, "Dean Wigmore has correctly pointed out that it is the level of pure abstraction. And he himself indicated that to be advantageously examined, it must be withdrawn into the realms of practical and humdrum affairs." Radin published another article a decade later in *Foreign Affairs* that drew on a different aspect of the *Treatise*—its comfort with contradiction. He appreciated that Wigmore refused to gloss over the inconsistencies of law. In a discussion on confessions, Radin related, "Dean Wigmore in his classic treatise on Evidence has given the history of the controversy and has shown how confused the discussion has been in part and how easily one can substantiate from our greatest legal authorities . . . the doctrine first, that confession is the least reliable, and next, that it is the most reliable kind of evidence."[57]

Herman Oliphant (1884–1939) also lauded Wigmore for countenancing the law's murky realities. Oliphant taught law at the University of Chicago and at Columbia, founded the short-lived Institute of Law at Johns Hopkins, and eventually left academia for the Treasury during Franklin Roosevelt's administration. His 1924 article in the *American Law School Review* insisted that "existing ambiguity" in the law "involves more than a mere difficulty of pedagogy." He continued, "It means an inadequate and confused body of knowledge to be taught." Oliphant complained that "scarcely more than a beginning has been made" on that front. "Comprehensive reanalyses of most subjects such as Thayer and Wigmore have given Evidence are needed." In the manner of Pound and Cardozo, Oliphant saw the *Treatise* as an apotheosis for others to imitate. Elsewhere, Oliphant referred to Wigmore as "a pioneer" who had "had to blaze the way."[58]

Like Oliphant, Hessel Yntema (1891–1966) praised Wigmore's *Treatise* as a unique contribution to the legal fraternity. Yntema taught law at Columbia and at Michigan, and joined Oliphant in founding the Institute of Law. In a 1934 piece in the *Columbia Law Review* entitled "Legal Science and Reform," Yntema expressed the classic modernist frustration that "legal science" displayed "indifference to the actualities of justice." He called on fellow scholars to emphasize the law's "actual operation." Yntema blamed this state of affairs on the "speculative tradition of jurisprudence, engrossed in the formal analysis of abstract rights." He then singled out Wigmore for his exceptional emphasis on law as it existed in the realm of the real: "With the exception of Dean Wigmore's massive treatise on evidence, for example, legal scholarship has yet to produce a critical, systematic study of procedure, of the administration of justice, indeed of the law in action."[59]

Rare was the leading modernist who did not acclaim Wigmore's *Treatise*. Years before the publication of the tome, Wigmore worked briefly in private practice and had received business thanks to Louis Brandeis. Wigmore later recalled how Brandeis "showed me several acts of kindness, as an elder to a younger brother, in starting my practice," and Brandeis later expressed support for Wigmore's contribution to evidence law. In fact, Wigmore solicited Brandeis's advice in preparing the first draft of the *Treatise*. "I have read with much interest the proof of the chapter on Cross-examination which you sent me," Brandeis informed the author in 1904. "As I anticipated, I find that there is little which I can suggest." The future Supreme Court justice added, "I am glad that we may look forward to an early publication of your book." Moreover, In 1912, Wesley Hohfeld, a scholar at Stanford and later Yale who would help recast property as a social construct, praised Wigmore's recent book on torts as "a work which I now keep as handy on my shelves as a certain well-known Treatise on *Evidence*."[60]

The Model Code of Evidence

At the twilight of his life, Wigmore publicly disavowed a proposed Model Code of Evidence, a rebuke indicative of his abiding legal modernism. In the late 1930s and early 1940s, the American Law Institute formulated and promoted the Model Code, which promised to convert evidence law into a binding legislative code. Wigmore originally contributed to the enterprise but ultimately renounced the work of the ALI.[61]

The Model Code was preceded by earlier reform efforts in the field of evidence law. In 1920, the Commonwealth Fund, a philanthropic organization, underwrote an examination of the field; Wigmore was a member of the committee tasked with the study, and Yale Law's Edmund Morgan served as its chair. Citing its satisfaction with the existing system, conceding that a code lay beyond its ambit, and predicting that the legal profession would not accept reform, the committee decided against the formulation of a code. In the 1930s, however, the successful codification of the rules of civil procedure reanimated professional interest in a code for evidence. The ALI received a grant in 1939 from the Carnegie Foundation to formulate a full-fledged code. Morgan, now at Harvard, headed the initiative, with Wigmore as its lead consultant. The two evidence scholars entertained conflicting views on the direction of the Model Code, and Wigmore disassociated himself from the project. As Wigmore explained to Morgan, "we do agree, substantially on the legal tenor of almost all rules. But in respect to classification, method, and style, we approach those rules from entirely opposite directions." For instance, Morgan wanted a relatively brief and simple code of legally binding rules that afforded broad judicial discretion, whereas Wigmore supported detailed rules that were advisory in nature and would provide the bench clear guidelines while affording judges flexibility to accommodate the demands of idiosyncratic cases.[62]

In a piece in the *American Bar Association Journal*, Wigmore delineated his reasons for disavowing the Model Code and illustrated his enduring commitment to modernist principles. According to Wigmore, the code indulged in "abstractions" rather than "specifically deal[t] with all the concrete rules." Wigmore was concerned with "practicability": "the number of novel changes, towards an ideal code, is so great that the Bars of our States, when made aware of them beforehand, would not accept them." He further criticized the Model Code for its "frequent use of novel terms," "long sentences," and "involved syntax," which failed "on their face [to] convey clearly their application to the every-day situation which they seek to govern." Here was Wigmore's preference for law-in-action over academic pedantry. (In fairness to Morgan, Wigmore's own critics had faulted his *Treatise* for its use of unfamiliar and pedantic language).[63]

Wigmore's *ABAJ* article reflected his view that the legal fraternity must accept the murky reality of the law. He was, for instance, piqued at the Model Code's suggested mandate that "all provisions of the common law or statutes of this State dealing with the subject matter of any of these Rules, or inconsistent with any provision of these Rules, are hereby abrogated." He derided this rule as incoherent because a sweeping dictate could not apply to a self-contradicting body of law. "No two authoritative authors, and no two original state codes, for a century past, have agreed on the topical classification and arrangement of the Evidence rules," Wigmore observed. "How then can there be certainty in identifying the 'subject-matter' that tells what is here repealed?" In other words, Wigmore rejected any universal and unbending metaprinciple because he saw it as inherently inconsonant with the nuanced, conflicting, and unsettled character of evidence law. There was another, more self-serving, rationale behind Wigmore's divorce from the Model Code. In a moment of candor, he relayed to Morgan that his endorsement of a code so divergent from his own treatise "would be fatal to the status of my own" work.[64]

Wigmore's opposition to the Model Code was instrumental to its demise. In 1940, Morgan predicted that if the code "cannot stand honest criticism from the man [i.e., Wigmore] who has devoted more time and study to the subject and has attained a position of greater authority in the subject than any other living man, then it ought to fail of adoption by the Institute as well as by legislatures." Morgan proved partially prescient. The ALI *did* support Morgan's ideas over Wigmore's objections, but not one state legislature adopted the Model Code. When the California bar first considered and then roundly rejected Morgan's code, it referenced Wigmore's commentary in the *ABAJ* in support of its conclusions. Such a devastating critique from the leading authority on evidence law was a death sentence.[65]

In the wake of the Model Code's downfall, Wigmore remained the un-challenged authority on evidence doctrine—a supremacy that would endure well his past his untimely death in 1943. Pragmatism may have lost its cachet beginning with World War II, but the *Treatise*, a consummate application of pragmatist thought, continued to dominate the law of evidence for decades. In 1963, Frankfurter affirmed the enduring value of Wigmore's magnum opus in a letter to the editor in chief of the Northwestern University Law Review: "Wigmore's treatise on the law of evidence is unrivalled as the greatest treatise on any subject of the law." Reformers eventually revisited the prospect of codification and ultimately secured passage of the Federal Rules of Evidence in 1975. But even the adoption of the FRE failed to render the *Treatise* obsolete. In our own time, more than a century since its publication, American judges still look to Wigmore's tome. While the *Treatise* will inevitably complete its transition from the domain of the practitioner to that of the historian, that day is hardly within our sights.[66]

Epilogue

If the law of evidence was indeed central to modern legal thought, then why has the story of legal modernism failed to account for this vital branch of law? The answer lies partly in the nature of professional legal education, which produces the lion's share of legal historians and privileges conclusions of law over findings of fact. Future professors are indoctrinated into a legal culture wherein the serious intellectual work concerns the attachment of legal consequences to a set of facts already given. As Jerome Frank lamented in 1949, "One of the principal reasons for the backwardness of judicial fact-finding is that the law schools have shirked their obligation to teach those skills. Moreover, thanks to their disregard of the trial court, the legal profession is not sufficiently alive to the need of improving fact-finding."[1] Unlike Frank, I imply no criticism by my observation; after all, the majority of lawyers pursue careers divorced from the courtroom. Still, the law school emphasis on substantive rather than procedural law permeates general histories of American legal thought. It comes as little surprise that this body of scholarship neglects the law of evidence.

Yet another reason why latter-day scholars inaccurately depict Wigmore as a formalist is that they echo some of Wigmore's contemporaries who made the same error. Recall from chapter 1 how Underhill Moore, a Columbia Law professor, spuriously claimed in 1923 that Wigmore essentialized the concept of rationality when, in fact, Wigmore openly treated rationality as a social construct. More than sixty years later, William Twining would point to Moore's commentary as an indication of "Wigmore's divorce from the mainstream of American Legal Realism."[2] Similarly, as discussed in chapter 6, Felix S. Cohen described Wigmore in misleadingly formalistic terms. According to Cohen, Wigmore's *Treatise* was enthralled with "the taxonomy of legal concepts" as well as with "the systematic explication of principles of 'justice' and 'reason,' buttressed by 'correct' cases." Wigmore was, allegedly, not attuned to "the hidden springs of judicial decision."[3] However, even a cursory reading of Wigmore's scholarship (as Jerome Frank recognized) revealed that its author was relentless in throwing back the veil of judicial explanation and exposing the reality of judicial practice.

Why did Underhill Moore and Felix Cohen rebuke Wigmore for promoting the very formalist positions that Wigmore explicitly repudiated? It might be tempting to interpret this kind of jurisprudential mudslinging as a proxy for liberal discontent with Wigmore's political conservatism on issues ranging from wartime speech freedoms to the Sacco-Vanzetti affair. But the two jurists who took the brunt of Wigmore's jingoistic lashings—Oliver Wendell Holmes Jr. for his famous *Abrams* dissent, and Frankfurter for supporting Sacco and Vanzetti— were foremost in recognizing Wigmore as a leading modernist when it came to the philosophy of law.

The attacks on Wigmore by the likes of Moore and Cohen, then, were less likely a specific reaction to Wigmore's politics than part of a broader attack on an older generation by younger scholars seeking to make names for themselves. When Moore and Cohen took on Wigmore in the 1920s and 1930s, Wigmore was a senior leader in the academy whereas Moore and Cohen were among the Young Turks of modernist jurisprudence. Legal scholars at that time—no less than scholars in other disciplines, no less then than now— prized originality of thought, or at least the appearance of it. For an enter- prising junior scholar anxious to ascend the steps of the ivory tower, taking aim at the revered figures of the generation ahead was an obvious move. If misreading the work of those established figures helped create the illusion of one's own ingenuity, so be it.

Wigmore's close friend Roscoe Pound offers perhaps the best example of this kind of oedipal complex because he was both a perpetrator of and vic- tim to the practice. In 1908, when Pound was still in his thirties and trying to build a national reputation, he published his acclaimed article "Mechanical Jurisprudence." Pound chided the older, reigning generation for its supposed fixation with "conceptions"—that is, for treating law as a bloodless abstraction while ignoring the actual consequences of their hollow logic:

> The jurisprudence of conceptions tends to decay. Conceptions are fixed. The premises are no longer to be examined. Everything is reduced to simple de- duction from them. Principles cease to have importance.[4]

But Pound's juxtaposition of his realistic jurisprudence with the formalism of the older generation was specious. At that time, it was a commonplace truism in the legal world that the law was too complex for the bench to treat cases as facile exercises in syllogistic reasoning.[5]

Pound's critique in "Mechanical Jurisprudence" of the *Lochner* decision is instructive. He castigated the majority on the US Supreme Court for its exaltation of the principle of liberty of contract and its failure to consider the facts on the ground. "The conception of freedom of contract is made the basis of a logical deduction," Pound contended. "The court does not inquire what the effect of such a deduction will be, when applied to the actual situation." In reality, the Court neither enshrined liberty of contract as sacrosanct in *Lochner* nor disregarded the facts of the case. Writing for the majority, Rufus Peckham candidly granted that the police power of the state could justify legislative encroachment on liberty of contract, provided that the legislation was "fair, reasonable and appropriate." Peckham merely found dubious the factual claim that limiting bakers' working hours had an effect on health. The issue, then, was not one of a jurisprudence of "conceptions" oblivious to facts versus a jurisprudence of realism immersed in facts. Each side looked to the facts, but merely read them differently.[6]

Pound's meteoric rise from obscure Nebraska professor to renowned Harvard Law dean indicates his success in convincing the legal academy that he was an innovative thinker fearlessly exposing the perils of the supposedly dominant formalists. But sons eventually turn into fathers, and by 1930, the fifty-nine-year-old Pound had become an enticing target for younger scholars. It was in that year that a thirty-six-year-old Columbia Law professor named Karl Llewellyn instigated a public back-and-forth with Pound that historian N. E. H. Hull has called "perhaps the most famous controversy in the history of American jurisprudence" and "in part a contest of wills between the king and a would-be usurper."[7]

In the *Columbia Law Review*, Llewellyn published, "A Realistic Jurisprudence— The Next Step." The "Next Step" in this proposed "Realistic Jurisprudence" was strikingly unoriginal, calling as it did for an emphasis on real-world outcomes rather than law as it existed in theory:

> The rules and precepts and principles which have hitherto tended to keep the limelight should be displaced, and treated with severe reference to their bearing upon that area of contact—in order that paper rules may be revealed for what they are, and rules with real behavior correspondences come into due importance.

Llewellyn's article chided Pound for scholarship that was "at times *on the level of bedtime stories for the tired bar.*"

Pound's response in the *Harvard Law Review* pointed out that Llewellyn and his band of young legal realists were hardly unique. In Pound's words, "After the actualities of the legal order have been observed and recorded, it remains to do something with them. What does realism propose to do with them which we had not been doing in the past?" In considering the legal thought of his own generation alongside that of Llewellyn, Pound rightly concluded, "There is as much actuality in the old picture as in the new." It was fitting that Pound's reply appeared in a special issue of the *Harvard Law Review* dedicated to Holmes; after all, if Pound had said it all twenty years earlier, Holmes had done so fifty years earlier.[8]

Wigmore was different from both Pound and Llewellyn. His desire to claim some real estate on crowded jurisprudential turf did not translate into an oedipal tendency to tear down his father's generation. Wigmore was more interested in influencing legal practitioners who yearned for stability in law than he was in impressing fellow academics who valued unorthodoxy in ideas. It would hardly have served Wigmore's purposes to present himself as an iconoclast railing against revered elders of the legal fraternity. Whereas Pound and Llewellyn were too eager to highlight their own originality, Wigmore actually downplayed the newness of his thought. In so doing, Wigmore rendered his suggestions for reform palatable to the less progressive elements of the bench and bar. In an article about Wigmore's efforts to revamp Illinois state law, Robert Burns explains, "Like any good reformer addressing a conservative audience, Wigmore could minimize the novelty of the rules he was proposing."[9]

But there also may have been a deeper psychological reason for Wigmore's aversion to scholarly oedipalism. As he broke free of his biological parents' control, and consequently endured their disapproval, he saw in older jurists not targets but father figures. That is not to say that Wigmore never critiqued seasoned judges and scholars—indeed he sometimes found fault with Holmes and even Thayer—but Wigmore was predisposed to acknowledge, not efface, intellectual debt in a manner that distinguished him from Pound and Llewellyn. He built his career by cultivating rather than caricaturing his elders. An exceptionally cerebral person, Wigmore fulfilled his human longing for companionship by finding intellectual common ground with others, both older and younger, both mentors and protégés. Wigmore's life reveals that the story of legal thought is a deeply human one.

Notes

Introduction

1. John Henry Wigmore, *A Treatise on the System of Evidence in Trials at Common Law: Including the Statutes and Judicial Decisions of All Jurisdictions of the United States*, 4 vols. (Boston: Little, Brown, 1904–1905). Hereafter referred to as the *Treatise*. The second edition appeared in 1923 and the third in 1940.

2. An exception is Brian Tamanaha, who twice mentions an 1892 law review article on evidence by John Henry Wigmore in *Beyond the Formalist-Realist Divide: The Role of Politics in Judging* (Princeton, NJ: Princeton University Press, 2009), 37, 47.

3. William Twining, *Theories of Evidence: Bentham and Wigmore* (London: Weidenfeld & Nicolson, 1985), 229–30n46, 18, 141–42; Annelise Riles, "Encountering Amateurism: John Henry Wigmore and the Uses of American Formalism," in *Rethinking the Masters of Comparative Law*, ed. Annelise Riles (Portland, OR: Hart Publishing, 2001), 97.

4. Michael Ariens mentions that Wigmore had an impact on Pound's jurisprudence in "Progress Is Our Only Product: Legal Reform and the Codification of Evidence," *Law & Social Inquiry* 17 (Spring 1992): 220–21.

5. William M. Wiecek, *The Lost World of Classical Legal Thought: Law and Ideology in America, 1886–1937* (New York: Oxford University Press, 1998), 5, 8–11, 13, 52, 81–82, 87, 99, 154; Morton J. Horwitz, *The Transformation of American Law, 1870–1960: The Crisis of Legal Orthodoxy* (Oxford: Oxford University Press, 1992), 16–17, 27, 33, 59–60, 193; Robert W. Gordon, "Legal Thought and Legal Practice in the Age of American Enterprise, 1870–1920," in *Professions and Professional Ideologies in America*, ed. Gerald L. Geison (Chapel Hill: University of North Carolina Press, 1983), 89–90; Neil Duxbury, *Patterns of American Jurisprudence* (Oxford: Clarendon Press, 1995), 6, 23, 30.

6. Wiecek, *Lost World*, 185, 188–89, 193, 195, 198, 199–204; Horwitz, *Transformation of American Law*, 6, 18, 33–34, 50, 72, 104, 110, 128, 129–31, 142, 156, 195–98, 200–201; Duxbury, *American Jurisprudence*, 47, 58, 80, 89–96, 105, 145; Gordon, "Legal Thought and Legal Practice," 94–95; James E. Herget, *American Jurisprudence, 1870–1970: A History* (Houston, TX: Rice University Press, 1990), 3, 7, 156–59.

7. Wiecek, *Lost World*, 83, 104–7, 123–26, 157, 175–76; Horwitz, *Transformation of American Law*, 4–5, 30, 66; Tamanaha, *Formalist-Realist Divide*, 1.

8. See generally Tamanaha, *Formalist-Realist Divide*; David Rabban, *Law's History: American Legal Thought and the Transatlantic Turn to History* (Cambridge: Cambridge University Press, 2013).

9. Morton White documents the shared modernist tendencies between contemporary law, philosophy, economics, politics, and history in his classic text *Social Thought in America: The Revolt against Formalism* (New York: Viking Press, 1949). White does not discuss the law of evidence.

10. For descriptions of contemporary alternatives to modernism in philosophy, history, and economics, see, respectively, J. David Hoeveler, *The New Humanism: A Critique of Modern America, 1900–1940* (Charlottesville: University Press of Virginia, 1977), 30–31; Charles A. Beard, *An Economic Interpretation of the Constitution of the United States* (1913; repr., New York: Macmillan, 1948), 1–2; Rick Tilman, *Thorstein Veblen and His Critics, 1891–1963: Conservative, Liberal and Radical Perspectives* (Princeton, NJ: Princeton University Press, 1992), 18–46. For antimodernism more generally, see T. J. Jackson Lears, *No Place of Grace: Antimodernism and the Transformation of American Culture, 1880–1920* (New York: Pantheon, 1981).

11. White, *Social Thought in America*, 3; John Patrick Diggins, *The Promise of Pragmatism: Modernism and the Crisis of Authority* (Chicago: University of Chicago Press, 1994), 386; Louis Menand, *The Metaphysical Club* (New York: Farrar, Straus and Giroux, 2001), 441.

12. For the varieties of intellectual modernism, see Jean B. Quandt, *From the Small Town to the Great Community: The Social Thought of Progressive Intellectuals* (New Brunswick, NJ: Rutgers University Press, 1970); Daniel T. Rodgers, *Atlantic Crossings: Social Politics in a Progressive Age* (Cambridge, MA: Harvard University Press, Belknap, 1998); Leslie Butler, *Critical Americans: Victorian Intellectuals and Transatlantic Liberal Reform* (Chapel Hill: University of North Carolina Press, 2007); James Turner, *The Liberal Education of Charles Eliot Norton* (Baltimore, MD: Johns Hopkins University Press, 1999).

13. Wiecek, *Lost World*, 198; Horwitz, *Transformation of American Law*, 169, 208–9; Duxbury, *American Jurisprudence*, 64–65; Tamanaha, "Understanding Legal Realism," *Texas Law Review* 87 (March 2009): 737–38; N. E. H. Hull, *Roscoe Pound and Karl Llewellyn: Searching for an American Jurisprudence* (Chicago: University of Chicago Press, 1997), 174–75.

Chapter 1 Wigmore's Life

1. Recollections, Beatrice Wigmore Hunter, 1–2, Box 17, Folder 11, John Henry Wigmore (1863–1943) Papers, 1868–2006, Series 17/20, Northwestern University Archives, Evanston, Illinois (hereinafter all manuscripts can be assumed to be in this collection, unless otherwise stated); Recollections, Francis Marion Wigmore, 1, Box 18, Folder 2.

2. Gunther Barth, *Instant Cities: Urbanization and the Rise of San Francisco and Denver* (New York: Oxford University Press, 1975), 119, 218–20, 135, 146.

3. Recollections, Hunter, 2–3, Box 17, Folder 11.

4. William R. Roalfe, *John Henry Wigmore: Scholar and Reformer* (Evanston, IL: Northwestern University Press, 1977), 8–17; Recollections, F. Wigmore, 3, Box 18, Folder 2.

5. Tal Golan, "Revisiting the History of Scientific Expert Testimony," *Brooklyn Law Review* 73 (Spring 2008): 902.

6. Bruce A. Kimball, *The Inception of Modern Professional Education: C. C. Langdell, 1826–1906* (Chapel Hill: University of North Carolina Press, 2009), 2, 6–7.

7. John H. Wigmore, "The Recent Cases Department," *Harvard Law Review* 50 (April 1937): 862; John Henry Schlegel writes, "a succession of individuals, of whom John Henry Wigmore and Nathan Abbott [of Stanford] are among the most notable, effectively conquered the law schools west of the Appalachians in the name of Langdell and his system," in *American Legal Realism and Empirical Social Science* (Chapel Hill: University of North Carolina Press, 1995), 26.

8. Recollections, Hunter, 3, Box 17, Folder 11; Recollections, Louis B. Wehle, 1, Box 18, Folder 2; Recollections, Lawrence Egbert, 2–3, Box 17, Folder 10; Recollections, Agnes F. Bradley, 3, Box 17, Folder 10.

9. Roalfe, *Wigmore*, 8–20, 71, 244; Recollections, F. Wigmore, 3, Box 18, Folder 2; Recollections, Edward A. Harriman, 2, Box 17, Folder 11; Recollections, Nathan William MacChesney, 57, Box 18, Folder 1; Recollections, Hunter, 3, Box 17, Folder 11. Quotation appears in MacChesney. Note that Wigmore moved to Japan in 1889 but did not begin his official duties until 1890.

10. Albion Small to Wigmore, July 29, 1889, 2, Box 105, Folder 21. Lester Ward, *Dynamic Sociology, or Applied Social Science as Based upon Statistical Sociology and the Less Complex Sciences* (New York: D. Appleton, 1883). See also Edward C. Rafferty, *Apostle of Human Progress: Lester Frank Ward and American Political Thought, 1841–1913* (Lanham, MD: Rowman and Littlefield, 2003), 1, 262.

11. See generally Box 105, Folder 21. On the primacy of *Dynamic Sociology*, see Louis Menand, *The Metaphysical Club* (New York: Farrar, Straus and Giroux, 2001), 303.

12. Neil Pedlar, *The Imported Pioneers: Westerners Who Helped Build Modern Japan* (New York: St. Martin's Press, 1990), 13–14, 16, 23.

13. H. J. Jones, *Live Machines: Hired Foreigners and Meiji Japan* (Vancouver: University of British Columbia Press, 1980), 55; Kenneth W. Abbott, "Wigmore: The Japanese Connection," *Northwestern University Law Review* 75 (February 1981 Supplement): 10; Takayanagi Kenzô, "John Henry Wigmore" (1966), in *Law and Justice in Tokugawa Japan: Materials for the History of Japanese Law and Justice under the Tokugawa Shogunate 1603–1867*, ed. Wigmore, 9 vols. (Tokyo: University of Tokyo Press, 1969), 1:xx, n1.

14. Pedlar, *Imported Pioneers*, 187, 189; Wigmore, "Legal Education in Modern Japan," *Green Bag* 5 (1893): 17–18; Wigmore, "Parliamentary Days in Japan," *Scribner's Magazine* 10 (August 1891): 245.

15. Quotation appears in Kenzô, "John Henry Wigmore," in Wigmore, *Law and Justice in Tokugawa Japan*, 1:xviii. See also Wigmore, "Legal Education," 19; Sakata Yoshio, "The Beginning of Modernization in Japan," in *The Modernizers: Overseas Students, Foreign*

Employees, and Meiji Japan, ed. Ardath W. Burks (Boulder, CO: Westview Press, 1985), 76, 82n17; Wigmore, "Legal Education," 31.

16. Quoted in Roalfe, *Wigmore,* 22.

17. Quoted in Annelise Riles, "Encountering Amateurism: John Henry Wigmore and the Uses of American Formalism," in *Rethinking the Masters of Comparative Law,* ed. Riles (Portland, OR: Hart, 2001), 101. For Eliot's role in Wigmore's placement, see Wigmore, "Comparative Law: Jottings on Comparative Legal Ideas and Institutions," *Tulane Law Review* 6 (Part I: December 1931; Part II: February 1932): 48. For Wigmore's preparations, see Abbott, "Wigmore," 11.

18. Abbott, "Wigmore," 11; Wigmore, "Legal Education," 79; Roalfe, *Wigmore,* 24.

19. Wigmore, "Foreign Jurisdiction in Japan," *The Nation,* January 12, 1893, 26–27.

20. Wigmore, ed. *Materials for the Study of Private Law in Old Japan,* 4 vols. (Tokyo: Asiatic Society of Japan, 1892), 1:2.

21. Wigmore, *A Panorama of the World's Legal Systems,* 3 vols. (Saint Paul, MN: West Publishing, 1928), 1:xv. For playing shortstop, see Roalfe, *Wigmore,* 24.

22. Jerome Hall, *Comparative Law and Social Theory* (Baton Rouge: Louisiana State University Press, 1963), 10; Riles, "Wigmore's Treasure Box: Comparative Law in the Era of Information," *Harvard International Law Journal* 40 (Winter 1999): 282; David S. Clark, "The Modern Development of American Comparative Law: 1904–1945," *American Journal of Comparative Law* 55 (Fall 2007): 607.

23. Wigmore, *Materials,* 1:6; Wigmore, "Legal Education," 21–22; Wigmore, "Comparative Law," 48.

24. Wigmore, "Preface" (1941), in Wigmore, *Law and Justice in Tokugawa Japan,* 1:xii.

25. Wigmore, "Comparative Law," 262–63.

26. Wigmore, "The Legal System of Old Japan," *Green Bag* 4 (Part I: September 1892; Part II: October 1892): 403.

27. Wigmore, "Legal System of Old Japan," 403, 409.

28. Wigmore, *Materials,* 1:22. See also Abbott, "Wigmore," 12.

29. Riles, "Encountering Amateurism," 108; Wigmore, "Legal System of Old Japan," 403; Wigmore, "The Pledge Idea: A Study in Comparative Legal Ideas," *Harvard Law Review* 10 & 11 (Part I: January 1897; Part II: February 1897; Part III: April 1897): 39. In the same vein, Wigmore wrote in his 1941 book on comparative law, "Whether the professional individual tribunal or the popular group-tribunal is the better in policy for securing fair and effective trial procedure seems to depend on the period, the place, and the person." Wigmore, *A Kaleidoscope of Justice: Containing Authentic Accounts of Trial Scenes from All Times and Climes* (Washington, DC: Washington Law Book, 1941), 722.

30. Wigmore, "Legal Education," 85.

31. Wigmore, *Materials,* 1:24–25. Although Riles sees Wigmore as a universalist, she still recognizes that "Wigmore was committed to the importance of law in social context." See Riles, "Wigmore's Treasure Box," 264. See also Riles, "Encountering Amateurism," 110.

32. Wigmore, "Legal System of Old Japan," 408.

33. Duane B. Simmons and Wigmore, *Notes on Land Tenure and Local Institutions in Old Japan* (1891; repr., Washington, DC: University Publications of America, 1979), 37–38, 46.

34. Wigmore, "Legal Education," 17.

35. Wigmore, "The Administration of Justice in Japan," *American Law Register and Review* 45 (Part I: July 1897; Part II: August 1897; Part III: October 1897): 632–33. See also Kenzô, "John Henry Wigmore," in Wigmore, *Law and Justice in Tokugawa Japan*, 1:xx; Roalfe, *Wigmore*, 28.

36. Wigmore, "Legal System of Old Japan," 404, 479; Wigmore, *Materials*, 1:15–16.

37. Wigmore, "Legal Education," 78.

38. Wigmore, "Comparative Law," 48. See also Roalfe, *Wigmore*, 29.

39. Harold M. Mayer and Richard C. Wade, with the assistance of Glen E. Holt, *Chicago: Growth of a Metropolis* (Chicago: University of Chicago Press, 1969), 208–10, 230, 193, 273–74, 256, 242; William Cronon, *Nature's Metropolis: Chicago and the Great West* (New York: W. W. Norton, 1991), 367.

40. Harold F. Williamson and Payson S. Wild, *Northwestern University: A History, 1850–1975* (Evanston, IL: Northwestern University, 1976), 71–74. See also F. B. Crossley, "Northwestern University Law School," in *History of Northwestern University and Evanston*, ed. Robert D. Sheppard and Harvey B. Hurd (Chicago: Munsell, 1906): 105–8.

41. Roalfe, *Wigmore*, 37; Wigmore, "The Four-Year Law Course," *American Bar Association Journal* 3 (1917): 14–20; Wigmore, "A Course on 'The Profession of the Bar,'" *American Law School Review* 7 (December 1931): 273–80; Williamson and Wild, *Northwestern*, 118; and Recollections, Charles B. Elder, 4, Box 17, Folder 10; Recollections, Elder, 3, Box 17, Folder 10.

42. Recollections, Charles H. Watson, 1, Box 18, Folder 2.

43. Recollections, Elder, 1, Box 17, Folder 10.

44. Recollections, F. Wigmore, 7–8, Box 18, Folder 2.

45. Recollections, Anne George Millar, 1, Box 18 Folder 1; Recollections, Edwin C. Austin, 1, Box 17, Folder 10; Recollections, Hall, 2, Box 17, Folder 11; Recollections, Fred D. Fagg Jr., 5, Box 17, Folder 11.

46. Recollections, Francis S. Philbrick, 21, Box 18, Folder 2; Recollections, Manley O. Hudson, 5, Box 17, Folder 11.

47. Recollections, MacChesney, 37–38, Box 18, Folder 1. Note that there are two versions of MacChesney's recollections. In this book, I cite only the version that spans fifty-nine pages rather than forty-seven.

48. Roalfe, *Wigmore*, 279, 76; Recollections, Sarah B. Morgan, 25, Box 18, Folder 1; Recollections, F. Wigmore, 4, Box 18, Folder 2. Roalfe inaccurately wrote that the Tokugawa Shogunate series was sixteen volumes, likely because Wigmore himself anticipated that the series would amount to that number; see "Bibliography," *Northwestern University Law Review* 75 (February 1981 supplement): 56. Ultimately the series filled nine volumes.

49. Holmes to Wigmore, October 24, 1902, Box 65, Folder 25; Recollections, F. Wigmore, 7, Box 18, Folder 2. For Emma's investment in her husband's productivity, see Recollections, Watson, 1, Box 18, Folder 2.

50. Recollections, Egbert, Box 17, Folder 10; Recollections, Robert Wyness Millar, 1, Box 18, Folder 1; Recollections, Morgan, 28, Box 18, Folder 1.

51. Wigmore, *Treatise*, 2:1951–52.

52. Wigmore, *Treatise*, 3:2173–76. Quotation appears on 3:2173. The bench's rationale for rejecting scientific treatises was that the texts were hearsay if unaccompanied by the testimony of their respective authors.

53. Wigmore, *Treatise*, 3:2187–88.

54. Samuel Haber, *The Quest for Authority and Honor in the American Professions, 1750–1900* (Chicago: University of Chicago Press, 1991), 212.

55. Roalfe, *Wigmore*, 107, 112.

56. Wigmore, "Organizing the Power of the American Bar," *American Bar Association Journal* 17 (June 1931): 391.

57. The quotation belongs to Judge J. Weston Allen, Chairman of the Committee on Award of the American Bar Association Medal, and appears in "American Bar Association Medal Presented," *American Bar Association Journal* 18 (November 1932): 741.

58. Wigmore, *Treatise*, 1:782. Still, Wigmore entrusted the bench to screen for expert qualifications. For codes of ethics, see Haber, *Authority and Honor*, 211, 266–67; for self-policing, see Thomas L. Haskell, *The Emergence of Professional Social Science: The American Social Science Association and the Nineteenth-Century Crisis of Authority* (Urbana: University of Illinois Press, 1977), 67.

59. Wigmore, "Should the Standards for Bar Preparation Be More Exacting?" *Tennessee Law Review* 11 (February 1933): 103. Burton J. Bledstein writes, "As many professions as feasible would locate the center of their authority within university schools," in *The Culture of Professionalism: The Middle Class and the Development of Higher Education in America* (New York: W. W. Norton, 1976), 325. See also Kimball, *The "True Professional Ideal" in America* (Cambridge, MA: Blackwell, 1992), 248.

60. Recollections, Watson, 3–4, Box 18, Folder 2.

61. Recollections, Stuart S. Ball, 7, Box 17, Folder 10.

62. Roalfe, *Wigmore*, 70–71.

63. Ibid., 16, 117, 232–33.

64. Recollections, Morgan, 24, Box 18, Folder 1.

65. Recollections, Elder, 7–8, Box 17, Folder 10.

66. Recollections, Hudson, 2, Box 17, Folder 11; Roalfe, *Wigmore*, 113, 120–23.

67. Roalfe, *Wigmore*, 114; Recollections, F. Wigmore, 5, Box 18, Folder 2; Recollections, Association of American Law Schools, 4, Box 18, Folder 3.

68. Wigmore to James Bradley Thayer, May 6, 1894, Box 19, Folder 6, James Bradley Thayer Papers, Harvard Law School Library (hereinafter Thayer Papers); Recollections,

Philbrick, 21, Box 18, Folder 2. Bruce Kuklick argues for the importance of temper-
ament in shaping intellectual outlook in *The Rise of American Philosophy: Cambridge,
Massachusetts, 1860–1930* (New Haven, CT: Yale University Press, 1977), xvii. For ex-
amples of other AAUP members who were swept up in wartime fervor, see Carol S.
Gruber, *Mars and Minerva: World War I and the Uses of the Higher Learning in America*
(Baton Rouge: Louisiana State University Press, 1975), 163–212.

69. Roalfe, *Wigmore*, 146–47. The Supreme Court came to embrace Holmes's reasoning fifty years later in Brandenburg v. Ohio, 395 U.S. 444 (1969).

70. Abrams v. United States, 250 U.S. 616 (1919); Wigmore, "Abrams *v.* U.S.: Freedom
of Speech and Freedom of Thuggery in War-time and Peace-time," *Illinois Law Review*
14 (March 1920): 549–51.

71. *Abrams*, 250 U.S. 616; Holmes to Wigmore, March 16, 1915, Reel 39, Frame 39,
Oliver Wendell Holmes Jr. Papers, Harvard Law School Library (hereinafter Holmes
Papers); Wigmore, "Abrams *v.* U.S.," 546.

72. *Abrams*, 250 U.S. 616; Wigmore, "Abrams *v.* U.S.," 552.

73. "Holmes to Pollock, April 25, 1920," in *Holmes-Pollock Letters: The Correspondence
of Mr. Justice Holmes and Sir Frederick Pollock, 1874–1923,* ed. Mark DeWolfe Howe, 2
vols. (Cambridge, MA: Harvard University Press, 1942), 2:42; Holmes to Wigmore, May
29, 1929, Reel 39, Frame 75, Holmes Papers.

74. Moshik Temkin, *The Sacco-Vanzetti Affair: America on Trial* (New Haven, CT: Yale
University Press, 2009), 1, 9–12.

75. Temkin, *Sacco-Vanzetti Affair*, 22–36.

76. Felix Frankfurter, "The Case of Sacco and Vanzetti," *Atlantic Monthly* 139 (March
1927): 431–32. See also Temkin, *Sacco-Vanzetti Affair*, 31–32.

77. Wigmore to Webster Thayer, March 31, 1927, Box 47, Folder 26.

78. Wigmore, "The Sacco-Vanzetti Verdict—A Reply," *Boston Evening Transcript*, May
10, 1927, 15. For other articles in the Wigmore-Frankfurter exchange, see Wigmore,
"John Henry Wigmore Answers Frankfurter Attack on Sacco-Vanzetti Verdict," *Boston
Evening Transcript*, April 25, 1927; Frankfurter, "Prof. Frankfurter Replies to Dean
Wigmore," *Boston Evening Transcript*, April 26, 1927, 15; Frankfurter, "Frankfurter Says
Wigmore Admits Sacco Inaccuracy," *Boston Herald*, May 11, 1927, 3.

79. Frankfurter, "Wigmore Admits Sacco Inaccuracy," 3.

80. See, for instance, Alden P. White [Judge, Probate and Insolvency Courts, Essex
County], April 26, 1927; Gleason L. Archer [Dean, Suffolk Law School] to Wigmore,
April 26, 1927; Oscar A. Marden [Justice, District Court of Southern Norfolk] to
Wigmore, April 26, 1927; Charles A. Cushman [lawyer, Cambridge] to Wigmore, April
26, 1927; Harlow M. Davis [attorney, Boston] to Wigmore, April 26, 1927; Daniel
Buckley [counselor at law, Boston] to Wigmore, April 26, 1927; Homer Albers [Dean,
Boston University Law School] to Wigmore, April 27, 1927; Eugene C. Upton [attor-
ney, Boston] to Wigmore, April 27, 1927, Box 47, Folder 26.

81. W. Thayer to Wigmore, May 4, 1927, Box 47, Folder 26.

82. Temkin, *Sacco-Vanzetti Affair*, 78–79.

83. Frankfurter, *Felix Frankfurter Reminisces* (London: Secker & Warburg, 1960), 217.

84. Walter Dill Scott to Wigmore, May 25, 1927, Box 47, Folder 26; Wigmore to Chief of the Bureau of Investigation [i.e., J. Edgar Hoover], March 31, 1927, Box 47, Folder 26. See also Roalfe, *Wigmore*, 152.

85. Wigmore, "John Henry Wigmore Answers Frankfurter Attack," 1. As Temkin writes, "Relatively little of Wigmore's much-anticipated piece . . . dealt with the legal matters that Frankfurter had discussed, or even with Wigmore's own area of expertise, evidence." Temkin, *Sacco-Vanzetti Affair*, 77. Similarly, N. E. H. Hull details that Wigmore was "more polemical than legal," in *Roscoe Pound and Karl Llewellyn: Searching for an American Jurisprudence* (Chicago: University of Chicago Press, 1997), 157.

86. Wigmore and Albert Kocourek, eds., *Rational Basis of Legal Institutions* (New York: Macmillan, 1923); William Twining, *Theories of Evidence: Bentham and Wigmore* (London: Weidenfeld & Nicolson, 1985), 229–30n46. Schlegel writes, "Perversely, in reviewing the book at length, Moore ignored its manifest content but took its title at face value," in "American Legal Realism and Empirical Social Science: The Singular Case of Underhill Moore," *Buffalo Law Review* 29 (Spring 1980): 203.

87. Underhill Moore, "Rational Basis of Legal Institutions," *Columbia Law Review* 23 (November 1923): 612.

88. Wigmore, *Treatise*, 1:31, 34.

89. Moore, "Rational Basis of Legal Institutions," 614–15.

90. Quoted in Schlegel, "Singular Case of Underhill Moore," 238n259.

91. Rick Tilman, *Thorstein Veblen, John Dewey, C. Wright Mills and the Generic Ends of Life* (Lanham, MD: Rowman & Littlefield, 2004), 12. For the history of the New School, see Peter M. Rutkoff and William B. Scott, *New School: A History of the New School for Social Research* (New York: Free Press, 1986).

92. Holmes to Wigmore, January 10, 1923, Reel 39, Frame 63, Holmes Papers. Thorstein Veblen, *The Theory of the Leisure Class* (1899; repr., New York: Macmillan, 1912).

93. Wigmore and Kocourek, "Editorial Preface," in *Rational Basis*, xxi.

94. Roalfe, *Wigmore*, 183, 187.

95. Wigmore, *Panorama*, 1:xi, 3:1123.

96. Wigmore, "Comparative Law," 51, 52, 264.

97. Wigmore, "Preface," in Wigmore, *Law and Justice in Tokugawa Japan*, 1:xv. For background on the translation project, see Kenzô, "John Henry Wigmore," in Wigmore, *Law and Justice in Tokugawa Japan*, 1:xxi.

98. Wigmore, "Comparative," 60.

99. Abbott, "Wigmore," 14–15.

100. Recollections, Fagg, 1, Box 17, Folder 11.

101. Recollections, Association of American Law Schools, 1, Box 18, Folder 3; Roalfe, *Wigmore*, 275–77; quotation appears in Recollections, Margaret G. Belknap, 11, Box 17, Folder 10.

Chapter 2 Intellectual Influences

1. Jay Hook, "A Brief Life of James Bradley Thayer," *Northwestern University Law Review* 88 (1993–1994): 1–8. Thayer is among the most important figures of American legal history without a biography. On Thayer as one of four full-time Harvard Law faculty members, see G. Edward White, *Justice Oliver Wendell Holmes: Law and the Inner Self* (New York: Oxford University Press, 1993), 198. Ralph Waldo Emerson was another famous intellectual associated with Thayer; the latter married the niece of the celebrated poet.

2. Wigmore to Mrs. Thayer, February 16, 1902, Box 25, Folder 9, Thayer Papers. On Wigmore's strained relationship with his family, see William R. Roalfe, *John Henry Wigmore: Scholar and Reformer* (Evanston, IL: Northwestern University Press, 1977), 20.

3. Thayer to Wigmore, January 3, 1889, Box 108, Folder 27; Thayer to Wigmore, August 2, 1889, Box 108, Folder 27; Thayer to Wigmore, September 3, 1893, Box 108, Folder 27; Wigmore to Mrs. Thayer, February 16, 1902.

4. Wigmore to Thayer, November 3, 1895, Box 19, Folder 6, Thayer Papers. For Wigmore seeking advice from Thayer on scholarship and hiring, see Wigmore to Thayer, May 31, 1896, Box 19, Folder 6, Thayer Papers; Wigmore to Thayer October 17, 1897, Box 19, Folder 6, Thayer Papers; Wigmore to Thayer, January 13, 1902, Box 19, Folder 6, Thayer Papers; Wigmore to Thayer, May 6, 1894, Box 19, Folder 6, Thayer Papers; Wigmore to Thayer, March 4, 1895, Box 19, Folder 6, Thayer Papers; Thayer to Wigmore, February 28, 1895, Box 108, Folder 27; and Thayer to Wigmore, May 30, 1895, Box 108, Folder 27.

5. Wigmore to Thayer, December 30, 1894, Box 19, Folder 6, Thayer Papers; Wigmore to Thayer, September 23, 1900, Box 19, Folder 6, Thayer Papers. James Bradley Thayer, *Select Cases on Evidence at Common Law* (Cambridge, MA: Charles W. Sever, 1892). For Wigmore's citation of *Cases on Evidence*, see John Henry Wigmore, *A Treatise on the System of Evidence in Trials at Common Law: Including the Statutes and Judicial Decisions of All Jurisdictions of the United States*, 4 vols. (Boston: Little, Brown, 1904–1905), 2:1879n1, 2:1940n4.

6. Thayer to Wigmore, September 23, 1899, Box 108, Folder 27; Thayer to Wigmore, September 28, 1899, Box 108, Folder 27; Thayer to Wigmore, February 8, 1900, Box 108, Folder 27; Wigmore to Thayer, September 23, 1900. For Thayer's referencing of Wigmore's edition of *Greenleaf*, see Thayer, *A Selection of Cases on Evidence at the Common Law*, 2nd ed. (Cambridge, MA: Charles W. Sever, 1900), 728.

7. Thayer, *Preliminary Treatise on Evidence at the Common Law* (Boston: Little, Brown, 1898), 511.

8. Wigmore to Thayer, November 23, 1898, Box 19, Folder 6, Thayer Papers.

9. Thayer, *Preliminary Treatise*, 267; Oliver Wendell Holmes Jr., *The Common Law* (Boston: Little, Brown, 1881), 1; Thayer, *Preliminary Treatise*, 3–4, 273, 514.

10. Thayer, *Preliminary Treatise*, 319, 518.

11. Ibid., 251–52, 204, 297, 265.

12. Ibid., 536, 273–74, 529. Louis Menand credits Thayer with imparting an anti-universalist ethic in the famous modernist judge, Learned Hand; see Menand, *The Metaphysical Club* (New York: Farrar, Straus and Giroux, 2001), 425.

13. Thayer, *Preliminary Treatise*, 428–29; Wigmore, *Treatise*, 4:3481.

14. Thayer, *Preliminary Treatise*, 48, 292, 181–82. For Wigmore's citation of Thayer, see Wigmore, *Treatise*, 3:2179n2.

15. Thayer, *Preliminary Treatise*, 528, 526, 258, 309. For Wigmore's citation of Thayer, see Wigmore, *Treatise*, 4:3601.

16. Thayer, *Preliminary Treatise*, 531; Thayer, "The Origin and Scope of the American Doctrine of Constitutional Law," *Harvard Law Review* 7 (1893): 144. On the significance of Thayer's article, see White, "Revisiting James Bradley Thayer," *Northwestern University Law Review* 88 (1993–1994): 48–49.

17. Lochner v. New York, 198 U.S. 45 (1905); William M. Wiecek, *The Lost World of Classical Legal Thought: Law and Ideology in America, 1886–1937* (New York: Oxford University Press, 1998), 152; Morton J. Horwitz, *The Transformation of American Law, 1870–1960: The Crisis of Legal Orthodoxy* (Oxford: Oxford University Press, 1992), 33; Neil Duxbury, *Patterns of American Jurisprudence* (Oxford: Clarendon, 1995), 30–31; David E. Bernstein, "*Lochner* Era Revisionism, Revised: *Lochner* and the Origins of Fundamental Rights Constitutionalism," *Georgetown Law Journal* 92 (November 2003): 1.

18. *Lochner*, 198 U.S. 45. For scholarship that challenges the traditional view of *Lochner*, see Stephen A. Siegel, "*Lochner* Era Jurisprudence and the American Constitutional Tradition," *North Carolina Law Review* 70 (November 1991): 15–21; and Brian Tamanaha, *Beyond the Formalist-Realist Divide: The Role of Politics in Judging* (Princeton, NJ: Princeton University Press, 2010), 36.

19. *Lochner*, 198 U.S. 45. For Herbert Spencer's work, see *Social Statics, or The Conditions essential to Happiness specified, and the First of them Developed* (New York: D. Appleton, 1872).

20. Wigmore, *Treatise*, 2:1657.

21. Ibid., 2:1672

22. Thayer, *Preliminary Treatise*, 226.

23. Ibid., 524–25; Wigmore, *Treatise*, 3:2552–53. The notion that what we choose to label "facts" are in fact "inferences" is consistent with the commonplace proposition in the philosophy of science that our perception of the world is theory-laden; see, for instance, Norwood Russell Hanson, *Patterns of Discovery: An Inquiry into the Conceptual Foundations of Science* (Cambridge: Cambridge University Press, 1958), 19.

24. Thayer, *Preliminary Treatise*, 274, 271, 343, 376.

25. Ibid., 447, 382, 274.

26. See Box 11, Folders 2–4, Thayer Papers.

27. Wigmore to Thayer, November 23, 1898; Wigmore to Thayer, May 9, 1900, Box 19, Folder 6, Thayer Papers; Thayer to Wigmore, May 13, 1900, Box 108, Folder 27; Thayer to Wigmore, September 19, 1900, Box 108, Folder 27; Wigmore to Thayer,

January 23, 1902, Box 19, Folder 6, Thayer Papers. For the dedication, see Wigmore, *Treatise*, 1:v. For the reference to Thayer as "the great master," see Wigmore, *Treatise*, 1:31. The *Treatise* was also dedicated to Charles Doe, onetime chief justice of the New Hampshire Supreme Court. Holmes was surprised by Wigmore's affection for Doe. "I thought there was not a great deal of brandy in his water," Holmes once remarked to Wigmore; see Holmes to Wigmore, January 14, 1910, Reel 39, Frame 20, Holmes Papers.

28. White, *Oliver Wendell Holmes, Jr.*, 2nd ed. (New York: Oxford University Press, 2006), 6–23. Note that White authored more than one biography of Holmes; this source is distinct from White's *Justice Oliver Wendell Holmes: Law and the Inner Self*, cited elsewhere.

29. White, *Oliver Wendell Holmes, Jr.*, 27–43.

30. Ibid., 50, 63; Horwitz, *Transformation of American Law*, 140; Wiecek, *Lost World*, 181. Holmes published "The Path of the Law" in the *Harvard Law Review* shortly after his speech; see Holmes, "The Path of the Law," *Harvard Law Review* 10 (March 1897): 457–478.

31. White, *Oliver Wendell Holmes, Jr.*, 75–77, 113–18, 125–29; Menand, *Metaphysical Club*, 65–67. On Holmes's role as class poet, see White, *Law and the Inner Self*, 182. James Kent, *Commentaries on American Law*, ed. Holmes, 12th ed. (Boston: Little, Brown, 1873).

32. White, *Law and the Inner Self*, 95, 125–26, 197, 200, 205–7; Menand, *Metaphysical Club*, 338; White, *Oliver Wendell Holmes, Jr.*, 41. Given Thayer's perpetual assistance, he was understandably upset when Holmes abruptly left the Harvard Law faculty for the Massachusetts Supreme Judicial Court without first consulting either university president Charles William Eliot or his colleagues on the faculty, who learned of Holmes's resignation in the newspaper.

33. Felix Frankfurter to Arthur Schlesinger, June 18, 1963, in *Roosevelt and Frankfurter: Their Correspondence, 1928–1945*, ed. Max Freedman (London: Bodley Head, 1967), 25; Holmes, "The Path of the Law," 474; Holmes, "The Theory of Legal Interpretation," *Harvard Law Review* 12 (January 1899): 417; *Lochner*, 198 U.S. 45.

34. Holmes to Wigmore, November 3, 1887, Box 65, Folder 25. For Wigmore's articles, see Wigmore, "The Boycott and Kindred Practices as Ground for Damages," *American Law Review* 21 (July–August 1887): 509–32; and Wigmore, "Interference with Social Relations," *American Law Review* 21 (September–October 1887): 764–78.

35. Holmes to Wigmore, December 19, 1891, Box 65, Folder 25; Holmes to Wigmore, May 3, 1894, Box 65, Folder 25; Wigmore to Holmes, November 1, 1892, Box 65, Folder 25; and Wigmore to Holmes, March 6, 1931, Reel 39, Frames 203 & 204, Holmes Papers. See also Wigmore to Holmes, March 7, 1934, Reel 39, Frames 211 & 212, Holmes Papers.

36. Wigmore to Holmes, August 19, 1902, Box 65, Folder 25. For the Tremont House, see Recollections, Nathan William MacChesney, 29, Box 18, Folder 1. For Holmes's traveling west of the Alleghenies, see Wigmore's preface to "Address of Mr. Justice

Oliver Wendell Holmes" (address, Northwestern University School of Law, Chicago, IL, October 20, 1902) repr.; January 12, 1932, Box 65, Folder 25.

37. Wigmore to Holmes, November 9, 1902, Box 65, Folder 25; Holmes to Wigmore, October 31, 1902, Box 65, Folder 25. See also "The Northwestern University Law School Building Dedicated—Address by Oliver Wendell Holmes, Chief Justice of the Supreme [Judicial] Court of Massachusetts," *Chicago Legal News* 35, no. 10 (October 1902), Box 65, Folder 25.

38. Wigmore to Holmes, June 14, 1902, Box 65, Folder 25; "Address of Mr. Justice Oliver Wendell Holmes"; Holmes to Lady Pollock, October 24, 1902, *Holmes Pollock Letters: The Correspondence of Mr. Justice Holmes and Sir Frederick Pollock, 1874 1923*, ed. Mark DeWolfe Howe (Cambridge, MA: Harvard University Press, 1942), 1:108. Menand writes that "Holmes was a famously brilliant talker on any subject—it was a gift he inherited from his father," in *Metaphysical Club*, 204.

39. Holmes, *Common Law*, 1. Holmes lifted the opening from a book review he had published earlier; see "Book Notices," *American Law Review* 14 (March 1880): 234.

40. White, *Law and the Inner Self*, 148–53, 170, 183–85; Tamanaha, "Understanding Legal Realism," *Texas Law Review* 87 (March 2009): 748; James E. Herget, *American Jurisprudence, 1870–1970: A History* (Houston, TX: Rice University Press, 1990), 46.

41. Wigmore to Holmes, June 7, 1924, Box 65, Folder 27; and Wigmore to Holmes, January 12, 1932, Reel 39, Frame 202, Holmes Papers. For Wigmore's comment on the enduring value of *The Common Law*, see Wigmore to Holmes, December 23, 1910, Reel 39, Frame 126, Holmes Papers. For the popularity of *The Common Law* only decades after its publication, see White, *Law and the Inner Self*, 149; and Wiecek, *Lost World*, 182. For Wigmore gifting Beale a copy of Holmes's book, see Wigmore to Holmes, March 18, 1909, Reel 39, Frame 121, Holmes Papers.

42. Holmes, *Common Law*, 111, 162. See also David Rosenburg, *The Hidden Holmes: His Theory of Torts in History* (Cambridge, MA: Harvard University Press, 1995), 2–3, 13, 51–52; Frederic R. Kellogg, *Oliver Wendell Holmes, Jr., Legal Theory and Judicial Restraint* (New York: Cambridge University Press, 2007), 88–90, 108, 125.

43. Wigmore, *Treatise*, 4:3374, 4:3389, 4:3375, 4:3389–90, 4:3390n2, 4:3375.

44. Holmes, "Privilege, Malice, and Intent," *Harvard Law Review* 8 (April 1984): 1–14; Wigmore to Holmes, April 29, 1894, Box 65, Folder 25; Holmes to Wigmore, May 3, 1894; Wigmore, "Responsibility for Tortious Acts: Its History," *Harvard Law Review* 7 (March 1894): 315–37; Wigmore, "The Tripartite Division of Torts," *Harvard Law Review* 8 (November 1894): 200–210; Wigmore, "A General Analysis of Tort Relations," *Harvard Law Review* 8 (February 1895): 377–95; Holmes to Wigmore, March 25, 1895, Box 65, Folder 25. For a discussion of the exchange between Holmes and Wigmore concerning torts, see Rosenburg, *Hidden Holmes*, 147–49.

45. Holmes, *Common Law*, 152; Wigmore, *Treatise*, 4:3592, 4:3592n1. See also Rosenburg, *Hidden Holmes*, 67. For Holmes's appreciation of combat expertise, see Menand, *Metaphysical Club*, 58.

46. Wigmore, *Treatise*, 1:528. Holmes's words come from an 1887 decision, Reeve v. Dennett, 145 Mass. 23, 28, 11 N.E. 938, 944 (1887).

47. Wigmore, *Treatise*, 4:3479, 4:3481; Goode v. Riley, 153 Mass. 585, 28 N.E. 228 (1891). While sympathetic to Holmes's reasoning, Wigmore still insisted on a flexible approach. "The truth," asserted Wigmore, "is that whatever virtue and strength lies in the argument for the antique rule leads not to a fixed rule of law, but only to a general maxim of prudent discretion," in *Treatise*, 4:3481. Holmes, the eternal skeptic, almost certainly would have appreciated Wigmore's qualification.

48. Holmes, "Theory of Legal Interpretation," 417, 419; Wigmore, *Treatise*, 4:3475n1, 4:3479n13.

49. Holmes, "Path of the Law," 469; Wigmore, *Treatise*, 1:vi. See also Wigmore to Holmes, April 1, 1921, Reel 39, Frame 186, Holmes Papers.

50. Holmes, "Path of the Law," 460–61.

51. Adair v. United States, 208 U.S. 161 (1908); Tamanaha, *Beyond the Formalist-Realist Divide*, 101.

52. Wigmore, *Treatise*, 3:2461.

53. Holmes, "Privilege, Malice, and Intent," 3; Horwitz, *Transformation of American Law*, 131. Holmes reiterated these ideas in "The Path of the Law": "Behind the logical form lies a judgment as to the relative worth and importance of competing legislative grounds. . . . There is a concealed, half conscious battle on the question of legislative policy, and if any one thinks that it can be settled deductively, or once for all, I only can say that I think he is theoretically wrong," 466–67.

54. Wigmore to Holmes, April 29, 1894.

55. *Lochner*, 198 U.S. 45; Menand, *Metaphysical Club*, 61; Rosenburg, *Hidden Holmes*, 16.

56. Holmes, "Path of the Law," 466; "Address of Mr. Justice Oliver Wendell Holmes," 7.

57. Holmes, *Common Law*, 310–11; Wigmore, *Treatise*, 4:3407n3; "Address of Mr. Justice Oliver Wendell Holmes"; Holmes to Lady Pollock, October 24, 1902, *Holmes Pollock Letters*, 1:108; Holmes, "Ideals and Doubts," *Illinois Law Review* 10 (1915–1916): 3. Note that *Northwestern University Law Review* was titled *Illinois Law Review* from 1906 to 1952. For Wigmore's solicitation of the article, see Wigmore to Holmes, March 25, 1915, Reel 39, Frames 169 & 170, Holmes Papers.

58. Peter J. King, *Utilitarian Jurisprudence in America: The Influence of Bentham and Austin on American Legal Thought in the Nineteenth Century* (New York: Garland, 1986), 3; John Dinwiddy, *Bentham: The Selected Writings of John Dinwiddy*, ed. William Twining (Stanford, CA: Stanford University Press, 2004), 12–13.

59. Jeremy Bentham, *A Fragment on Government* (London: T. Payne, 1776), ii; King, *Utilitarian Jurisprudence in America*, 5; Twining, *Rethinking Evidence: Exploratory Essays*, 2nd ed. (Cambridge: Cambridge University Press, 2006), 41–45.

60. Wigmore, *Treatise*, 1:28, 4:3092, 2:1171, 4:3016.

61. C. J. W. Allen, *The Law of Evidence in Victorian England* (Cambridge: Cambridge University Press, 1997), 4–7, 182–86.

62. David Armitage, *The Declaration of Independence: A Global History* (Cambridge, MA: Harvard University Press, 2008), 79; Philip Schofield, *Utility and Democracy: The Political Thought of Jeremy Bentham* (Oxford: Oxford University Press, 2006), 159; Bentham to Andrew Jackson, June 14, 1830, in *Correspondence of Andrew Jackson*, ed. John Spencer Bassett, 7 vols. (Washington, DC: Carnegie Institution, 1926–1937), 4:146.

63. King, *Utilitarian Jurisprudence in America*, 63; Schofield, *Utility and Democracy*, 244–46; quotation appears on p. 246. On Bentham's lack of influence in the antebellum South, see Michael O'Brien, *Conjectures of Order: Intellectual Life and the American South, 1810–1860*, 2 vols. (Chapel Hill: University of North Carolina Press, 2004), 2:1039–40.

64. King, *Utilitarian Jurisprudence in America*, 270–73, 325.

65. Allen, *Law of Evidence in Victorian England*, 10–11.

66. Kyong Whan Ahn and Jongcheol Kim, "Bentham, Modernity and the Nineteenth Century Revolution in Government," *Pophak: Seoul Law Journal* 35 (1994): 136, 147–50; David Philips, "'A Just Measure of Crime, Authority, Hunters and Blue Locusts': The 'Revisionist' Social History of Crime and the Law in Britain, 1780–1850," in *Social Control and the State*, ed. Stanley Cohen and Andrew Scull (New York: St. Martin's, 1983), 65–66; Max Rheinstein, ed., *Max Weber on Law in Economy and Society* (Cambridge, MA: Harvard University Press, 1954), 62; Tamanaha, *Beyond the Formalist-Realist Divide*, 25–26. Quotations appear in Ahn and Kim.

67. Bentham, *The Works of Jeremy Bentham*, ed. John Bowring, 11 vols. (Edinburgh: W. Tait, 1843), 7:370; Wigmore, *Treatise*, 3:2449–50, 3:2403. For Wigmore's citation of Bentham, see *Treatise*, 3:2403n4, 3:2425n1.

68. Bentham, *Works of Jeremy Bentham*, 7:185, 7:186; Wigmore, *Treatise*, 4:3627. For Wigmore's citation of Bentham, see *Treatise*, 4:3627n1.

69. Bentham, *Works of Jeremy Bentham*, 6:573; Wigmore, *Treatise*, 3:2001–2. For Wigmore's citation of Bentham, see *Treatise*, 3:2002n4. Schofield writes that "Bentham did not object to religious institutions as such, but rather to official religious establishments, funded by taxation which, by definition, was extracted by coercion," in *Utility and Democracy*, 198.

70. Twining, *Theories of Evidence: Bentham and Wigmore* (London: Weidenfeld & Nicolson, 1985), 45. Federal Rule of Evidence 403 would later reflect these same concerns: "The court may exclude relevant evidence if its probative value is substantially outweighed by a danger of one or more of the following: unfair prejudice, confusing the issues, misleading the jury, undue delay, wasting time, or needlessly presenting cumulative evidence."

71. Bentham, *Works of Jeremy Bentham*, 7:532; Wigmore, *Treatise*, 3:2521. To qualify, Bentham opposed greater judicial discretion in substantive law even as he supported it in adjective law; see Twining, *Rethinking Evidence*, 43.

72. Bentham, *Works of Jeremy Bentham*, 7:366–67; Wigmore, *Treatise*, 4:3366.

73. Bentham, *Works of Jeremy Bentham*, 7:521; Wigmore, *Treatise*, 3:2710. For Wigmore's citation of Bentham, see *Treatise*, 3:2708–9. For Wigmore's discussion of numerical rules, see *Treatise*, 3:2707. Additional examples of Wigmore's advocacy of Benthamite causes

include (1) their shared opposition to the rule proscribing the impeachment of one's own witness (Bentham, *Works of Jeremy Bentham*, 6:401; Wigmore, *Treatise*, 2:1021–23); and (2) their joint denunciation of the privilege against providing answers to questions on the stand that would elicit disgrace (Bentham, *Works of Jeremy Bentham*, 7:464; Wigmore, *Treatise*, 2:1120). For Bentham's unqualified opposition to fixed rules, see *Works of Jeremy Bentham*, 7:563.

74. Wigmore, *Treatise*, 4:2965–67, including Wigmore's quotation of Bentham.

75. For Wigmore's quotation, see *Treatise*, 3:2376, and for Bentham cited in Wigmore, see *Treatise*, 3:2376–77.

76. For an alternative discussion of the similarities and differences between Bentham and Wigmore, see Twining, *Theories of Evidence*, 115–18.

77. Wigmore, *Treatise*, 2:1243–46.

78. Ibid., 2:1345n1.

79. Bentham, *Works of Jeremy Bentham*, 6:309; Wigmore, *Treatise*, 3:2363. For Wigmore's citation of Bentham, see *Treatise*, 3:2363n1.

80. Bentham, *Works of Jeremy Bentham*, 7:179; Wigmore, *Treatise*, 3:2917. For Wigmore's citation of Bentham, see *Treatise*, 3:2917n1.

81. For quotations from both Bentham and Wigmore, see Wigmore, *Treatise*, 4:3199–201, 4:3202–4.

82. Bentham, *Works of Jeremy Bentham*, 7:452. For Wigmore's citation of Bentham, see *Treatise*, 4:3093.

83. Wigmore, *Treatise*, 4:3095–97.

Chapter 3 Wigmore's Treatise

1. In addition to William Twining's work cited elsewhere, the limited historiography on this subject includes John H. Langbein, "Historical Foundations of the Law of Evidence: A View from the Ryder Sources," *Columbia Law Review* 96 (June 1996): 1168–202; T. P. Gallanis, "The Rise of Modern Evidence Law," *Iowa Law Review* 84 (March 1999): 499–560; and Frederick Schauer, "On the Supposed Jury-Dependence of Evidence Law," *University of Pennsylvania Law Review* 155 (November 2006): 165–202. For standards of proof (as opposed to the admissibility of evidence), see Barbara J. Shapiro, *Beyond Reasonable Doubt and Probable Cause: Historical Perspectives on the Anglo-American Law of Evidence* (Berkeley: University of California Press, 1991); and James Q. Whitman, *The Origins of Reasonable Doubt: Theological Roots of the Criminal Trial* (New Haven, CT: Yale University Press, 2008). For evidence doctrine antedating evidence as a discrete branch, see Twining, *Rethinking Evidence: Exploratory Essays*, 2nd ed. (Cambridge: Cambridge University Press, 2006), 37.

2. Simon Greenleaf, *A Treatise on the Law of Evidence*, rev. John Henry Wigmore, 16th ed., 3 vols. (Boston: Little, Brown, 1899), 1:v.

3. Samuel March Phillips, *A Treatise on the Law of Evidence*, 2nd ed. (London: A. Strahan, 1815); Thomas Starke, *A Practical Treatise on the Law of Evidence, and Digest of Proofs, in Civil and Criminal Proceedings*, ed. Theron Metcalf (Philadelphia: Wells and Lilly,

1826); Twining, *Rethinking Evidence*, 53. Only one evidence treatise by an American author appeared before 1842: Zephaniah Swift, *A Digest of the Law of Evidence, in Civil and Criminal Cases. And a Treatise on Bills of Exchange, and Promissory Notes* (Hartford, CT: Oliver D. Cooke, 1810). This work did little to replace Phillips and Starke, who continued, collectively, to monopolize the American market.

4. Greenleaf, *Law of Evidence*, 1:v–vi. Neither of the two American treatises on evidence from the latter half of the nineteenth century posed a serious challenge to Greenleaf's dominance: (1) John Appleton, *The Rules of Evidence: Stated and Discussed* (Philadelphia: T. & J. W. Johnson, 1860); and (2) Alexander M. Burrill, *A Treatise on the Nature, Principles, and Rules of Circumstantial Evidence: Especially That of the Presumptive Kind in Criminal Cases* (New York: Baker, Voorhis, 1868). Twining writes that the former did prove successful "in enabling the accused to give evidence in criminal cases" while the latter "does not seem to have made much impact," in *Rethinking Evidence*, 55.

5. Greenleaf, *Law of Evidence*, 1:828. For industrialization and tort law, see G. Edward White, *Tort Law in America: An Intellectual History* (Oxford: Oxford University Press, 2003), 16. For the judiciary's acceptance of intent as germane to tort law, see Wigmore, *A Treatise on the System of Evidence in Trials at Common Law: Including the Statutes and Judicial Decisions of All Jurisdictions of the United States*, 4 vols. (Boston: Little, Brown, 1904–1905), 4:3374–75, 4:3389–90, 4:3390n2.

6. Greenleaf, *Law of Evidence*, 1:881; Wigmore, *Treatise*, 1:703–5.

7. Greenleaf, *Law of Evidence*, 1:850–51.

8. William Reynolds, "National Codification of the Law of Evidence: Its Advantages and Practicability," *American Law Review* 16 (January 1882): 4; James Bradley Thayer, *Preliminary Treatise on Evidence at the Common Law* (Boston: Little, Brown, 1898), 511, 531; Tal Golan, *Laws of Men and Laws of Nature: The History of Scientific Expert Testimony in England and America* (Cambridge, MA: Harvard University Press, 2004), 143.

9. Wigmore, "Circumstantial Evidence in Poisoning Cases," *Medico-Legal Journal* 6 (1888): 292–313; Wigmore, "Scientific Books in Evidence," *American Law Review* 26 (May–June 1892): 390–403 (repeated in Wigmore, *Treatise*, 3:2173–76); Wigmore, "Proof by Comparison of Handwriting; Its History," *American Law Review* 30 (July–August 1896): 481–99; Wigmore, "Proof of Character by Personal Knowledge or Opinion: Its History," *American Law Review* 32 (September–October 1898): 713–30 (reiterated in Wigmore, *Treatise*, 3:2637–44). Other articles on evidence from Wigmore in the 1890s include "Confessions: A Brief History and a Criticism," *American Law Review* 33 (May–June 1899): 376–95; and "A View of the Parol Evidence Rule," *American Law Register* 47 (June 1899): 337–54, 432–47, 683–90. For Wigmore using his prize money to purchase an engagement ring, see William R. Roalfe, *John Henry Wigmore: Scholar and Reformer* (Evanston, IL: Northwestern University Press, 1977), 16.

10. Wigmore, "Scientific Books," 392; Wigmore, "Proof of Comparison," 497; Wigmore, "Scientific Books," 399; Wigmore, "Proof of Comparison," 481; Wigmore, "Scientific Books," 402.

11. Greenleaf, *Law of Evidence*, 1:vi–ix. Wigmore's original chapters were IV, V, and XI. For the Ames Prize, see Roalfe, *Wigmore*, 43.

12. Wigmore to Thayer, September 23, 1900, Box 19, Folder 6, Thayer Papers; Wigmore to Thayer, November 30, 1901, Box 19, Folder 6, Thayer Papers.

13. Wigmore, "Sequestration of Witnesses," *Harvard Law Review* 14 (March 1901): 475–95; Wigmore, "Required Number of Witnesses; a Brief History of the Numerical System in England," *Harvard Law Review* 15 (June 1901): 83–108; Wigmore, "Expert Opinion as to Insurance Risk," *Columbia Law Review* 2 (February 1902): 67–78; "The Privilege against Self-Crimination; Its History," *Harvard Law Review* 15 (April 1902): 610–37 (an earlier version was published as "Nemo Tenetur Seipsum Prodere," *Harvard Law Review* 5 [May 1891]: 71–88); Wigmore, "New Trials for Erroneous Rulings on Evidence; a Practical Problem for American Justice," *Columbia Law Review* 3 (November 1903): 433–46; Wigmore, "Putting in One's Own Case on Cross-Examination," *Yale Law Journal* 14 (November 1904): 26–42; Wigmore, "A Brief History of the Parol Evidence Rule," *Columbia Law Review* 4 (May 1904): 338–55; Wigmore, "The History of the Hearsay Rule," *Harvard Law Review* 17 (May 1904): 437–58. For his publisher's interest in a new treatise, see Roalfe, *Wigmore*, 42. For the timing of the publication of the *Treatise*'s various volumes, see Postcard, "Wigmore on Evidence," circa 1904, Little, Brown, Box 228, Folder 6.

14. While the legislature could revise the rules of evidence, Wigmore wrote that it could only do so to enhance the credibility of fact-finding. Laws that would hamstring fact-finding constituted a legislative encroachment on a judicial function; see Wigmore, *Treatise*, 1:23. For the lengthy footnote, see *Treatise*, 1:591–629.

15. Ibid., 4:3589–92.

16. Ibid., 1:31–79. Quotations appear on 1:49–50.

17. Ibid., 1:40, 1:84, 4:3542–45. See also ibid., 4:3534.

18. Ibid., 1:91–92.

19. Ibid., 1:11, 1:920, 3:2801, 4:3067. Quotation appears on 1:11.

20. Wigmore, *Treatise*, 3:2562, 1:860. See also Twining, *Rethinking Evidence*, 212–13.

21. For examples of historians' conflation of classification/induction with formalism, see Neil Duxbury, *Patterns of American Jurisprudence* (Oxford: Clarendon, 1995), 15; Morton J. Horwitz, *The Transformation of American Law, 1870–1960: The Crisis of Legal Orthodoxy* (Oxford, Oxford University Press, 1992), 17–18; White, *Tort Law in America*, 27; James E. Herget, *American Jurisprudence, 1870–1970: A History* (Houston, TX: Rice University Press, 1990), 101. Conversely, Brian Tamanaha writes, "To say that law should be organized rationally . . . and to engage in this process are not to say that legal rules are immutable or autonomous, or that only logic matters in the development and application of the law," in *Beyond the Formalist-Realist Divide* (Princeton, NJ: Princeton University Press, 2009), 52.

22. Thayer, *Preliminary Treatise*, 264–65; Wigmore, *Treatise*, 1:31–35.

23. Wigmore, *Treatise*, 1:268

24. Quoted in Roalfe, *Wigmore*, 183.

25. Wigmore, *Treatise*, 1:1–581.

26. Ibid., 1:582–1002; 2:1003–343.

27. Ibid., 2:1344–74.

28. Ibid., 2:1673–974; 3:1975–2273.

29. Ibid., 3:2347–950.

30. Ibid., 4:2951–3629.

31. Twining, *Theories of Evidence: Bentham and Wigmore* (London: Weidenfeld & Nicolson, 1985), viii; Wigmore, *Treatise*, 1:127.

32. Wigmore, *Treatise*, 1:893.

33. Ibid., 2:1566, 2:1697–98, 3:2386–87.

34. Ibid., 3:2727–28; Schauer, "On the Supposed Jury-Dependence of Evidence Law," 171.

35. Shapiro, *Beyond Reasonable Doubt*, 4–5; Schauer, "On the Supposed Jury-Dependence of Evidence Law," 173–75.

36. Edmund M. Morgan, "The Jury and the Exclusionary Rules of Evidence," *University of Chicago Law Review* 4 (February 1937): 248, 250–51, 254.

37. Joseph Henry Beale, "Book Reviews," *Harvard Law Review* 18 (April 1905): 478; and see generally "What is Thought of Wigmore on Evidence," Little, Brown, circa 1905, Box 228, Folder 6. Quotations appear on pages 6, 7, and 1. This document, a part of the publisher's promotional materials for the *Treatise*, combines excerpts from several law reviews.

38. E. A. Harriman to Wigmore, January 13, 1905, Box 225, Folder 5; "What is Thought of Wigmore on Evidence," 3–4, 7, Little, Brown, circa 1905, Box 228, Folder 6.

39. Ibid., 1, 6, 2.

40. *The Law Book Bulletin* 67 (October 1924) [published by Little, Brown], 5, Box 228, Folder 6; "Wigmore on Evidence—*Second Edition*," promotion materials, Little, Brown, circa 1923, Box 228, Folder 6; "Improvements in Wigmore on Evidence," promotional materials, Little, Brown, circa 1923, Box 228, Folder 6.

41. Quoted in *The Law Book Bulletin* 67 (October 1924) [published by Little, Brown], 2, 3, 4.

42. Quoted in ibid., 3, 4.

43. Leigh Bienen, "A Question of Credibility: John Henry Wigmore's Use of Scientific Authority in Section 924a of the Treatise on Evidence," *California Western Law Review* 19 (1983): 237, 245–55; Wigmore, *Supplement 1923–1933 to the Second Edition (1923) of a Treatise on the System of Evidence in Trials at Common Law* (Boston: Little, Brown, 1934), 379.

44. Wigmore, *Treatise*, 3rd ed., 1:vii–xii. Quotations appear on vii and xii.

45. Wilbur H. Cherry, "Book Reviews," *Minnesota Law Review* 25 (February 1941): 395; James H. Chadbourn, "Book Reviews," *University of Pennsylvania Law Review and American Law Register* 89 (December 1940): 256; Morgan, "Book Reviews," *Boston University Law Review* 20 (November 1940): 793.

46. Michael Ariens, "Progress Is Our Only Product: Legal Reform and the Codification of Evidence," *Law & Social Inquiry* 17 (Spring 1992): 226; Eileen A. Scallen, "Analyzing 'The Politics of [Evidence] Rulemaking,'" *Hastings Law Journal* 53 (April 2002): 847; Wigmore, *A Pocket Code of the Rules of Evidence in Trials at Law* (Boston: Little, Brown, 1910), ix; Wigmore, ed., *A Selection of Cases on Evidence: For the Use of Students of Law* (Boston: Little, Brown, 1906); Wigmore, *A Student's Textbook on the Law of Evidence* (Brooklyn, NY: Foundation, 1935).

47. Francis L. Wellman, *The Art of Cross-Examination* (New York: Macmillan, 1903); Charles C. Moore, *A Treatise on Facts or the Weight and Value of Evidence* (Northport, NY: Edward Thompson, 1908); Albert S. Osborn, *The Problem of Proof Especially as Exemplified in Disputed Document Trials* (New York: Matthew Bender, 1922); Twining, *Rethinking Evidence*, 72. Another Thayer disciple, Charles Frederick Chamberlayne, published a treatise on evidence in the second decade of the twentieth century that failed to disturb Wigmore's monopoly on the field; see Twining, *Rethinking Evidence*, 68.

Chapter 4 Law & Society

1. John Henry Wigmore, *Treatise on the System of Evidence in Trials at Common Law: Including the Statutes and Judicial Decisions of All Jurisdictions of the United States*, 4 vols. (Boston: Little, Brown, 1904–1905), 4:2984.

2. Ibid., 4:3187.

3. Ibid., 1:995–98.

4. Ibid., 1:703. Wigmore also argued that the advent of cross-examination made the admission of questionable witnesses less threatening; see ibid., 1:704.

5. Ibid., 2:1900, 2:1803.

6. Ibid., 1:28.

7. Ibid., 4:3035.

8. Ibid., 4:3415–16.

9. Ibid., 3:2362–64.

10. Ibid., 2:1017–23. Quotation appears on

11. Ibid., 2:1023, 3:2063. For the contemporary prominence of teleological historiography, see Peter Novick, *That Noble Dream: The "Objectivity Question" and the American Historical Profession* (New York: Cambridge University Press, 1998), 85.

12. Wigmore, *Treatise*, 1:844.

13. "1598, *William Shakespeare*, King John, Act I, Scene I," cited in Wigmore, *Treatise*, 1:219–20; "Circa 1595, *King John, V*, 4," cited in Wigmore, *Treatise*, 2:1804n1. For the literary contents of Wigmore's briefcase, see Recollections, Sarah B. Morgan, 25, Box 18, Folder 1.

14. "Henry VI, pt. II, Act IV, Sc. 2," cited in Wigmore, *Treatise*, 3:2890.

15. "1837, *Mr. Charles Dickens*, The Pickwick Papers, c. XXXIV," cited in Wigmore, *Treatise*, 1:872–73.

16. "1852, *Charles Dickens*, Bleak House, c. XI," cited in Wigmore, *Treatise*, 3:2359. For Wigmore and Train, see William R. Roalfe, *John Henry Wigmore: Scholar and Reformer* (Evanston, IL: Northwestern University Press, 1977), 102–3.

17. "*The Judgment of Solomon*, First Book of Kings, III, 16," cited in Wigmore, *Treatise*, 1:340. For the Bible in Wigmore's briefcase, see Recollections, Sarah B. Morgan, 25, Box 18, Folder 1.

18. "*The History of Susanna*," cited in Wigmore, *Treatise*, 3:2381–82.

19. "Analects, book II;" and "Essay on Spiritual Laws;" both cited in Wigmore, *Treatise*, 2:1958. For Quintilian and Trollope, see "Quintilian, De Institutione Oratoria, lib. V, c. VII," cited in Wigmore, *Treatise*, 1:860n; "1857, Mr. Anthony Trollope, *The Three Clerks*, c. XL," cited in Wigmore, *Treatise*, 1:873.

20. Wigmore, *Treatise*, 2:1703, 3:2764, 4:3037; Robert Southey, "The Battle of Blenheim," in *Parodies of the Works of English and American Authors*, ed. Walter Hamilton, 6 vols. (London: Reeves and Turner, 1884–1889), 3:163. The anonymous proverb is often mistakenly attributed to Euripides.

21. Wigmore, *Treatise*, 4:2967.

22. Ibid.

23. Ibid., 4:2967–68.

24. Ibid., 2:1170, 2:1768–69.

25. Ibid., 4:3005, 4:3102.

26. Ibid., 4:3005.

27. George H. Daniels, "An American Defense of Bacon: A Study in the Relations of Scientific Thought, 1840–1845," *Huntingdon Library Quarterly* 28 (August 1965): 323–28, 336; Theodore Dwight Bozeman, *Protestants in an Age of Science: The Baconian Ideal and Antebellum American Religious Thought* (Chapel Hill: University of North Carolina Press, 1977), 160, 162, 166; Paul Jerome Croce, *Science and Religion in the Era of William James* (Chapel Hill: University of North Carolina Press, 1995), 90; Curt J. Ducasse, "Francis Bacon's Philosophy of Science," in *Theories of Scientific Method: The Renaissance through the Nineteenth Century*, ed. Edward H. Madden (1960; repr., New York: Gordon and Breach, 1989), 54.

28. Daniel, "American Defense of Bacon," 324; Bozeman, *Protestants in an Age of Science*, 167; Croce, *Science and Religion*, 90–91; Julie Reuben, *The Making of the Modern University: Intellectual Transformation and the Marginalization of Morality* (Chicago: University of Chicago Press, 1996), 37–48.

29. Wigmore, *Treatise*, 1:529–30, 1:565. The inner quotation on p. 1:565 comes from Justice Charles Doe.

30. Ibid., 1:758, 1:762–63.

31. Ibid., 1:902, 1:223. For the scientific litmus test for truth, see Reuben, *Making of the Modern University*, 49.

32. Wigmore, *Treatise*, 2:1905, 4:3629. For truth as open to revision, see Reuben, *Making of the Modern University*, 37, 42, 44; John H. Roberts and James Turner, *The Sacred*

and the Secular University (Princeton, NJ: Princeton University Press, 2000), 38. At the twilight of his life, Wigmore reiterated his view of the role of contingency in the law: "It behooves us, as a matter of sound policy, to make and keep the trial system a subject of prominent and careful attention, with a view to adapting it to other progressive changes in communal life. At present the United States is in a period of such attention. But that period was preceded by a century of careless inattention. Hereafter the attention should be constant and unceasing." Wigmore, *A Kaleidoscope of Justice: Containing Authentic Accounts of Trial Scenes from All Times and Climes* (Washington, DC: Washington Law Book, 1941), 717.

33. Roberts and Turner write, "This doctrine of the cumulative and self-correcting nature of science enabled partisans of scientific inquiry to turn a seemingly formidable weakness—science's liability to error—into a source of strength," in *Sacred and the Secular*, 39. See also Reuben, *Making of the Modern University*, 44, 49.

34. Wigmore, *Treatise*, 3:2169–70.

35. Ibid., 1:88, 1:90.

36. N. E. H. Hull, *Roscoe Pound and Karl Llewellyn: Searching for an American Jurisprudence* (Chicago: University of Chicago Press, 1997), 80; Wigmore, *Treatise*, 1:462, 1:508.

37. Wigmore, *Treatise*, 1:545–46; 1:539.

38. Ibid., 1:669.

39. Ibid., 2:1968, 3:2208. For the classification of official documents, see ibid., 3:1992, 3:2056.

40. Ibid., 1:467, 3:2193.

41. Ibid., 1:227–28.

42. For examples, see ibid., 1:350, 2:1862–63.

43. Ibid., 1:280.

44. Ibid., 1:285.

45. Ibid., 1:699.

46. Ibid., 2:1957.

47. Ibid., 1:574, 1:814.

48. Ibid., 3:2585–86. Wigmore did not attribute the inside quotations to any source; they appear to be his own words and the use of quotations a rhetorical device.

49. Ibid., 4:2952.

50. Ibid., 4:3165. For an additional example of a social construct, see Wigmore's discussion of sanity and insanity on 1:278. Although modernist jurists were not centrally concerned with race, modernist logic would dictate that race was socially constructed rather than inherent. Yet many modernists, including Wigmore, oscillated between constructivist and essentialist views of race. For an example of Wigmore treating race as socially constructed, see Wigmore, "The Legal System of Old Japan," *Green Bag* 4 (Part I: September 1892; Part II: October 1892): 407–8. For an example of Wigmore employing an essentialist conception of race, see Wigmore, "American Naturalization and the Japanese," *American Law Review* 28 (November–December 1894): 820–21, 827.

For inconsistent views on race among contemporary modernists, see Carl N. Degler, *In Search of Human Nature: The Decline and Revival of Darwinism in American Social Thought* (New York: Oxford University Press, 1991), 17–19.

51. Wigmore, *Treatise*, 3:2206, 3:2315.

52. Ibid., 2:1475–76.

53. Ibid., 2:1956. See also ibid., 1:121–22.

54. Ibid., 3:2899. See also ibid., 1:799–801.

55. Ibid., 4:3117, 1:419–20.

56. Ibid., 1:501–2.

57. Ibid., 1:632, 1:668. See also 1:810.

58. Ibid., 2:1206, 3:2821, 3:2889.

59. Ibid., 1:931.

60. Hugo Münsterberg, *On the Witness Stand: Essays on Psychology and Crime* (New York: Doubleday, Page, 1909), 10–11.

61. Wigmore, "Professor Muensterberg and the Psychology of Testimony," *Illinois Law Review* 3 (February 1909): 407–22. Quotations appear on pp. 407, 415, and 422.

62. Ibid., 418–30; Recollections, Robert H. Gault, 4, Box 17, Folder 11; Tal Golan, *Laws of Men and Laws of Nature: The History of Scientific Expert Testimony in England and America* (Cambridge, MA: Harvard University Press, 2004), 242; Roalfe, *Wigmore*, 96; William Twining, *Theories of Evidence: Bentham and Wigmore*, (London: Weidenfeld & Nicolson, 1985), 136.

63. Wigmore to Münsterberg, January 3, 1913, Box 92, Folder 16. Jill Lepore argues similarly, "Despite his feud with Münsterberg, Wigmore believed that no science was more important to the law than psychology and that no aspect of psychology was more important to judicial proof than the study of testimony," in *The Secret History of Wonder Woman* (New York: Alfred A. Knopf, 2014), 64. For Wigmore's use of *On the Witness Stand*, see Wigmore, *The Principles of Judicial Proof: As Given by Logic, Psychology, and General Experience and Illustrated in Judicial Trials* (Boston: Little, Brown, 1913), 568–71. Wigmore delivered a speech to the Iowa State Bar Association in which he called on the legal profession to appreciate the relevance to criminal law of fields such as psychology, sociology, and penology. Still, he was not prepared to advocate specific legal reforms based on social scientific research. When Wigmore proposed to his audience a series of improvements to the law of evidence, he merely reiterated suggestions that he had made in the *Treatise*; see Wigmore, "Science of Criminology—Rules of Evidence in Criminal Cases," *Proceedings of the Iowa State Bar Association* (1909): 114–19.

64. John Henry Schlegel, *American Legal Realism and Empirical Social Science* (Chapel Hill: University of North Carolina Press, 1995), 255, 253.

Chapter 5 Judging

1. John Henry Wigmore, *Treatise on the System of Evidence in Trials at Common Law: Including the Statutes and Judicial Decisions of All Jurisdictions of the United States*, 4 vols. (Boston: Little, Brown, 1904–1905), 3:2887.

2. Ibid., 2:1264, 3:2844, 3:2908, 2:1405.

3. Ibid., 2:1808–9, 2:1892, 3:2067, 3:2256–57.

4. Ibid., 1:779, 1:776, 1:861–62. Leading questions were permitted during cross-examination; see ibid., 1:866. An expert witness was not supposed to offer an opinion on the "ultimate issue" before the jury because the stating of such an opinion would arrogate the jury's prerogative; however, judges often bypassed that legal doctrine by permitting hypothetical questions, the premises of which the jury could accept or reject; see Tal Golan, "Revisiting the History of Scientific Expert Testimony," *Brooklyn Law Review* 73 (Spring 2008): 921–22. Federal Rule of Evidence 704 reversed Wigmore's course and generally allows expert testimony on the ultimate issue.

5. Wigmore, *Treatise*, 2:1146, 1:890–91, 2:1084.

6. Ibid., 1:849–50, 1:837.

7. Ibid., 1:348, 1:290–93, 1:785.

8. Ibid., 3:2825, 3:2853.

9. Ibid., 4:3233–34, 4:3262.

10. Ibid., 2:1755.

11. Ibid., 2:1192, 2:1212.

12. Ibid., 1:556–57, 3:2465–66. Simplicative rules prohibited evidence that obscured rather than illuminated the truth; see ibid., 3:2459.

13. Ibid., 3:2378, 3:2530, 3:2491.

14. Ibid., 1:345, 1:394, 2:1918, 1:965.

15. Ibid., 1:198, 1:532.

16. Ibid., 1:745, 1:753.

17. Ibid., 1:882–83, 1:77.

18. Ibid., 2:1117.

19. Ibid., 3:2747, 4:3282–83.

20. Ibid., 1:674, 1:639.

21. Ibid., 1:781, 1:789, 3:2675.

22. Ibid., 1:774–80.

23. Ibid., 2:1604. For the definition of attesting witnesses, see ibid., 2:1567. For an attesting witness's privilege against testifying, see ibid., 2:1607.

24. Ibid., 1:865, 1:877, 1:882, 2:1081, 2:1203, 3:2487.

25. Ibid., 2:1503.

26. Ibid., 3:2392–95, 3:2471, 3:2479.

27. Ibid., 1:277, 1:462, 1:480, 1:487, 2:1068, 1:403, 1:517. For additional examples of judicial discretion in the realm of time, see ibid., 1:795 and 2:1433.

28. Ibid., 2:1845, 3:2214.

29. Ibid., 3:2236.

30. Ibid., 1:308–9, 2:1953. The Federal Rules of Evidence reject the "overt act" limitation on reputation evidence against the victim. For additional examples of Wigmore's support for judicial discretion, see 1:273–74, 1:276–77, 1:279, 1:450, 1:984–85, 2:1357, 3:2174, 3:2760, 3:2842, 3:2902, and 4:3597.

31. Ibid., 3:2518, 3:2520–21.

32. Ibid., 2:1147–50. Note that a party could always call one expert witness to impugn another's *opinion* on some data, but that is a distinct issue from the one here discussed.

33. Ibid., 2:1354.

34. Ibid., 2:1359, 2:1364.

35. Ibid., 2:1895, 4:2998.

36. Ibid., 1:868, 2:1746.

37. Ibid., 3:2379.

38. Ibid., 4:3001–2.

39. Ibid., 1:937, 4:3026, 2:1827.

40. Ibid., 2:1057. See also 2:1111–12.

41. Ibid., 2:1513–24. Quotation appears on 2:1518.

42. Ibid., 2:1834, 2:1838.

43. Ibid., 3:1978, 4:3543–44, 4:3177.

44. Ibid., 2:1344–45.

45. Ibid., 4:3313, 4:3226.

46. Ibid., 2:1444, 4:3329, 2:1452, 3:1977.

47. Ibid., 4:3003–4, 4:3340, 4:3340–41.

48. Ibid., 1:183, 1:265.

49. Ibid., 1:363.

50. Ibid., 3:2377.

51. Ibid., 4:3257. Note that this is distinct from the privilege against testifying against one's spouse. For instance, a wife could learn a fact about her husband that the husband did not disclose to her, and this evidence would not be protected by the former doctrine but would be by the latter. See ibid., 4:3258 for Wigmore's elaboration on the difference.

52. Ibid., 2:1605.

53. Ibid., 4:3350.

54. Oliver Wendell Holmes Jr., *The Common Law* (Boston: Little, Brown, 1881), 1; Wigmore, *A Supplement to a Treatise on the System of Evidence in Trials at Common Law*, 2nd ed. (Boston: Little, Brown, 1915), ix. Note that this latter source is the second edition of the supplement to the first edition of the *Treatise*.

55. Wigmore, *Treatise*, 1:771–72.

56. Ibid., 1:306–8.

57. Ibid., 2:1064.

58. Ibid., 1:72–74, 4:3037.

59. Ibid., 1:492, 1:526–29.

60. Ibid., 1:349, 2:1041–42.

61. Ibid., 4:3037, 4:3177, 4:3220.

62. Ibid., 1:585–86, 1:821.

63. Ibid., 2:1697; 1:878–79.

64. Ibid., 3:2495–99.

65. Ibid., 2:1378, 3:2460.
66. Ibid., 3:2250, 2:1807.
67. Ibid., 1:301, 1:344, 1:360.
68. Ibid., 1:122, 1:330–31, 2:1889.
69. Ibid., 2:1098, 2:1173.
70. Ibid., 1:100–106.
71. Ibid., 1:88, 1:583.
72. Ibid., 2:1695.
73. Ibid., 1:784–85.
74. Ibid., 2:1888–89, 2:1896.
75. Ibid., 1:305–6.
76. Ibid., 1:336. See 1:509 and 2:1004 for additional examples of practical classification.
77. Ibid., 1:747–8, 3:2795, 4:3135.
78. Ibid., 2:1473, 3:2107–9, 3:2919.
79. Ibid., 3:1987–89, 3:2068.
80. Ibid., 1:1443, 3:2643, 4:3113–14.

Chapter 6 Contemporary Recognition

1. In contrast to my findings, Annelise Riles disputes the affinity of Wigmore's thought with legal modernism, but she still concedes that "early critics of nineteenth century classicism in the United States and Europe readily recognized Wigmore as one of their own"; see Riles, "Encountering Amateurism: John Henry Wigmore and the Uses of American Formalism," in *Rethinking the Masters of Comparative Law*, ed. Riles (Portland, OR: Hart, 2001), 114.

2. Herbert Hovenkamp, "Evolutionary Models in Jurisprudence," *Texas Law Review* 64 (December 1985): 678, 682; James E. Herget, *American Jurisprudence, 1870–1970: A History* (Houston, TX: Rice University Press, 1990), 5–7, 147–70; Neil Duxbury, *Patterns of American Jurisprudence* (Oxford: Clarendon, 1995), 55–59, 96; William M. Wiecek, *The Lost World of Classical Legal Thought: Law and Ideology in America, 1886–1937* (New York: Oxford University Press: 1998), 191–92; David M. Rabban, "The Historiography of Late Nineteenth-Century American Legal History," *Theoretical Inquiries in Law* 4 (2003): 577.

3. David Wigdor, *Roscoe Pound: Philosopher of Law* (Westport, CT: Greenwood, 1974), 3, 6–15, 18, 24–25, 31, 44–47, 71.

4. Ibid., 71, 103, 106–9; N. E. H. Hull, *Roscoe Pound and Karl Llewellyn: Searching for an American Jurisprudence* (Chicago: University of Chicago Press, 1997), 7–8.

5. Wigdor, *Roscoe Pound*, 182, 203–4, 233.

6. Brandeis to Wigmore, May 8, 1912, Box 38, Folder 33; Chafee, Hand, and Cardozo quotations appear in Wigdor, *Roscoe Pound*, on 201, 204, and 233. Chafee legitimated free speech by its service to society rather than as a natural right, providing the intellectual substance for Holmes's classic *Abrams* dissent; see Rabban, *Free Speech in Its Forgotten Years* (Cambridge: Cambridge University Press, 1997), 4–7.

7. Morton J. Horwitz, *The Transformation of American Law, 1870–1960: The Crisis of Legal Orthodoxy* (Oxford: Oxford University Press, 1992), 171–75, 217–20; Duxbury, *American Jurisprudence*, 60–63; Wigdor, *Roscoe Pound*, 255–81. Hull writes, "Apparently at odds, Pound and [Karl] Llewellyn were searching for the same grail, and their search had taken them roughly in the same direction," in *Roscoe Pound and Karl Llewellyn*, 223.

8. Pound, "Do We Need a Philosophy of Law?" *Columbia Law Review* 5 (May 1905), 346; Wigmore, *A Treatise on the System of Evidence in Trials at Common Law: Including the Statues and Judicial Decisions of All Jurisdictions of the United States*, 4 vols. (Boston: Little, Brown, 1904–1905), 4:2967–68; Pound to Wigmore, May 11, 1905, Box 98, Folder 7; Recollections, Roscoe Pound, 2, Box 98, Folder 7. In fact, "Do We Need a Philosophy of Law" was Pound's second—not first—article to appear in the *Columbia Law Review*. A few months earlier, he had published "The Decadence of Equity," *Columbia Law Review* 5 (January 1905): 20–35.

9. Pound, "The Causes of Popular Dissatisfaction with the Administration of Justice," reprinted in *Journal of the American Judicature Society* 20 (February 1937): 181–86; Wigmore, *Treatise*, 1:882; Pound to Wigmore, November 10, 1906, Box 98, Folder 7. The phrase "slaughterhouse of reputations" actually comes from an unnamed judge whom Wigmore quoted in the *Treatise*, 2:1112. For instances of Pound referencing the "sporting theory," see Pound, *The Spirit of the Common Law* (Boston: Marshall Jones, 1921), 127; and Pound, "Canons of Procedural Reform," *American Bar Association* 12 (August 1926): 543.

10. Wigmore to Holmes, September 5, 1907, Reel 39, Frame 114, Holmes Papers; Wigmore, "Roscoe Pound's St. Paul Address of 1906: The Spark that Kindled the White Flame of Progress," *Journal of the American Judicature Society* 20 (February 1937): 176–78.

11. Pound to Wigmore, April 11, 1907, Box 98, Folder 7; Holmes to Wigmore, April 6, 1907, Box 65, Folder 25; Holmes to Pollock, December 31, 1911, in *Holmes-Pollock Letters: The Correspondence of Mr. Justice Holmes and Sir Frederick Pollock, 1874–1923*, ed. Mark DeWolfe Howe, 2 vols. (Cambridge, MA: Harvard University Press, 1942), 1:187. See also Holmes to Wigmore, March 28, 1907, Box 65, Folder 25. For Holmes's earlier letter to Wigmore regarding Pound's scholarship, see Holmes to Wigmore, November 8, 1905, Box 65, Folder 25.

12. Wigmore to A. W. Harris, April 15, 1907, Box 98, Folder 7.

13. Quoted in Wigdor, *Roscoe Pound*, 135.

14. Wigmore form letter, April 15, 1937, Box 98, Folder 7.

15. Wigmore, *Treatise*, 3:2169–82; Pound, "Mechanical Jurisprudence," *Columbia Law Review* 8 (1908): 620.

16. Pound to Wigmore, April 22, 1909, Box 98, Folder 7; Wigmore to Pound, April 26, 1909, Box 98, Folder 7; Pound to Wigmore, April 26, 1909, Box 98, Folder 7. For Wigmore's willingness to resign as dean and for Amidon's quotation, see Wigdor, *Roscoe Pound*, 146–47.

17. Pound, "Some Principles of Procedural Reform," *Illinois Law Review* 4 (Jan–Feb 1910): 391, 503, 503n76.

18. Ibid., 506–7.

19. Pound, "A Practical Program for Procedural Reform," *Green Bag* (August 1910): 449, 454–55; Wigmore, *A Pocket Code of the Rules of Evidence in Trials at Law* (Boston: Little, Brown, 1910), 27–28.

20. A. Lawrence Lowell to Wigmore, February 7, 1910, Box 98, Folder 7; Wigmore to Lowell, February 9, 1910, Box 98, Folder 7 (note that this document is a draft but Wigdor's description of the letter suggests the draft reflects the contents of the actual letter; see Wigdor, *Roscoe Pound*, 182); Pound to Harlan F. Stone, October 13, 1921, Box 98, Folder 7.

21. Pound, "The Scope and Purpose of Sociological Jurisprudence," *Harvard Law Review* 25 (April 1912): 515, 515n100; Pound, ed., *Readings on the History and System of the Common Law*, 2nd ed. (Boston: Boston Book, 1913), v, 136–37; Pound to Wigmore, April 5, 1913, Box 98, Folder 7; Pound, *Interpretations of Legal History* (New York: Macmillan, 1923), v; Pound to Wigmore, July 31, 1922, Box 98, Folder 7.

22. Pound, "Taught Law," *American Law School Review* 3 (November 1912): 169.

23. Pound to Wigmore, April 6, 1919, Box 98, Folder 7.

24. Pound, "What Can Law Schools Do for Criminal Justice?" *Iowa Law Review* 12 (February 1927): 107, 113; Pound, "New Possibilities of Old Materials of American Legal History," *West Virginia Law Quarterly and the Bar* 40 (April 1934): 209; Pound, *The Formative Era of American Law* (Boston: Little, Brown, 1938), 165. For general praise of Wigmore from Pound, see Pound, "Jurisprudence," in *Research Methods in the Social Sciences, Its Fundamental Methods and Objectives*, ed. Wilson Gee (New York: Macmillan, 1929), 201; Pound, "A Generation of Law Teaching," *Michigan Law Review* 38 (November 1939): 22; Pound, *The History and System of the Common Law* (New York: P. F. Collier & Son, 1939), 86.

25. Pound to Wigmore, October 25, 1932, Box 98, Folder 7; Wigmore to Pound, November 11, 1932, Reel 99, Frame 109, Roscoe Pound Papers, Harvard Law School Library (hereinafter Pound Papers). For Wigmore and Pound entertaining colleagues at the ABA, see Wigdor, *Roscoe Pound*, 134–45; William R. Roalfe, *John Henry Wigmore: Scholar and Reformer* (Evanston, IL: Northwestern University Press, 1977), 211. For Pound winning the ABA medal, see Wigmore to Pound, September 22, 1940, Reel 99, Frame 135, Pound Papers.

26. E. A. Gilmore to Wigmore, October 6, 1941, Box 98, Folder 7; Foreword to the Pound Lectures on Administrative Law, Box 98, Folder 7; Pound to Wigmore, June 8, 1936, Box 98, Folder 7. For Wigmore's fundraising for the Pound Professorship, see Wigmore form letter, April 15, 1937. For Pound's invitations to Wigmore to speak at Harvard, see Roalfe, *Wigmore*, 192–95.

27. Pound to Wigmore, June 17, 1940, Box 98, Folder 7; Wigmore to Pound, June 18, 1940, Reel 99, Frame 131, Pound Papers; Recollections, Roscoe Pound, Box 98, Folder 7.

28. Richard A. Posner, *Cardozo: A Study in Reputation* (Chicago: University of Chicago Press, 1990), 1–7.

29. Andrew L. Kaufman, *Cardozo* (Cambridge, MA: Harvard University Press, 1998), 199–219; Richard Polenberg, *The World of Benjamin Cardozo: Personal Values and the Judicial Process* (Cambridge, MA: Harvard University Press, 1997), 86–87; G. Edward White, *Tort Law in America: An Intellectual History* (Oxford: Oxford University Press, 2003), 119–23; Brian Tamanaha, *Beyond the Formalist-Realist Divide* (Princeton, NJ: Princeton University Press, 2009), 21; Herget, *American Jurisprudence, 1870–1970*, 172.

30. Benjamin N. Cardozo, *The Nature of the Judicial Process* (New Haven, CT: Yale University Press, 1921).

31. Palsgraf v. Long Island Railroad, 248 N.Y. 339 (1928); Horwitz, *Transformation of American Law*, 61; Wiecek, *Lost World*, 202–3; White, *Tort Law in America*, 98, 126.

32. Matter of Fowles, 222 N.Y. 222 (1918); Wigmore, *Treatise*, 4:3497; Matter of Smith, 254 N.Y. 283 (1930). For Cardozo's tendency to cite legal treatises, see Polenberg, *World of Benjamin Cardozo*, 85.

33. Wigmore, *Treatise*, 2nd ed., 1:637; People v. Gerks, 243 N.Y. 166 (1926).

34. Cardozo, "To Rescue 'Our Lady of the Common Law,'" *American Bar Association Journal* 10 (1924): 347–48.

35. People v. Miller, 257 N.Y. 54 (1931); Wigmore, *Treatise*, 2nd ed., 5:153.

36. Wigmore, *Treatise*, 2nd ed., 5:442; Morrison v. California, 291 U.S. 82 (1934).

37. Cardozo, *The Growth of the Law* (New Haven, CT: Yale University Press, 1924), 10–11. Samuel Williston, a Harvard Law professor, wrote the dominant treatise of the era on contract law: *The Law of Contracts*, 5 vols. (New York: Baker, Voorhis, 1920–1922). See also Polenberg, *World of Benjamin Cardozo*, 85.

38. Cardozo to Wigmore, February 1, 1932, Box 41, Folder 21; Cardozo to Wigmore, February 18, 1932, Box 41, Folder 21; Cardozo to Wigmore, February 9, 1936, Box 41, Folder 21.

39. Holmes to Wigmore, December 21, 1905, Reel 39, Frame 14, Holmes Papers; Wigmore to Holmes, March 6, 1911, Reel 39, Frame 130, Holmes Papers; Holmes to Wigmore, March 8, 1911, Reel 39, Frame 26, Holmes Papers.

40. Holmes to Wigmore, March 8, 1915, Reel 39, Frame 37, Holmes Papers; Wigmore, "Justice Holmes and the Law of Torts," *Harvard Law Review* 29 (April 1916): 601; Holmes to Wigmore, April 13, 1916, Reel 39, Frame 49, Holmes Papers; Holmes to Wigmore, March 16, 1917, Reel 39, Frame 54, Holmes Papers. In 1910, Holmes lamented to Wigmore that he had "been broken in by importune death who has been busy with my friends. . . . If I had seen you I should have realized that not all my friends have departed," Holmes to Wigmore, October 6, 1910, Reel 39, Frame 21, Holmes Papers.

41. Holmes to Wigmore, March 12, 1911, Reel 39, Frame 27, Holmes Papers; Holmes to Wigmore, March 14, 1920, Reel 39, Frame 58, Holmes Papers; Holmes to Wigmore, March 9, 1925, Reel 39, Frame 65, Holmes Papers; Holmes to Wigmore, February 27, 1929, Reel 39, Frame 73, Holmes Papers.

42. Wigmore, *Treatise*, 4:3070; Holmes to Wigmore, December 21, 1905; Wigmore to Holmes, December 31, 1905, Reel 39, Frame 108, Holmes Papers; Oliver Wendell

Holmes Jr., *The Common Law* (Boston: Little, Brown, 1881), 1; Holmes, "Introduction," in *A General Survey of Events, Sources, Persons and Movements in Continental Legal History*, ed. Wigmore (Boston: Little, Brown, 1912), xxxii. For Wigmore and Holmes's common approach to torts, see David Rosenburg, *The Hidden Holmes: His Theory of Torts in History* (Cambridge, MA: Harvard University Press, 1995), 147–49. For Holmes's praise of another historical analysis from Wigmore, but one unrelated to evidence law, see Holmes to Wigmore, August 15, 1915, Reel 39, Frame 41, Holmes Papers.

43. Donnelly v. United States, 228 U.S. 243 (1913); Wigmore, *Treatise*, 2:1838–39.

44. Wigmore, *Pocket Code*, v–vi; Wigmore to Holmes, August 15, 1909, Reel 39, Frame 125, Holmes Papers; Holmes to Wigmore, January 14, 1910, Reel 39, Frame 20, Holmes Papers; Wigmore to Holmes, February 2, 1930, Reel 39, Frame 197, Holmes Papers; Holmes to Wigmore, February 5, 1913, Reel 39, Frame 32, Holmes Papers.

45. Wigmore to Morris Cohen, February 6, 1920, Box 45, Folder 29 (this letter came in response to M. Cohen's article, "Communal Ghosts and Other Perils in Social Philosophy," *Journal of Philosophy, Psychology and Scientific Methods* 16 [December 1919]: 673–90); Wigmore to M. Cohen, February 11, 1933, Box 45, Folder 29. Although M. Cohen was neither a law professor nor judge, I discuss him in conjunction with legal modernists here rather than with nonlegal modernists in chapter 1 because his sustained interest in the law has led historians to group him with legal modernists; see, for instance, Wiecek, *Lost World*, 193. For M. Cohen's life, see generally David A. Hollinger, *Morris R. Cohen and the Scientific Ideal* (Cambridge, MA: MIT Press, 1975). For Cohen's research at Northwestern, see M. Cohen to Wigmore, April 12, 1914, Box 45, Folder 29.

46. Wigmore, *Treatise*, 4:3470; M. Cohen, "The Process of Judicial Legislation," *American Law Review* 48 (March–April 1914): 187n53.

47. M. Cohen, "The Place of Logic in the Law," *Harvard Law Review* 29 (April 1916): 622–24.

48. Jerome Frank, *Law and the Modern Mind* (1930; repr., New York: Tudor, 1935), 42; Neil Duxbury, "Jerome Frank and the Legacy of Legal Realism," *Journal of Law and Society* 18 (Summer 1991): 176–77; Horwitz, *Transformation of American Law*, 177; Duxbury, "Jerome Frank," 176; Tamanaha, "Understanding Legal Realism," *Texas Law Review* 87 (March 2009): 769–70.

49. Felix S. Cohen, "Transcendental Nonsense and the Functional Approach," *Columbia Law Review* 35 (June 1935): 833.

50. Wigmore, *Treatise*, 3:2248; Frank, "Short of Sickness and Death: A Study of Moral Responsibility in Legal Criticism," *N.Y.U. Law Review* 26 (October 1951): 600–601, n167.

51. Frank, "Modern and Ancient Legal Pragmatism—John Dewey & Co. vs. Aristotle: I," *Notre Dame Lawyer* 25 (Winter 1950): 232, 243.

52. Frank, *Courts on Trial: Myth and Reality in American Justice* (Princeton, NJ: Princeton University Press, 1949), 132, 49.

53. John Henry Schlegel, *American Legal Realism and Empirical Social Science* (Chapel Hill: University of North Carolina Press, 1995), 268; Lee J. Strang and Bryce G. Poole,

"Historical (In)Accuracy of the Brandeis Dichotomy: An Assessment of the Two-Tiered Standard of Stare Decisis for Supreme Court Precedents," *North Carolina Law Review* 86 (May 2008): 982; Stone to Wigmore, November 23, 1922, Box 107, Folder 40.

54. United States v. Trenton Potteries Company, 273 U.S. 392 (1927); Wigmore, *Treatise*, 3:2564.

55. District of Columbia v. Clawans, 300 U.S. 617 (1937); Wigmore, *Treatise*, 2nd ed., 2:332–33.

56. Felix Frankfurter to Holmes, January 13, 1943, Box 57, Folder 20; Frankfurter, "The Law and the Law Schools," *American Bar Association Journal* 1 (1915): 538; Frankfurter to Wigmore, November 9, 1923?, Box 57, Folder 20; Frankfurter to Wigmore, May 24, 1914, Box 57, Folder 20; Frankfurter to Wigmore, March 9, 1912, Box 57, Folder 20.

57. Max Radin, "The Privilege of Confidential Communication between Lawyer and Client," *California Law Review* 16 (September 1928): 490n11, 491; Radin, "The Moscow Trials: A Legal View," *Foreign Affairs* 16 (October 1937): 71. For commentary on Radin's contribution to legal modernism, see William O. Douglas, "Max Radin," *California Law Review* 36 (June 1938): 163–65.

58. Herman Oliphant, "Course in Brief Making and Legal Argument," *American Law School Review* 4 (Winter 1917): 295; Oliphant, "Legal Research in Law Schools," *American Law School Review* 5 (March 1924): 295. For Oliphant's career path, see Schlegel, *American Legal Realism*, 267.

59. Hessel Yntema, "Legal Science and Reform," *Columbia Law Review* 34 (February 1934): 219–20. For Yntema's career path, see Schlegel, *American Legal Realism*, 269.

60. Wigmore, *The Advocate*, October 17, 1941, Box 38, Folder 33; Brandeis to Wigmore, August 1, 1904, Box 38, Folder 33; Wesley Hohfeld to Wigmore, October 28, 1912, Box 65, Folder 17. On Hohfeld's view of property as a social construct, see Horwitz, *Transformation of American Law*, 153–56; and Wiecek, *Lost World*, 193.

61. For histories of the Model Code, see Eileen A. Scallen, "Classical Rhetoric, Practical Reasoning, and the Law of Evidence," *American University Law Review* 44 (June 1995): 1732–37; Thomas M. Mengler, "The Theory of Discretion in the Federal Rules of Evidence," *Iowa Law Review* 74 (January 1989): 424–62; Robert P. Mostoller, "Evidence History, the New Trace Evidence, and Rumblings in the Future of Proof," *Ohio State Journal of Criminal Law* 3 (Spring 2006): 524; Scallen, "Analyzing 'The Politics of [Evidence] Rulemaking,'" *Hastings Law Journal* 53 (April 2002): 847–51.

62. Wigmore to Morgan, February 28, 1940, Box 29, Folder 4; Michael Ariens, "Progress Is Our Only Product: Legal Reform and the Codification of Evidence," *Law & Social Inquiry* 17 (Spring 1992): 224–32; Charles Alan Wright and Kenneth W. Graham Jr., *Federal Practice and Procedure*, 2nd ed., (St. Paul, MN: Thomson, West, 2005), 21:152–55, 21:157. Wigmore did not want evidence rules "handed over to

the discretion of each and every one of some 5,000 trial judges to administer as their momentary wisdom moves them. It is a virtual scrapping of the trial experience of generations." At the same time, he wanted rules to "be only *directory*, not *mandatory*"; see Wigmore, "The American Law Institute Code of Evidence Rules: A Dissent," *American Bar Association Journal* 28 (1942): 25–26.

63. Wigmore, "American Law Institute Code of Evidence Rules," 23–25, 27.

64. Ibid., 27; Wigmore to Morgan, February 28, 1940.

65. Morgan to Wigmore, March 2, 1940, Box 29, Folder 4; "Report of Committee on Administration of Justice on Model Code of Evidence," *Journal of the State Bar of California* 19 (July–August 1944): 262, 267; Ariens, "Progress Is Our Only Product," 231–32, 234; Scallen, "Analyzing 'The Politics of [Evidence] Rulemaking,'" 850.

66. Frankfurter to Craig Christensen, May 27, 1963, Box 47, Folder 26. A few states adopted the Uniform Rules of Evidence in the 1950s, but the passage of the Federal Rules of Evidence in 1975 marked the first significant codification of evidence law in the United States; see Ariens, "Progress Is Our Only Product," 246–52. William Twining describes "the period 1900–60" as "dominated by Wigmore," in *Rethinking Evidence: Exploratory Essays*, 2nd ed. (Cambridge: Cambridge University Press, 2006), 37. Twining appears to contradict this assertion when he suggests in an earlier publication, "From the early 1940s, Wigmore's general theory of evidence was widely thought to have been discredited," in *Theories of Evidence*, 111. In fact, there is no inconsistency; the latter comment alludes to Wigmore's relationship with other academics while the former refers to his abiding influence on legal practice. This depiction of Wigmore's continued dominance in legal practice but attenuated appeal to contemporary academics is further corroborated by Ariens, who writes, "Although his influence on the ALI's Evidence Editorial group was limited, to the legal profession Wigmore remained the preeminent authority on the law of evidence"; see Ariens, "Progress Is Our Only Product," 236–37. For a recent example of the judiciary's continued reliance on Wigmore's *Treatise*, see State v. Vail, 150 So. 3d 576 (La. App 3d Cir. 2014).

Epilogue

1. Jerome Frank, *Courts on Trial: Myth and Reality in American Justice* (1949; repr., Princeton, NJ: Princeton University Press, 1973), 246.

2. William Twining, *Theories of Evidence: Bentham and Wigmore* (London: Weidenfeld & Nicolson, 1985), 229–30n46.

3. Felix S. Cohen, "Transcendental Nonsense and the Functional Approach," *Columbia Law Review* 35 (June 1935): 833.

4. Roscoe Pound, "Mechanical Jurisprudence," *Columbia Law Review* 8 (December 1908): 612.

5. Brian Tamanaha, *Beyond the Formalist-Realist Divide: The Role of Politics in Judging* (Princeton, NJ: Princeton University Press, 2009), 27–43; David Rabban, *Law's History: American Legal Thought and the Transatlantic Turn to History* (New York: Cambridge University Press, 2013), 430.

6. Pound, "Mechanical Jurisprudence," 616; Lochner v. New York, 198 U.S. 45 (1905); David E. Bernstein, *Rehabilitating Lochner: Defending Individual Rights against Progressive Reform* (Chicago: University of Chicago Press, 2011), 34.

7. N. E. H. Hull, *Roscoe Pound and Karl Llewellyn: Searching for an American Jurisprudence* (Chicago: University of Chicago Press, 1997), 173.

8. Karl Llewellyn, "A Realistic Jurisprudence—The Next Step," *Columbia Law Review* 30 (April 1930): 464, 435n3; Pound, "The Call for a Realist Jurisprudence," *Harvard Law Review* 44 (March 1931): 697, 699.

9. Robert P. Burns, "A Wistful Retrospective on Wigmore and His Prescriptions for Illinois Evidence Law," *Northwestern University Law Review* 100 (2006): 145.

Bibliography

Manuscript Sources

Harvard Law School Library, Cambridge, Massachusetts.
    James Bradley Thayer Papers.
    Oliver Wendell Holmes Jr. Papers.
    Roscoe Pound Papers.
Northwestern University Archives, Evanston, Illinois.
    John Henry Wigmore (1863-1943) Papers, 1868-2006, Series 17/20.

Printed Primary Sources

Abrams v. United States, 250 U.S. 616 (1919).

Adair v. United States, 208 U.S. 161 (1908).

"American Bar Association Medal Presented." *American Bar Association Journal* 18 (November 1932): 741-42.

Appleton, John. *The Rules of Evidence: Stated and Discussed.* Philadelphia: T. & J. W. Johnson, 1860.

Beale, Joseph Henry. "Book Reviews." *Harvard Law Review* 18 (April 1905): 478-80.

Bentham, Jeremy. *A Fragment on Government.* London: T. Payne, 1776.

———. *The Works of Jeremy Bentham.* Edited by John Bowring. 11 vols. Edinburgh: W. Tait, 1843.

———, to Andrew Jackson, June 14, 1830. In *Correspondence of Andrew Jackson,* edited by John Spencer Bassett. 7 vols. Washington, DC: Carnegie Institution, 1926–1937.

Boas, Franz. *The Mind of Primitive Man.* 1911. Reprint, New York: Macmillan, 1921.

Brandenburg v. Ohio, 395 U.S. 444 (1969).

Burrill, Alexander M. *A Treatise on the Nature, Principles, and Rules of Circumstantial Evidence: Especially That of the Presumptive Kind in Criminal Cases.* New York: Baker, Voorhis, 1868.

Cardozo, Benjamin N. *The Growth of the Law*. New Haven, CT: Yale University Press, 1924.

———. *The Nature of the Judicial Process*. New Haven, CT: Yale University Press, 1921.

———. "To Rescue 'Our Lady of the Common Law.'" *American Bar Association Journal* 10 (1924): 347-49.

Chadbourn, James H. "Book Reviews." *University of Pennsylvania Law Review and American Law Register* 89 (December 1940): 256-57.

Cherry, Wilbur H. "Book Reviews." *Minnesota Law Review* 25 (February 1941): 395-96.

Cohen, Felix S. "Transcendental Nonsense and the Functional Approach." *Columbia Law Review* 35 (June 1935): 809-49.

Cohen, Morris R. "Communal Ghosts and Other Perils in Social Philosophy." *Journal of Philosophy, Psychology and Scientific Methods* 16 (December 1919): 673-90.

———. "The Place of Logic in the Law." *Harvard Law Review* 29 (April 1916): 622-39.

———. "The Process of Judicial Legislation." *American Law Review* 48 (March-April 1914): 161-98.

District of Columbia v. Clawans, 300 U.S. 617 (1937).

Donnelly v. United States, 228 U.S. 243 (1913).

Douglas, William O. "Max Radin." *California Law Review* 36 (June 1938): 163-68.

Ely, Richard T., Samuel Peter Orth, and Willford Isbell King. *Property and Contract in Their Relations to the Distribution of Wealth*. 2 vols. New York: Macmillan, 1914.

Federal Rules of Evidence.

Frank, Jerome. *Courts on Trial: Myth and Reality in American Justice*. Princeton, NJ: Princeton University Press, 1949.

———. *Law and the Modern Mind*. 1930. Reprint, New York: Tudor, 1935.

———. "Modern and Ancient Legal Pragmatism———John Dewey & Co. vs. Aristotle: I." *Notre Dame Lawyer* 25 (Winter 1950): 207-57.

———. "Short of Sickness and Death: A Study of Moral Responsibility in Legal Criticism." *New York University Law Review* 26 (October 1951): 545-633.

Frankfurter, Felix, to Arthur Schlesinger, June 18, 1963. In *Roosevelt and Frankfurter: Their Correspondence, 1928-1945*, edited by Max Freedman. London: Bodley Head, 1967.

———. "The Case of Sacco and Vanzetti." *Atlantic Monthly* 139 (March 1927): 409-32.

———. *Felix Frankfurter Reminisces*. London: Secker & Warburg, 1960.

———. "Frankfurter Says Wigmore Admits Sacco Inaccuracy." *Boston Herald*, May 11, 1927.

———. "John Henry Wigmore: A Centennial Tribute." *Northwestern University Law Review* 58 (September-October 1963): 443.

———. "The Law and the Law Schools." *American Bar Association Journal* 1 (1915): 532-40.

———. "Prof. Frankfurter Replies to Dean Wigmore." *Boston Evening Transcript,* April 26, 1927.

Goode v. Riley, 153 Mass. 585, 28 N.E. 228 (1891).

Greenleaf, Simon. *A Treatise on the Law of Evidence*, revised by John Henry Wigmore. 16th ed. 3 vols. Boston: Little, Brown, 1899.

Holmes, Jr., Oliver Wendell. "Book Notices." *American Law Review* 14 (March 1880): 233-36.

———. *The Common Law*. Boston: Little, Brown, 1881.

———. "Ideals and Doubts." *Illinois Law Review* 10 (1915-1916): 1-4.

———. "Introduction." In *A General Survey of Events, Sources, Persons and Movements in Continental Legal History*, edited by John H. Wigmore, xlv-xlvii. Boston: Little, Brown, 1912.

———. "Privilege, Malice, and Intent." *Harvard Law Review* 8 (April 1984): 1-14.

———. "The Path of the Law." *Harvard Law Review* 10 (March 1897): 457-78.

———. "The Theory of Legal Interpretation." *Harvard Law Review* 12 (January 1899): 417-20.

———, and Frederick Pollock. *Holmes-Pollock Letters: The Correspondence of Mr. Justice Holmes and Sir Frederick Pollock, 1874-1923*, edited by Mark DeWolfe Howe. 2 vols. Cambridge, MA: Harvard University Press, 1942.

Kent, James. *Commentaries on American Law*. Edited by Oliver Wendell Holmes Jr. 12th ed. Boston: Little, Brown, 1873.

Kenzô, Takayanagi. "John Henry Wigmore" (1966). In *Law and Justice in Tokugawa Japan: Materials for the History of Japanese Law and Justice under the Tokugawa Shogunate 1603-1867*, edited by John Henry Wigmore, 1:xvii-xxiv. 9 vols. Tokyo: University of Tokyo Press, 1969.

Llewellyn, Karl. "A Realistic Jurisprudence———The Next Step." *Columbia Law Review* 30 (April 1930): 431-65.

Lochner v. New York, 198 U.S. 45 (1905).

Matter of Fowles, 222 N.Y. 222 (1918).

Matter of Smith, 254 N.Y. 283 (1930).

Moore, Charles C. *A Treatise on Facts or the Weight and Value of Evidence*. Northport, NY: Edward Thompson, 1908.

Moore, Underhill. "Rational Basis of Legal Institutions." *Columbia Law Review* 23 (November 1923): 609-17.

Morgan, Edmund M. "Book Reviews." *Boston University Law Review* 20 (November 1940): 776-93.

Morrison v. California, 291 U.S. 82 (1934).

Münsterberg, Hugo. *On the Witness Stand: Essays on Psychology and Crime.* New York: Doubleday, Page, 1909.

Oliphant, Herman. "Course in Brief Making and Legal Argument." *American Law School Review* 4 (Winter 1917): 258-72.

———. "Legal Research in Law Schools." *American Law School Review* 5 (March 1924): 293-99.

Osborn, Albert S. *The Problem of Proof Especially as Exemplified in Disputed Document Trials.* New York: Matthew Bender, 1922.

Palsgraf v. Long Island Railroad, 248 N.Y. 339 (1928).

Pennsylvania Coal Co. v. Mahon, 260 U.S. 393 (1922).

People v. Gerks, 243 N.Y. 166 (1926).

People v. Miller, 257 N.Y. 54 (1931).

Phillips, Samuel March. *A Treatise on the Law of Evidence.* 2nd ed. London: A. Strahan, 1815.

Pound, Roscoe. "The Call for a Realist Jurisprudence." *Harvard Law Review* 44 (March 1931): 697-711.

———. "Canons of Procedural Reform." *American Bar Association* 12 (August 1926): 290-303.

———. "The Causes of Popular Dissatisfaction with the Administration of Justice." Reprinted in *Journal of the American Judicature Society* 20 (February 1937): 178-86.

———. "The Decadence of Equity." *Columbia Law Review* 5 (January 1905): 20-35.

———. "Do We Need a Philosophy of Law?" *Columbia Law Review* 5 (May 1905): 339-53.

———. *The Formative Era of American Law.* Boston: Little, Brown, 1938.

———. "A Generation of Law Teaching." *Michigan Law Review* 38 (November 1939): 16-29.

———. *The History and System of the Common Law.* New York: P. F. Collier & Son, 1939.

———. *Interpretations of Legal History.* New York: Macmillan, 1923.

———. "Jurisprudence." In *Research Methods in the Social Sciences, Its Fundamental Methods and Objectives*, edited by Wilson Gee, 181-206. New York: Macmillan, 1929.

———. "Mechanical Jurisprudence." *Columbia Law Review* 8 (1908): 605-23.

———. "New Possibilities of Old Materials of American Legal History." *West Virginia Law Quarterly and the Bar* 40 (April 1934): 205-11.

———. "A Practical Program for Procedural Reform." *Green Bag* (August 1910): 438-56.

———, ed. *Readings on the History and System of the Common Law.* 2nd ed. Boston: Boston Book, 1913.

———. "The Scope and Purpose of Sociological Jurisprudence." *Harvard Law Review* 25 (April 1912): 489-516.

———. "Some Principles of Procedural Reform." *Illinois Law Review* 4 (Jan-Feb 1910): 388-407, 491-508.

———. *The Spirit of the Common Law*. Boston: Marshall Jones, 1921.

———. "Taught Law." *American Law School Review* 3 (November 1912): 164-73.

———. "What Can Law Schools Do for Criminal Justice?" *Iowa Law Review* 12 (February 1927): 105-13.

Radin, Max. "The Moscow Trials: A Legal View." *Foreign Affairs* 16 (October 1937): 64-79.

———. "The Privilege of Confidential Communication between Lawyer and Client." *California Law Review* 16 (September 1928): 487-97.

Reeve v. Dennett, 145 Mass. 23, 28, 11 N.E. 938 (1887).

"Report of Committee on Administration of Justice on Model Code of Evidence." *Journal of the State Bar of California* 19 (July-August 1944): 188-224.

Reynolds, William. "National Codification of the Law of Evidence: Its Advantages and Practicability." *American Law Review* 16 (January 1882): 1-15.

Rheinstein, Max, ed. *Max Weber on Law in Economy and Society*. Cambridge, MA: Harvard University Press, 1954.

Simmons, Duane B., and John H. Wigmore. *Notes on Land Tenure and Local Institutions in Old Japan*. 1891. Reprint, Washington, DC: University Publications of America, 1979.

Smith, Adam. *An Inquiry into the Nature and Causes of the Wealth of Nations*. 1776. Reprint, New York: Oxford University Press, 2008.

Southey, Robert. "The Battle of Blenheim." In *Parodies of the Works of English and American Authors*, edited by Walter Hamilton, 3:163. 6 vols. London: Reeves and Turner, 1884-1889.

Starke, Thomas. *A Practical Treatise on the Law of Evidence, and Digest of Proofs, in Civil and Criminal Proceedings*, edited by Theron Metcalf. Philadelphia: Wells and Lilly, 1826.

Swift, Zephaniah. *A Digest of the Law of Evidence, in Civil and Criminal Cases. And a Treatise on Bills of Exchange, and Promissory Notes*. Hartford, CT: Oliver D. Cooke, 1810.

Thayer, James Bradley, ed. *Letters of Chauncey Wright*. Cambridge, MA: John Wilson and Son, 1878.

———. "The Origin and Scope of the American Doctrine of Constitutional Law." *Harvard Law Review* 7 (1893): 129-56.

———. *Preliminary Treatise on Evidence at the Common Law*. Boston: Little, Brown, 1898.

———. *Select Cases on Evidence at Common Law*. Cambridge, MA: Charles W. Sever, 1892.

———. *A Selection of Cases on Evidence at the Common Law.* 2nd ed. Cambridge, MA: Charles W. Sever, 1900.

United States v. Trenton Potteries Company, 273 U.S. 392 (1927).

Veblen, Thorstein. *The Theory of the Leisure Class.* 1899. Reprint, New York: Macmillan, 1912.

Ward, Lester. *Dynamic Sociology, or Applied Social Science as Based upon Statistical Sociology and the Less Complex Sciences.* New York: D. Appleton, 1883.

Wellman, Francis L. *The Art of Cross-Examination.* New York: Macmillan, 1903.

Wigmore, John Henry. "Abrams *v.* U.S.: Freedom of Speech and Freedom of Thuggery in War-time and Peace-time." *Illinois Law Review* 14 (March 1920): 539-61.

———. "The Administration of Justice in Japan." *American Law Register and Review* 45 (Part I: July 1897; Part II: August 1897; Part III: October 1897): 437-49, 491-503, 628-41.

———. "The American Law Institute Code of Evidence Rules: A Dissent." *American Bar Association Journal* 28 (1942): 23-28.

———. "American Naturalization and the Japanese." *American Law Review* 28 (November-December 1894): 818-27.

———. "The Boycott and Kindred Practices as Ground for Damages." *American Law Review* 21 (July-August 1887): 509-32.

———. "A Brief History of the Parol Evidence Rule." *Columbia Law Review* 4 (May 1904): 338-55.

———. "Circumstantial Evidence in Poisoning Cases." *Medico-Legal Journal* 6 (1888): 292-313.

———. "Comparative Law: Jottings on Comparative Legal Ideas and Institutions." *Tulane Law Review* 6 (Part I: December 1931; Part II: February 1932): 48-68, 244-66.

———. "Confessions: A Brief History and a Criticism." *American Law Review* 33 (May-June 1899): 376-95.

———. "A Course on 'The Profession of the Bar.'" *American Law School Review* 7 (December 1931): 273-80.

———. "Expert Opinion as to Insurance Risk." *Columbia Law Review* 2 (February 1902): 67-78.

———. "Foreign Jurisdiction in Japan." *The Nation,* January 12, 1893.

———. "The Four-Year Law Course." *American Bar Association Journal* 3 (1917): 14-20.

———. "A General Analysis of Tort Relations." *Harvard Law Review* 8 (February 1895): 377-95.

———. "The History of the Hearsay Rule." *Harvard Law Review* 17 (May 1904): 437-58.

———. "Interference with Social Relations." *American Law Review* 21 (September-October 1887): 764-78.

———. "John Henry Wigmore Answers Frankfurter Attack on Sacco-Vanzetti Verdict." *Boston Evening Transcript,* April 25, 1927.

———. "Justice Holmes and the Law of Torts." *Harvard Law Review* 29 (April 1916): 601-16.

———. *A Kaleidoscope of Justice: Containing Authentic Accounts of Trial Scenes from All Times and Climes.* Washington, DC: Washington Law Book, 1941.

———, ed. *Law and Justice in Tokugawa Japan: Materials for the History of Japanese Law and Justice under the Tokugawa Shogunate 1603-1867.* 9 vols. Tokyo: University of Tokyo Press, 1969.

———. "Legal Education in Modern Japan." *Green Bag* 5 (1893): 17-33.

———. "The Legal System of Old Japan." *Green Bag* 4 (Part I: September 1892; Part II: October 1892): 403-11, 478-84.

———, ed. *Materials for the Study of Private Law in Old Japan.* 4 vols. Tokyo: Asiatic Society of Japan, 1892.

———. "Nemo Tenetur Seipsum Prodere." *Harvard Law Review* 5 (May 1891): 71-88.

———. "New Trials for Erroneous Rulings on Evidence; a Practical Problem for American Justice." *Columbia Law Review* 3 (November 1903): 433-46.

———. "Organizing the Power of the American Bar." *American Bar Association Journal* 17 (June 1931): 387-91.

———. "Our Naturalization Law: A Post-War International Problem." *American Bar Association Journal* 29 (June 1943): 313-15.

———. *A Panorama of the World's Legal Systems.* 3 vols. Saint Paul, MN: West Publishing, 1928.

———. "Parliamentary Days in Japan." *Scribner's Magazine* 10 (August 1891): 243-55.

———. "The Pledge Idea." In *Primitive and Ancient Legal Institutions,* edited by Albert Kocourek and John Henry Wigmore, 456-77. Boston: Little, Brown, 1915.

———. "The Pledge Idea: A Study in Comparative Legal Ideas." *Harvard Law Review* 10 & 11 (Part I: January 1897; Part II: February 1897; Part III: April 1897): 321-50, 389-417, 18-39.

———. *A Pocket Code of the Rules of Evidence in Trials at Law.* Boston: Little, Brown, 1910.

———. "Preface" (1941). In *Law and Justice in Tokugawa Japan: Materials for the History of Japanese Law and Justice under the Tokugawa Shogunate 1603-1867,* edited by John Henry Wigmore, 1:xi-xvi. 9 vols. Tokyo: University of Tokyo Press, 1969.

———. *The Principles of Judicial Proof: As Given by Logic, Psychology, and General Experience and Illustrated in Judicial Trials.* Boston: Little, Brown, 1913.

———. "The Privilege against Self-Crimination; Its History." *Harvard Law Review* 15 (April 1902): 610-37.

———. "Professor Muensterberg and the Psychology of Testimony." *Illinois Law Review* 3 (February 1909): 399-444.

———. "Proof by Comparison of Handwriting; Its History." *American Law Review* 30 (July-August 1896): 481-99.

———. "Proof of Character by Personal Knowledge or Opinion: Its History." *American Law Review* 32 (September-October 1898): 713-30.

———. "Putting in One's Own Case on Cross-Examination." *Yale Law Journal* 14 (November 1904): 26-42.

———. "The Recent Cases Department." *Harvard Law Review* 50 (April 1937): 862-67.

———. "Required Number of Witnesses; a Brief History of the Numerical System in England." *Harvard Law Review* 15 (June 1901): 83-108.

———. "Responsibility for Tortious Acts: Its History." *Harvard Law Review* 7 (March 1894): 315-37.

———. "Roscoe Pound's St. Paul Address of 1906: The Spark that Kindled the White Flame of Progress." *Journal of the American Judicature Society* 20 (February 1937): 176-78.

———. The Sacco-Vanzetti Verdict———A Reply. *Boston Evening Transcript*, May 10, 1927.

———. "Science of Criminology———Rules of Evidence in Criminal Cases." *Proceedings of the Iowa State Bar Association* (1909): 114-19.

———. "Scientific Books in Evidence." *American Law Review* 26 (May-June 1892): 390-403.

———, ed. *A Selection of Cases on Evidence: For the Use of Students of Law.* Boston: Little, Brown, 1906.

———. "Sequestration of Witnesses." *Harvard Law Review* 14 (March 1901): 475-95.

———. "Should the Standards for Bar Preparation Be More Exacting?" *Tennessee Law Review* 11 (February 1933): 103-4.

———. *A Student's Textbook on the Law of Evidence.* Brooklyn, NY: Foundation, 1935.

———. *Supplement 1923-1933 to the Second Edition (1923) of a Treatise on the System of Evidence in Trials at Common Law.* Boston: Little, Brown, 1934.

———. *A Supplement to a Treatise on the System of Evidence in Trials at Common Law.* 2nd ed. Boston: Little, Brown, 1915.

———. *A Treatise on the System of Evidence in Trials at Common Law: Including the Statutes and Judicial Decisions of All Jurisdictions of the United States.* 4 vols. Boston: Little, Brown, 1904-1905.

———. "The Tripartite Division of Torts." *Harvard Law Review* 8 (November 1894): 200-210.

———. "A View of the Parol Evidence Rule." *American Law Register* 47 (June 1899): 337-54, 432-47, 683-90.

————, and Albert Kocourek, eds. *Rational Basis of Legal Institutions*. New York: Macmillan, 1923.

Williston, Samuel. *The Law of Contracts*. 5 vols. New York: Baker, Voorhis, 1920-1922.

Wong v. Smith, 178 L. Ed. 2d 403 (2010).

Woolf, Virginia. *Mrs. Dalloway*. New York: Harcourt, Brace, 1925.

Yntema, Hessel. "Legal Science and Reform." *Columbia Law Review* 34 (February 1934): 207-29.

Secondary Sources

Abbott, Kenneth W. "Wigmore: The Japanese Connection." *Northwestern University Law Review* 75 (February 1981 Supplement): 10-16.

Ahn, Kyong Whan, and Jongcheol Kim. "Bentham, Modernity and the Nineteenth Century Revolution in Government." *Pophak: Seoul Law Journal* 35 (1994): 135-55.

Allen, C. J. W. *The Law of Evidence in Victorian England*. Cambridge: Cambridge University Press, 1997.

Ariens, Michael. "Progress Is Our Only Product: Legal Reform and the Codification of Evidence." *Law & Social Inquiry* 17 (Spring 1992): 213-55.

Armitage, David. *The Declaration of Independence: A Global History*. Cambridge, MA: Harvard University Press, 2008.

Barth, Gunther. *Instant Cities: Urbanization and the Rise of San Francisco and Denver*. New York: Oxford University Press, 1975.

Beard, Charles A. *An Economic Interpretation of the Constitution of the United States*. 1913. Reprint, New York: Macmillan, 1948.

Bernstein, David E. "*Lochner* Era Revisionism, Revised: *Lochner* and the Origins of Fundamental Rights Constitutionalism." *Georgetown Law Journal* 92 (November 2003): 1-60.

————. *Rehabilitating Lochner: Defending Individual Rights against Progressive Reform*. Chicago: University of Chicago Press, 2011.

"Bibliography." *Northwestern University Law Review* 75 (February 1981 supplement): 19-122.

Bienen, Leigh. "A Question of Credibility: John Henry Wigmore's Use of Scientific Authority in Section 924a of the Treatise on Evidence." *California Western Law Review* 19 (1983): 235-68.

Bledstein, Burton J. *The Culture of Professionalism: The Middle Class and the Development of Higher Education in America*. New York: W. W. Norton, 1976.

Bordogna, Francesca. *William James at the Boundaries: Philosophy, Science, and the Geography of Knowledge*. Chicago: University of Chicago Press, 2008.

Boutroux, Emile. *William James*. Translated by Archibald and Barbara Henderson. 2nd ed. New York: Longmans, Green, 1912.

Bozeman, Theodore Dwight. *Protestants in an Age of Science: The Baconian Ideal and Antebellum American Religious Thought.* Chapel Hill: University of North Carolina Press, 1977.

Burns, Robert P. "A Wistful Retrospective on Wigmore and His Prescriptions for Illinois Evidence Law." *Northwestern University Law Review* 100 (2006): 131-50.

Butler, Leslie. *Critical Americans: Victorian Intellectuals and Transatlantic Liberal Reform.* Chapel Hill: University of North Carolina Press, 2007.

Clark, David S. "The Modern Development of American Comparative Law: 1904-1945." *American Journal of Comparative Law* 55 (Fall 2007): 587-615.

Croce, Paul Jerome. *Science and Religion in the Era of William James.* Chapel Hill: University of North Carolina Press, 1995.

Cronon, William. *Nature's Metropolis: Chicago and the Great West.* New York: W. W. Norton, 1991.

Crossley, F. B. "Northwestern University Law School." In *History of Northwestern University and Evanston*, edited by Robert D. Sheppard and Harvey B. Hurd, 105-8. Chicago: Munsell, 1906.

Daniels, George H. "An American Defense of Bacon: A Study in the Relations of Scientific Thought, 1840-1845." *Huntingdon Library Quarterly* 28 (August 1965): 321-39.

Degler, Carl N. *In Search of Human Nature: The Decline and Revival of Darwinism in American Social Thought.* New York: Oxford University Press, 1991.

Diggins, John Patrick. *The Promise of Pragmatism: Modernism and the Crisis of Authority.* Chicago: University of Chicago Press, 1994.

Dinwiddy, John. *Bentham: The Selected Writings of John Dinwiddy*, edited by William Twining. Stanford, CA: Stanford University Press, 2004.

Ducasse, Curt J. "Francis Bacon's Philosophy of Science." In *Theories of Scientific Method: The Renaissance through the Nineteenth Century*, edited by Edward H. Madden, 50-74. 1960. Reprint, New York: Gordon and Breach, 1989.

Duxbury, Neil. "Jerome Frank and the Legacy of Legal Realism." *Journal of Law and Society* 18 (Summer 1991): 175-205.

———. *Patterns of American Jurisprudence.* Oxford: Clarendon, 1995.

Friedman, Lawrence M. *A History of American Law.* 3rd ed. New York: Simon & Schuster, 2005.

Gallanis, T. P. "The Rise of Modern Evidence Law." *Iowa Law Review* 84 (March 1999): 499-560.

Golan, Tal. *Laws of Men and Laws of Nature: The History of Scientific Expert Testimony in England and America.* Cambridge, MA: Harvard University Press, 2004.

———. "Revisiting the History of Scientific Expert Testimony." *Brooklyn Law Review* 73 (Spring 2008): 879-942.

Gordon, Robert W. "Legal Thought and Legal Practice in the Age of American Enterprise, 1870-1920." In *Professions and Professional Ideologies in America*, edited by Gerald L. Geison, 70-110. Chapel Hill: University of North Carolina Press, 1983.

Gruber, Carol S. *Mars and Minerva: World War I and the Uses of the Higher Learning in America*. Baton Rouge: Louisiana State University Press, 1975.

Haber, Samuel. *The Quest for Authority and Honor in the American Professions, 1750-1900*. Chicago: University of Chicago Press, 1991.

Hall, Jerome. *Comparative Law and Social Theory*. Baton Rouge: Louisiana State University Press, 1963.

Hanson, Norwood Russell. *Patterns of Discovery: An Inquiry into the Conceptual Foundations of Science*. Cambridge: Cambridge University Press, 1958.

Haskell, Thomas L. *The Emergence of Professional Social Science: The American Social Science Association and the Nineteenth-Century Crisis of Authority*. Urbana: University of Illinois Press, 1977.

Hawkins, Mike. *Social Darwinism in European and American Thought, 1860-1945: Nature as Model and Nature as Threat*. Cambridge: Cambridge University Press, 1997.

Herget, James E. *American Jurisprudence, 1870-1970: A History*. Houston, TX: Rice University Press, 1990.

Hoeveler, J. David. *The New Humanism: A Critique of Modern America, 1900-1940*. Charlottesville: University Press of Virginia, 1977.

Hollinger, David A. *Morris R. Cohen and the Scientific Ideal*. Cambridge, MA: MIT Press, 1975.

Hook, Jay. "A Brief Life of James Bradley Thayer." *Northwestern University Law Review* 88 (1993-1994): 1-8.

Horsman, Reginald. *Race and Manifest Destiny: The Origins of American Racial Anglo-Saxonism*. Cambridge, MA: Harvard University Press, 1981.

Horwitz, Morton J. *The Transformation of American Law, 1870-1960: The Crisis of Legal Orthodoxy*. Oxford: Oxford University Press, 1992.

Hovenkamp, Herbert. "Evolutionary Models in Jurisprudence." *Texas Law Review* 64 (December 1985): 645-85.

Hull, N. E. H. *Roscoe Pound and Karl Llewellyn: Searching for an American Jurisprudence*. Chicago: University of Chicago Press, 1997.

Hume, L. J. "Jeremy Bentham and the Nineteenth-Century Revolution in Government." *Historical Journal* 10 (1967): 361-75.

Jones, H. J. *Live Machines: Hired Foreigners and Meiji Japan*. Vancouver: University of British Columbia Press, 1980.

Kaufman, Andrew L. *Cardozo*. Cambridge, MA: Harvard University Press, 1998.

Kellogg, Frederic R. *Oliver Wendell Holmes, Jr., Legal Theory and Judicial Restraint*. New York: Cambridge University Press, 2007.

Kimball, Bruce A. *The Inception of Modern Professional Education: C. C. Langdell, 1826-1906*. Chapel Hill: University of North Carolina Press, 2009.

―――――. *The "True Professional Ideal" in America.* Cambridge, MA: Blackwell, 1992.

King, Peter J. *Utilitarian Jurisprudence in America: The Influence of Bentham and Austin on American Legal Thought in the Nineteenth Century.* New York: Garland, 1986.

Kuklick, Bruce. *The Rise of American Philosophy: Cambridge, Massachusetts, 1860-1930.* New Haven, CT: Yale University Press, 1977.

Langbein, John H. "Historical Foundations of the Law of Evidence: A View from the Ryder Sources." *Columbia Law Review* 96 (June 1996): 1168-202.

Lears, T. J. Jackson. *No Place of Grace: Antimodernism and the Transformation of American Culture, 1880–1920.* New York: Pantheon, 1981.

Lepore, Jill. *The Secret History of Wonder Woman.* New York: Alfred A. Knopf, 2014.

Martin, Jay. *The Education of John Dewey: A Biography.* New York: Columbia University Press, 2002.

Mayer, Harold M., and Richard C. Wade, with the assistance of Glen E. Holt. *Chicago: Growth of a Metropolis.* Chicago: University of Chicago Press, 1969.

Menand, Louis. *The Metaphysical Club.* New York: Farrar, Straus and Giroux, 2001.

Mengler, Thomas M. "The Theory of Discretion in the Federal Rules of Evidence." *Iowa Law Review* 74 (January 1989): 413-66.

Morgan, Edmund M. "The Jury and the Exclusionary Rules of Evidence." *University of Chicago Law Review* 4 (February 1937): 247-58.

Mostoller, Robert P. "Evidence History, the New Trace Evidence, and Rumblings in the Future of Proof." *Ohio State Journal of Criminal Law* 3 (Spring 2006): 523-42.

Novick, Peter. *That Noble Dream: The "Objectivity Question" and the American Historical Profession.* New York: Cambridge University Press, 1998.

O'Brien, Michael. *Conjectures of Order: Intellectual Life and the American South, 1810-1860.* 2 vols. Chapel Hill: University of North Carolina Press, 2004.

Pedlar, Neil. *The Imported Pioneers: Westerners Who Helped Build Modern Japan.* New York: St. Martin's, 1990.

Philips, David. "'A Just Measure of Crime, Authority, Hunters and Blue Locusts': The 'Revisionist' Social History of Crime and the Law in Britain, 1780-1850." In *Social Control and the State*, edited by Stanley Cohen and Andrew Scull, 50-75. New York: St. Martin's, 1983.

Polenberg, Richard. *The World of Benjamin Cardozo: Personal Values and the Judicial Process.* Cambridge, MA: Harvard University Press, 1997.

Posner, Richard A. *Cardozo: A Study in Reputation.* Chicago: University of Chicago Press, 1990.

Quandt, Jean B. *From the Small Town to the Great Community: The Social Thought of Progressive Intellectuals.* New Brunswick, NJ: Rutgers University Press, 1970.

Rabban, David. *Free Speech in its Forgotten Years*. Cambridge: Cambridge University Press, 1997.

———. "The Historiography of Late Nineteenth-Century American Legal History." *Theoretical Inquiries in Law* 4 (2003): 541-78.

———. *Law's History: American Legal Thought and the Transatlantic Turn to History*. Cambridge: Cambridge University Press, 2013.

Rader, Benjamin G. *The Academic Mind and Reform: The Influence of Richard T. Ely in American Life*. Lexington: University of Kentucky Press, 1966.

Rafferty, Edward C. *Apostle of Human Progress: Lester Frank Ward and American Political Thought, 1841-1913*. Lanham, MD: Rowman and Littlefield, 2003.

Richardson, Robert D. *William James: In the Maelstrom of American Modernism*. Boston: Houghton Mifflin, 2006.

Riles, Annelise. "Encountering Amateurism: John Henry Wigmore and the Uses of American Formalism." In *Rethinking the Masters of Comparative Law*, edited by Annelise Riles, 94-126. Portland, OR: Hart, 2001.

———. "Wigmore's Treasure Box: Comparative Law in the Era of Information." *Harvard International Law Journal* 40 (Winter 1999): 221-83.

Roalfe, William R. *John Henry Wigmore: Scholar and Reformer*. Evanston, IL: Northwestern University Press, 1977.

Roberts, John H., and James Turner. *The Sacred and the Secular University*. Princeton, NJ: Princeton University Press, 2000.

Rodgers, Daniel T. *Atlantic Crossings: Social Politics in a Progressive Age*. Cambridge, MA: Harvard University Press, Belknap, 1998.

Rosenburg, David. *The Hidden Holmes: His Theory of Torts in History*. Cambridge, MA: Harvard University Press, 1995.

Reuben, Julie. *The Making of the Modern University: Intellectual Transformation and the Marginalization of Morality*. Chicago: University of Chicago Press, 1996.

Rutkoff, Peter M., and William B. Scott. *New School: A History of the New School for Social Research*. New York: Free Press, 1986.

Scallen, Eileen A., "Analyzing 'The Politics of [Evidence] Rulemaking.'" *Hastings Law Journal* 53 (April 2002): 843-84.

———. "Classical Rhetoric, Practical Reasoning, and the Law of Evidence." *American University Law Review* 44 (June 1995): 1717-816.

Schauer, Frederick. "On the Supposed Jury-Dependence of Evidence Law." *University of Pennsylvania Law Review* 155 (November 2006): 165-202.

Schlegel, John Henry. *American Legal Realism and Empirical Social Science*. Chapel Hill: University of North Carolina Press, 1995.

———. "American Legal Realism and Empirical Social Science: The Singular Case of Underhill Moore." *Buffalo Law Review* 29 (Spring 1980): 195-323.

Schofield, Philip. *Utility and Democracy: The Political Thought of Jeremy Bentham*. Oxford: Oxford University Press, 2006.

Shapiro, Barbara J. *Beyond Reasonable Doubt and Probable Cause: Historical Perspectives on the Anglo-American Law of Evidence*. Berkeley: University of California Press, 1991.

Siegel, Stephen A. "*Lochner* Era Jurisprudence and the American Constitutional Tradition." *North Carolina Law Review* 70 (November 1991): 1–111.

Spencer, Herbert. *Social Statics, or The Conditions essential to Happiness specified, and the First of them Developed*. New York: D. Appleton, 1872.

Strang, Lee J., and Bryce G. Poole. "Historical (In)Accuracy of the Brandeis Dichotomy: An Assessment of the Two-Tiered Standard of Stare Decisis for Supreme Court Precedents." *North Carolina Law Review* 86 (May 2008): 969–1031.

Tamanaha, Brian. *Beyond the Formalist-Realist Divide: The Role of Politics in Judging*. Princeton, NJ: Princeton University Press, 2009.

———. "Understanding Legal Realism." *Texas Law Review* 87 (March 2009): 731–85.

Temkin, Moshik. *The Sacco-Vanzetti Affair: America on Trial*. New Haven, CT: Yale University Press, 2009.

Tilman, Rick. *Thorstein Veblen and His Critics, 1891–1963: Conservative, Liberal and Radical Perspectives*. Princeton, NJ: Princeton University Press, 1992.

———. *Thorstein Veblen, John Dewey, C. Wright Mills and the Generic Ends of Life*. Lanham, MD: Rowman and Littlefield, 2004.

Turner, James. *The Liberal Education of Charles Eliot Norton*. Baltimore, MD: Johns Hopkins University Press, 1999.

Twining, William. *Rethinking Evidence: Exploratory Essays*. 2nd ed. Cambridge: Cambridge University Press, 2006.

———. *Theories of Evidence: Bentham and Wigmore*. London: Weidenfeld & Nicolson, 1985.

White, G. Edward. *Justice Oliver Wendell Holmes: Law and the Inner Self*. New York: Oxford University Press, 1993.

———. *Oliver Wendell Holmes, Jr*. 2nd ed. New York: Oxford University Press, 2006.

———. "Revisiting James Bradley Thayer." *Northwestern University Law Review* 88 (1993–1994): 48–83.

———. *Tort Law in America: An Intellectual History*. Oxford: Oxford University Press, 2003.

White, Morton. *Social Thought in America: The Revolt against Formalism*. New York: Viking, 1949.

Whitman, James Q. *The Origins of Reasonable Doubt: Theological Roots of the Criminal Trial*. New Haven, CT: Yale University Press, 2008.

Wiecek, William M. *The Lost World of Classical Legal Thought: Law and Ideology in America, 1886-1937*. New York: Oxford University Press, 1998.

Wigdor, David. *Roscoe Pound: Philosopher of Law*. Westport, CT: Greenwood, 1974.

Williamson, Harold F., and Payson S. Wild. *Northwestern University: A History, 1850-1975.* Evanston, IL: Northwestern University Press, 1976.

Wright, Charles Alan, and Kenneth W. Graham Jr. *Federal Practice and Procedure.* 2nd ed. St. Paul, MN: Thomson, West, 2005.

Yoshio, Sakata. "The Beginning of Modernization in Japan." In *The Modernizers: Overseas Students, Foreign Employees, and Meiji Japan,* edited by Ardath W. Burks, 69-83. Boulder, CO: Westview, 1985.

Index